1001 Most Asked Texas Gardeni

1001 Most Asked Texas Gardening Questions

by

Neil Sperry

THE SUMMIT PUBLISHING GROUP

The Summit Publishing Group
One Arlington Centre, 1112 East Copeland Road, Fifth Floor
Arlington, Texas 76011
summit@dfw.net
www.summitbooks.com

Printed in the United States of America.

01 00 99 98 97   010   5 4 3 2 1

Library of Congress Cataloging-in-Publication Data

Sperry, Neil.
  1001 most asked Texas gardening questions / by Neil Sperry.
    p. cm.
  ISBN 1-56530-229-X
  1. Gardening--Texas--Miscellanea.   2.Gardening--
    Miscellanea. I. Title II. Title: One thousand one most
    asked Texas gardening questions.
SB453.2.T4S62 1997   635.9'09764--dc21
96-51263   CIP

Cover design by Dennis Davidson
Page design by Michael Melton
Illustrations by Georgene Wood
Project Editor June Ford
Cover photo by Truitt Rogers
Flap photo by Brian Sperry

To Lynn, Brian, Todd and Erin, the most
important parts of my garden.
In memory of Omer and Lois, who lent their
very great support all along the way.
God bless you all.

Contents

Note: The 101 most commonly asked questions are indicated by stars on each side of the question numbers.

Introduction

It was August, 1970. Lynn and I were motoring west out of Texarkana to my new job as Dallas County Extension horticulturist. Two years of teaching horticulture at Pioneer Vocational School in Shelby, Ohio, had already been as rewarding as anyone could ever have deserved in a young career. Now—on to this new job, which would entail a certain amount of work with the media. What would it be like? Would it be terrifying, or would it be a challenge? Would I be up to the task?

We had hardly entered the boundaries of my great home state of Texas when we tuned to 1080 on the AM radio dial at 7:00 PM that summer evening. Some program called *Ask the Experts* had an attorney answering callers' questions. "Who could be that confident?" I asked myself. "Who could expose himself to that kind of risk?" "Why would you take the chance?" Reasonable questions, it seemed at the time.

Those first thirty months I served in Dallas County found me answering the phone five or six hours each day. My record, probably never to be challenged, was nineteen consecutive elm leaf beetle questions one July afternoon. I took, on average, fifty calls per day all through those thirty months. We held lawn and garden clinics and answered more questions. Those were great learning months. They taught me never to be embarrassed if I didn't know an answer, but simply to make an honest promise to try to find out.

In 1972, I was invited to cohost a call-in, question-and-answer program on a Dallas radio station, and a few years later my friend and mentor, Super Handyman Al Carrell challenged me to try my hand at live radio. My trial balloon was Thanksgiving Day, 1977, opposite Dallas Cowboy football, on radio station WFAA in Dallas/Fort Worth. The management told me, "If you can pull against the Cowboys, we'll take you on." Well, that Thursday afternoon was hectic, and I started with them in January 1978.

I left WFAA in May 1980, because of a conflict I had with a product they expected me to advertise. Since that time I've been answering questions over, that's right, KRLD, 1080 AM, the place where I had first wondered about people who would do that kind of programming. A 180-degree turn in just ten years. From KRLD, my work extended on to its sister affiliate, the Texas State Radio Network. They have been great places to work all those years. The initial fright of 1970 long ago turned to joy and anticipation of each weekend morning.

I figured the other day that I have answered more than 250,000 questions in those years on radio and through my weekly question-and-answer newspaper columns, which began in 1971. Everywhere I go, folks have garden questions. Few of us are so blessed as to get to talk and write all day long about our favorite hobby. I truly feel confident that I have accurate answers to the most common questions.

Many of the questions I hear are one-of-a-kind types, but there are also many repeaters. So, it's with that latter group in mind that I write this volume. It's my hope that this will allow you to sort through all the confusion and cut right to the problems that bother your plants the most.

Having said all that, I think I hear my phone ringing. Probably a friend with a garden question. Might I suggest a book...?

Thanks, for reading...

And happy gardening!

Neil Sperry

Note: The 101 most commonly asked questions are indicated by stars on each side of the question numbers.

FUNDAMENTALS OF TEXAS GARDENING

TEMPERATURES AND THEIR EFFECTS ON GARDENING

"Hardening" vs. "Hardiness"

Q Why is it that plants can be killed by temperatures one time and not damaged at all by the very same temperature another time?

A There are several variables involved in the way temperatures affect plants. One is called "hardening," where a plant is gradually conditioned to lower and lower temperatures for several weeks before a really hard freeze. Using oleanders as an example, they can normally withstand temperatures to 15 degrees—if they have received prior conditioning at, say 30, 25, and 20 degrees over several weeks. However, if the first freeze hits 20 degrees, those same plants may be frozen to the ground or killed entirely. How much wind accompanies the cold also enters the picture, as will the number of hours that the minimum temperature is maintained. You'll see more damage in a citrus orchard, for example, if it's below freezing for 15 hours than you will if the same temperature is held for only 3 hours. You'll see more damage if you have applied a high-nitrogen fertilizer just a few weeks prior to the cold, and you'll see much more damage if the plants are in water stress when the low temperatures hit.

Q What does a "Hardiness Zone" mean when I'm buying plants?

A Plants have certain minimum temperatures below which they simply cannot survive. For tropical hibiscus, for example, it's 32° F. For rose of Sharon, a type of woody and hardy hibiscus, it's -10° F. Every plant has its limits. Years ago the United States Department of Agriculture cataloged all of the counties in the United States to determine their average lowest temperature of each winter, then they broke the country into 10 different zones. Four of those zones are represented in Texas. Keep in mind that the larger the zone number, the warmer the winters. The Texas Panhandle is

Zone 6 (-10⁰ F to 0), while much of the Trans-Pecos and North Central Texas fall into Zone 7 (0 to +10⁰ F). Central Texas, the Hill Country, and Big Bend are mostly in Zone 8 (10⁰ F to 20⁰ F), while deep South Texas is in Zone 9 (20⁰ F to 30⁰ F). When you go shopping you should buy only plants that are winter-hardy to your county's zone rating or northward. In other words, if you live in Zone 7, you should choose only plants suited to Zones 7, 6, 5, 4 and perhaps 3. Many of those really cold-hardy plants, from Zone 3, as counter-examples, have trouble with our heat, so they may or may not be good for the area.

Protecting Plants From Temperature Extremes

☆3☆

 I want to plant some cold-sensitive shrubs. Would they be best on the south or east side of my house?

 Actually, they'd be best on the north or northwest sides. This catches almost everyone off guard, but the explanation is fairly simple. Those tender plants on the south and east side of the house will stay vegetative and active farther into the fall, increasing the chance that a sudden and quick freeze might damage them. Remember, too, that our coldest nights are usually clear. That means that the sun will be bright the following morning, hitting those frozen leaves on the east-facing plants before they have a chance to gradually thaw out.

4

Can I cover tender plants to keep them from freezing? What type of covering is best?

If you're talking about tomatoes, marigolds and similar tender annual plants, they can be damaged by frost, even when it isn't actually freezing. Frost can form on exposed surfaces on clear, still nights, even at temperatures as warm as 38 to 40 degrees. You can prevent that kind of damage by covering the plants with old sheets or one of the lightweight nursery fabrics. If it's going below freezing, however, you'll need to add supplemental heating under the cover, so you might want to use plastic. You'll have to remove it early in the morning, however, or the plants will warm up much too quickly. By comparison, if you have tender shrubs or plants such as pansies, you can gain several degrees of protection from really cold temperatures by covering the plants securely with the lightweight horticultural fabrics you can buy at full-service retail garden centers. These products can be reused in future winters, and they're really great at saving your plants.

Soil Temperatures

5

 How critical are soil temperatures in my gardening activities? Would it help if I had a soil thermometer? Where are they sold?

 Many things are impacted by the temperature of the soil. A couple of prominent examples are sowing bermuda seed and planting caladiums, both of which should wait until soil temperatures exceed 70 degrees on a regular basis; and planting tulips after the soil temperature drops to the low 50s for three consecutive days in early winter. Many other plants are equally affected.

You can buy soil thermometers in well-stocked hardware stores, and they're also sold in specialty gardening tool catalogs. Many folks use a heating/air conditioning contractor's pocket thermometer. They're small, slender, and easily inserted into garden soil.

Frost-free Dates

6

 Where can I find the frost-free dates for my county, and how do I use them in planting my flowers and vegetables?

 Your county Extension office has the information for all 254 counties in Texas. Remember: The average date of the last killing frost in the spring only means that there is a 50 percent chance of another killing frost occurring on that date. To be secure in planting cold-sensitive plants such as tomatoes, peppers, beans, or marigolds, zinnias or moss rose, you need to wait a couple of weeks after the average date of the last killing freeze.

TEXAS'S SOILS AND COPING WITH THEM
••

Improving Soil

☆**7**☆

Q I have clay soil. How can I loosen it up so plants' roots can grow?

A Organic matter will help break up tight clay soils. Rototill to blend several inches of Canadian peat moss, well-rotted compost, finely shredded bark mulch and rotted manure, among other sources of organic matter, into the soil. As the organic matter breaks down it will act to loosen the clay. You'll need to supplement with fresh organic matter every year or two. You can also include a very thin layer (½ to 1 inch) of washed brick sand, but only with the organic matter. Sand alone won't improve clays. The clay will filter through the much larger sand particles.

☆**8**☆

Q I have a sandy soil. What can I use to help it better hold moisture and fertilizers?

A Oddly, the same organic matter that improves a clay soil will also help sandy soils. In this case, however, the organic matter will act to retain moisture and nutrients. It has a much greater total surface area than the sand particles.

9

Q Can I use my fireplace ashes in my garden or in the compost pile?

A The critical fact to remember is that ashes of all types are highly alkaline. If you live in the eastern 20 percent of Texas where soils are acidic, ashes might be of some benefit. However, for folks with alkaline soils and/or alkaline irrigation water, the highly alkaline fireplace ashes would be like pouring gasoline on an existing fire. Don't use the ashes there.

10

Q Can I use gypsum to loosen our tight clay soils? The product label claims it will do that.

A Gypsum doesn't seem to do a very good job of breaking up normal clay soils. Texas-based university research to back those claims is sparse, if it exists at all, and my own personal tests in treating a heavy clay soil with gypsum resulted in no visible changes in the soil's structure after one month or even one year. Incorporating organic matter is still the best method.

11

Q How much soil preparation will I need to do when I plant my trees and shrubs? How will that differ from what I do for my flowers and vegetables?

A The smaller the mature plant, the more you should be willing to give it heroic soil preparation prior to planting. That would mean you should always choose large shade trees that will grow willingly in your existing soil. There simply is no practical way of amending the soil for a tree's entire mature root system. Preparing special soil for the initial planting hole of, for example, an East Texas pine in alkaline soils of Central or West Texas, would only buy the tree a few years before its roots extended beyond the initial mix. In other words, don't try it! Large shrubs probably fall into the same category, but for smaller shrubs such as gardenias and azaleas, you can actually import their total planting mix. When you're preparing for small plants such as annual and perennial flowers and vegetables, you'll be able to provide anything they need. In fact, if your native soils are heavy clays, you'll probably want to develop a planting mix that resembles a commercial potting soil, and you'll certainly want to plant into raised beds to ensure good drainage.

Quack Soil Amendments

12

Q What can you tell me about a product that claimed it would result in superior plant growth? It didn't say anything about nutrients. It said only that it would "...stimulate microbes."

A This is a very important issue. There are garden writers and broadcasters who accept these junk products as advertisers, so stay alert and trust your intuition. Although most states do have laws regulating these quack soil additives, Texas has none. You need to be very careful or you may end up wasting money. Organic matter improves soil. Fertilizers improve plant growth. Good cultural practices of proper planting site, good drainage, attention to watering and prudent pest control all will yield better plants. These bogus soil amendments, however, perform no miracles. Ask questions, and look for documentation from Land Grant universities such as Texas A&M and Texas Tech. Don't put much weight in testimonial statements.

Fertilizers and When to Use Them

☆13☆

Q What type of plant food is best for my plant?

A The exact plant name changes, but the question is always the same. Really, it's been my experience that folks make more work out of picking fertilizers than is necessary. It's not that precise a science. You should have your soil tested every couple of years, just to be sure your plants' needs are being met. However, some general comments will at least get you started. Examine any product that claims to be a fertilizer and you'll see three numbers on its label. They stand, respectively, for:

- nitrogen (leaf and stem growth),

- phosphorus (roots, flowers and fruit), and

- potassium (summer and winter hardiness).

That would lead you to a high-nitrogen fertilizer for turfgrasses, lettuce and shade trees, for example. It would also suggest high-phosphate plant foods for roses, tomatoes and newly transplanted shrubs that need to regrow their root systems. What you may not know, however, is that Texas soil tests often show excessive amounts of phosphorus, especially after we have gardened in a specific area for several years, and especially if we've been adding high-phosphate fertilizers during that time. Don't be surprised if the soil tests suggest you use a lawn-type (high-nitrogen) fertilizer for many or all of your plantings. Trust the tests. One final thing: Check the fine print to see how much of the nitrogen in the bag is in a slow-release form. Ideally as much as one-half will be in a slow-release form.

14

Q What specific tips can you give me about having my soil tested?

A First, do it fairly often, at least every couple of years in soils in which you are actively gardening. Your county Extension office has the necessary collecting and mailing materials for your soil samples. You'll probably want to monitor the major elements and their levels in your soil, also the pH (acidity or alkalinity) and soluble mineral salts that have accumulated in the soil. Tell the testing laboratory what plants you're trying to grow, so they can better interpret your soil's needs. There is a charge for having the soil tested—payable when you send the sample to the laboratory at Texas A&M. Other labs can also test soil, and there are do-it-yourself kits in the marketplace. Collect small samples from several parts of any specific garden, to minimize the chance that an unusual circumstance in one area would sway the results. Collect separate samples from (a.) turf, groundcover and shrub areas and from (b.) flower and vegetable gardens.

15

Q How can I tell when my plants need to be fertilized?

They're going to give you the telltale symptoms.

- Nitrogen shortages will be the most common. The plants' growth will slow and their leaves won't be the deep, rich green you would normally expect. The yellowish-green color will be over all of the plant, not just on the new growth.

- Phosphorus deficiency is much less common. When it does show up, however, it will be seen as stunted growth with a purplish cast to the leaves. You'll see it on newly seeded bermuda lawns that have been kept too wet, but you'll rarely encounter it elsewhere.

- Iron deficiency will have symptoms of yellowed leaves with dark green veins, most prominently displayed on the newest growth first. Lots of other problems resemble iron deficiency, but they won't match all of those symptoms.

- Zinc deficiency is common only to pecans, and only west of Interstate 35. It causes a stunted dieback of the pecan branches, also referred to as witches' brooms.

As for timing of feedings, all of these elements will be most quickly assimilated by the plants if they're applied several weeks prior to vigorous growth. Most feedings will be made in early spring, late spring and early fall, but timing will vary with the crop.

Iron Deficiency ("Chlorosis")

☆16☆

 Why is it that my pines, azaleas, dogwoods, wisterias and hollies turn yellow? Someone has told me it was a lack of iron.

If your soil is alkaline (pH of 7.0 or greater), the iron that is in the soil changes form chemically, so that the plants' roots are unable to absorb it. Obviously, you should always start with plants which are less likely to show iron deficiency, if you're gardening in alkaline soils. Once they're in the ground and growing, however, you can add supplemental iron in the form of liquid or granular iron products. Keep the products off masonry and painted surfaces that could be stained by the iron. It's also a good idea to use a product containing sulfur, not so much because the plants need the extra sulfur, but more for what the sulfur can do to keep the iron in an "available" form. Sulfur forms an acid when it's mixed into the soil, lowering the soil pH. Spring and summer are the best times to apply the iron/sulfur additives, while your plants are most actively growing.

17

 Can I use iron filings to correct chlorosis in my plants?

 Iron filings are the wrong (insoluble) form of iron. They will have little, if any, impact on the chlorosis. You'll want to use chelated iron, iron sulfate or other available form of iron, along with sulfur soil acidifier to keep the iron in a soluble form.

Composting

18

 What is the best way to compost, and what can I include in my compost pile?

 To compost organic matter such as tree leaves, small twigs, grass clippings, manure, vegetable waste from the kitchen and garden stubble, you'll want it to be finely shredded, warm and moist. That means you'll probably need some type of enclosure, whether it's a bin made from treated pine or concrete blocks, or whether it's one of the many prefabricated bins you can buy from garden and home centers. Ideally the bin will face south, so the compost will absorb the winter sun. If it's an open pile, cover it with black plastic during the colder months to soak up solar energy. The organic matter should be run through your mower or through a grinder before you put it into the pile. Using the old hard-candy theory, it will break down much quicker if it has been "chewed up" initially. The layers should be 4 to 5 inches deep, and you can top each layer with 1 inch of topsoil, both to introduce microorganisms and also to conserve moisture. You might also want to add one cup of a complete-and-balanced fertilizer per cubic yard of compost. Keep the pile warm and moist and turn it with a spading fork every month or two. It will be ready for use when the component parts are no longer recognizable, usually in 6 to 8 months.

Mulches

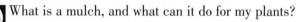

Q What is a mulch, and what can it do for my plants?

A Mulches are a gardener's salvation. They save plants, time, money, and a lot of hard work. Plus, they make the place look good. A mulch is any layer of covering over the top of the soil. It can be organic, such as ground pine bark, or it can be inorganic, such as the roll-type mulches you cut and fit around your plants. Mulches minimize the rate of temperature change in the soil. They reduce or eliminate weed growth. Mulches protect produce from splashing rains, and they also keep vegetables lifted off the soil surface. Mulches slow the movement of water across the soil surface so that more of it will penetrate into the root zone, and they also reduce the loss of topsoil in sandy, windy areas.

Grade Changes

Q I have low spots in my yard and I'd like to raise its grade. How will that impact my lawn and shade trees?

A Be really careful. You can actually take several inches of soil off the top of a tree's root system and do less damage than if you added the same amount. The majority of any tree's roots will be in the top foot of the soil, so adding soil risks oxygen depletion in the root zone. If you have to do significant grade changing, build a retaining wall and a well at the original grade. An arborist can consult with you to determine the size of the well for the specific tree and location. As a practical measure, however, you could add soil to one portion of the tree's root zone, so long as you don't cover more than 20 to 25 percent of the roots. As for the lawn, fill shallow low spots with washed brick sand. Use dry sand so it can filter down through the runners, and try not to use more than 1 inch of sand. If the low spots are deeper, dig the sod and put new topsoil in place before you replant the grass. April and May are ideal times to accomplish these changes.

PLANTING AND TRANSPLANTING

(See also more specific information in sections on Trees, Shrubs, Groundcovers, Annuals, Perennials, Turf, Fruits and Vegetables.)

21

 What sizes of plants should I buy?

Shade trees are available in containers from 1-gallon cans up to 200-gallon boxes. You can buy even larger shade trees that have been dug and balled-and-burlapped. You should determine your budget and buy a tree that is large enough to make an immediate statement, but that still fits into your overall allowances. Medium-sized trees establish quickly and take off handsomely. With shrubs, however, it's better to go somewhat larger than you might otherwise expect. Larger plants, say, from 3-, 5- and 10-gallon containers, have deeper roots, so there's a greater margin of error from drought during the summer. You'll also gain a year or two of growth, so your landscape will look more mature much more quickly. You'll also be more likely to space the plants at acceptable distances. Most of us overcrowd plants when we set out small transplants. As for groundcovers, use 4-inch or 1-gallon pots for the fastest good look. For annuals, 4-inch pots establish quickly and minimize the "down time" of your color beds.

22

 How important is "root stimulator" for new plants?

It's important for the first feeding of new annual flowers and vegetables, also nursery stock from containers. Because those plants have suffered no loss of roots when they were transplanted, just that one application should be sufficient. For balled-and-burlapped and bare-rooted trees, however, use the liquid root stimulator monthly for the first growing season.

23

Q I have ended up losing plants that seemed to be rootbound when I took them out of their pots. Is there an easy remedy so it won't happen again?

A Use a utility or paring knife to slice through the outer soil ball. Just as branches send out new shoots when they're cut, so do roots. That will break their circular pattern of growth.

24

Q We have a chance to move some trees and shrubs, due to a construction project. We know that winter is the best time to do it, but we have to do it now. Can they be moved at other seasons?

A With varying success. Some plants, such as crape myrtles, are notoriously forgiving. So long as you hold their soil in place as you transplant them, and if you trim them back to compensate for the shock, you can probably transplant crape myrtles in all but the hottest weather. Nonetheless, you always want to do your digging in the winter if you're given a choice. Other plants will be more difficult to move in spring, summer and fall. Don't spend a lot of money doing it, but try as many of the plants as you can. Keep them watered thoroughly and deeply after the move.

WATERING: TIMING, TOOLS, AND TECHNIQUES

Watering

☆ 25 ☆

 Q How often should I water my plants?

A That's the one question in this book that I won't try to answer. How often do *you* take a drink of water? Do the intervals vary? Of course, they vary due to your changing activities, temperatures, and other external conditions. You have learned to take a drink of water when you're thirsty, and that's exactly the way you should handle your plants. Learn to recognize their drought symptoms, then water them as needed.

26

Q I think I have overwatered my plants. They all seem to be dying, and it's many different types that are involved. What can I do now?

A Overwatering gets blamed for a lot of problems in which it really isn't involved. If I had a nickel for every time someone thought they had overwatered their plants, I'd be as wealthy as the Wrigleys with their gum. Usually, the plants have probably gotten too dry one time and the gardeners simply weren't aware of it. Plants that are consistently too wet will be wilted, even though the soil is still wet. Symptoms will vary with conditions and plant types, but overly wet plants will usually wilt all over, and all of their leaves will turn yellow and hang in place. Best rule of thumb: Never water when the soil is already moist, no matter how wilted the plant might be. If you follow that rule you'll never have to worry about overwatering your plants.

27

Q I live in a low spot where the soil is very poorly drained. What steps can I take to correct it?

A Determine where the water is coming from. If it's off your roof, consider guttering and downspouts that could redirect the flow of the water away from your planting beds. If it's coming down a hill from the neighbors' houses, you might be able to build a low berm or cut a shallow swale to redirect the incident water. A French drain installed under the bed could carry the water away rather than letting it stand in the soil. Finally, plant in raised beds so that your plants' roots will be above the water table at all times. You can determine whether your soil is waterlogged by digging a post hole, then watching it for a few days after a heavy rain. If the hole remains filled with water two or three days later, you have a problem.

28

Q I see a residue on my shrubs and groundcovers after the sprinklers have run. Some of the plants' leaves are turning brown around the edges. What could the problem be?

A It sounds like soluble mineral salts. Some of our waters have excessive amounts of sodium, for example, and plants may show symptoms of burning because of it. It's essentially the same thing that happens when we overfertilize a plant. The soil becomes so saturated with the mineral salts that water is actually drawn out of the root systems, causing the scorching and burning. It might help to incorporate gypsum into your soil. It replaces the sodium with non-threatening calcium, without changing the soil pH. Try to keep irrigation water off your plants' leaves, in the meanwhile.

☆ 29 ☆

Q My plants have brown edges around their leaves. It starts at the tips of the leaves and works its way completely to the bottoms of the leaves. Is that a disease?

A Diseases and insects will always be random in their effects. Anytime you see marginal or tip burn of leaves, you have to know that somehow it is related to moisture stress. If you think about the human circulation system, it can help explain what has happened to your plants. Those edges and tips are the points farthest from the roots, so they're where the plant will dry out first and will get water last. Either you have let the plants get far too dry at least once, or they have suffered root damage. You may have overfertilized them, or they may have some type of stem damage that inhibits their uptake of water. That kind of burn can be caused by sudden hot and dry winds, also by taking a plant that has become accustomed to moist, shady conditions and putting it into a hot, sunny location. Whatever the exact cause, it's related to the plant's inability to get water clear out to the tips of its leaves.

30

 Is it better to water frequently and not to use as much at a watering, or less often and more heavily?

Definitely the latter. If you "sprinkle" the soil lightly you'll be encouraging shallow roots that will stay near the soil surface where the water is hitting. Watering more deeply, then letting the soil dry out somewhat before watering again, will encourage your plants to develop much deeper roots, helping them to better withstand periods of drought.

Watering Tools

31

 What types of sprinklers are best?

All you want a sprinkler to do is to distribute water uniformly over a specified area. If it does it quickly, that's better. If it's not terribly expensive, that's even better. But the uniform distribution is critical. Rotary sprinklers are probably easier to use if you have lots of wind, because their water droplets are larger. However, they water in circles, so it's harder to get a uniform coverage. If you're dealing with a sprinkling system, be sure the heads are all correctly positioned, clean and functioning properly.

32

 What size of garden hose is best?

Most 1/2-inch hoses are cheaply made and won't last, and 3/4-inch hoses are too heavy when they're filled with water. As a compromise, look for a quality 5/8-inch hose that will retain its flexibility even in colder weather. Measure the distance from your faucets to the most distant points to determine length. Don't leave your hose attached to the faucet during freezing weather. Not only will the hose be brittle when it's filled with ice, but you also risk freezing the pipes in the outer walls of your house.

33

 What can you tell me about the sweating pipes that are sold to be buried in the ground? They're supposed to water uniformly, with absolutely no evaporation or runoff. I think they're made of old, ground-up rubber tires.

 Be careful. There are several pitfalls. First, how can the watering be uniform over the entire area when the lines are 18 or 24 inches apart? It stands to reason that some areas will be soaked, while others are still waiting for water. You'll also be crowding all of the oxygen out of the soil as you saturate the ground; plus, you'll have no way of leaching out excess mineral salts. These hoses would be great if they could be laid on top of the ground, but they're apparently not stable in all the Texas sunlight.

34

I'd like to cut my water bills. What tricks can you give?

Not too many tricks, just lots of common sense.

- Choose plants that don't require excessive amounts of water to stay healthy.
- Be sure your watering system is functioning properly, whether you use an automatic system or a hose with a sprinkler.
- Mulch your plants liberally, preferably with compost or shredded bark, and likely in combination with a roll-type mulch.
- Water early in the morning, when evaporation will be at its lowest, and if you have an automatic system, as we've mentioned elsewhere, leave it in the "manual" mode.
- Learn to recognize drought symptoms in your plants, then turn the water on manually. Usually, you'll have one or two plants that will be the first to wilt.
- Drip irrigation is the very best way to cut water bills—use it wherever it's practical.

PRUNING
....

Timing the Pruning

☆35☆

 When do I prune my various plants?

 That's a generic question, with many correct answers. In general terms, however, you should prune these plants in late winter: shade trees, evergreen shrubs, summer-flowering shrubs, bush roses, fruit trees and grape vines. Prune climbing roses and other spring-flowering shrubs and vines immediately after they finish blooming. Winter pruning of those plants would remove all or many of their buds. Prune blackberries immediately after harvest. Minor pruning to correct irregular growth can be done at any time during the year.

Pruning Techniques, Supplies

36

What do you mean when you refer to "pinching" plants?

That's a horticulturist's way of describing a very light job of pruning. Using coleus or chrysanthemums as examples, both tend to grow tall and leggy if they're not pruned in some way. The very best way is to prune them frequently and lightly, removing only the growing shoot tip, perhaps 1/4-inch long. That will make the plants branch out, keeping them more compact. Since you can easily do that pruning with your thumbnail and index finger, it's called "pinching."

37

I've heard talk about pruning to an "outward-facing" bud. What does that mean?

Any dormant bud on a limb or trunk has to face one particular direction. If you want to encourage open, more spreading growth, you would always prune just beyond a bud that was on the opposite side of the stem from the main trunk, or an "outward-facing" bud. That's critical technique when pruning roses, peaches and plums, for example, since you want them to spread. If you were to prune them just beyond a bud that faced back into the center of the plant, you'd get tight, congested growth.

38

 Is pruning paint all that helpful? I've heard that it isn't necessary.

 Pruning sealant dries to a hard, protective coating over cut surfaces. However, there is good research that shows that it can actually inhibit the regrowth of bark over the wound. If you do use it, keep it away from the outer edge of the cut. One place where you would want to use it: on any oak pruning that you do during the growing season, since insects that transmit diseases are attracted to the freshly cut wood. In areas where oaks are falling victim to oak wilt and other diseases, you may even want to use pruning sealant during the winter.

39

 Can I use roofing asphalt instead of the nursery pruning paint?

No. It's better to stick with the product that is made specifically for the job.

40

What is the purpose of whitewash I see on trees' trunks?

That used to be a method of inhibiting insect invasion. They were repulsed by the reflective white surface. It was used especially for protection against borers such as the damaging peach tree borer. However, today we have much better products that are far more effective. There still are some people who like the unnatural "white sidewall" look whitewash gives their trees, regardless of any pest-controlling properties.

Pruning Shrubs

☆41☆

 If I wanted to prune some of my shrubs back drastically, how much could I cut off, and when should I do it? Is it practical?

You can prune shrubs back rather heavily, but you do need to keep their genetic potential in mind. How tall would they be if you never pruned them at all? Try not to cut them lower than 50 percent of that height. Now, to your exact question, major pruning as you described should be done in late winter. That way you'll be looking at stubble for the minimum time, plus the plants will be able to devote maximum energy to regrowing in early spring. You could probably remove as much as 30 to 40 percent of their top growth, but try to leave some foliage in place.

42

 I have a row of redtip photinias that are up to the eaves. Can I prune them back, or should I just move them?

Redtip photinias grow to 12 to 15 feet when they're left unpruned. That means they should be kept no shorter than 6 to 8 feet. At those heights you'll have to prune them 5 or 6 times each summer. It's not a pretty picture. On the other hand, if you were to try digging those plants and moving them, you'd probably need chiropractic help before the day was over. If you really wanted big photinias somewhere else in your garden, you could probably get them more easily and quickly if you just started with new plants.

43

We have a hedge screening our property from the neighbors. How should we prune it to keep it dense? It seems to be thinning out.

Hedges should be pruned wider at their bases than they are at their tops. That ensures maximum sunlight can reach the bottom leaves. In reality, it's best to let the plants grow naturally so you don't get into the routine of regular trimming. If at all possible, do your pruning with lopping shears rather than hedge shears or power trimmers. Shrubs will also stay more compact and denser clear to the ground if they're not crowded together. For most shrub types that means you'll want them planted almost as far apart as they'll be allowed to grow in height.

44

 I have a large shrub that I'd like to train as an espalier. How would I go about doing that?

 You might not want to bother. Since a plant does most of its growing at the tips of its branches, it's usually easier to get an espalier to fill in at its base if you complete it one level at a time from the ground up. It's very hard to go back into an older, overgrown plant and retrofit it into a two-dimension form.

Pruning Trees

45

 I have a new tree that isn't growing very well. It was dug this past winter, but it has very few leaves. Should it have been pruned when it was dug?

 Absolutely. That pruning is done to compensate for the roots that were lost in the digging. You need to thin any tree of that sort out by 30 to 40 percent, or you can remove part of the top growth, or a combination of the two.

46

 I have a limb of my oak tree that has become a hazard at an intersection. Can I remove it during the growing season?

 Yes. The reason winter pruning of oaks is recommended is because of the diseases that are carried by insects that are active in the growing season. However, if you seal the cut wound immediately after you prune the limb, there won't be any threat to the tree.

47

 How much can I cut my shade tree back? It's too tall for where it's growing.

That sounds dangerously like "topping" a shade tree. If any plant is too big for its available space, you need to consider either moving it or removing it entirely. That's doubly true with shade trees, because cutting them back repeatedly to keep them in bounds will result in distorted growth and a ruined shape. The tree will never achieve its genetic potential. Fortunately, topping trees like mimosas and fruitless mulberries is almost unheard of today, compared to 20 and 30 years ago. Of course, if you needed to remove one errant limb that had grown out of the tree's basic canopy toward the roof of your house, you could certainly do that.

48

 We have a large limb we need to remove from one of our shade trees. What is the best way to do it?

 You need to follow the three-step approach to major pruning.

- Make your first cut 18 to 24 inches away from the trunk, cutting up from beneath the limb. Cut ¼ to ⅓ of the way into the limb from below.

- Move 6 inches farther out on the limb and cut completely through it from the top down. As the weight of the limb causes it to break and peel back, it will only strip the bark away to the point of the undercut.

- Cut the rest of the limb off where it attaches to the trunk.

49

 How much of a stub is too much when you're removing a tree limb?

If you look closely at any large limb, you'll notice that it swells just as it attaches to the main trunk. That's an area known as the "branch collar," and it's a very important part of the healing process. Rather than cutting exactly flush with the trunk, you need to leave that 1/16th-inch branch collar in place. Any more stub than that and you risk decay setting back into the trunk.

50

Someone told us we should "root prune" our shade tree before we try to move it. What is that, and how beneficial would it be?

Root pruning really is good business. It's the process of cutting the lateral roots so that the new root growth will all be within the eventual soil ball. It results in far less transplant shock, provided you give the plant enough lead time to regrow its roots. Ideally you'd want to do the root pruning no later than early fall for a mid-winter transplanting. If you could do the root pruning the prior winter, so much the better.

PLANNING THE LANDSCAPE

GENERAL QUESTIONS ABOUT LANDSCAPING

Budget

51

 How much should I plan on spending on my landscape?

That's a question without a good answer. How much would you spend on your *interior* decor? In fact, how much are you including in the "landscape"? Are you including hard surfaces, fences and the swimming pool, or just the plants themselves? How about the sprinkler system, and what about your patio improvements? It would be easy to run the bill up quite high, when, in reality, only a small part of it was actually the "green and growing" part of the garden.

52

 I have a limited budget. What parts of the landscape should go in first?

The slower, most permanent plants are first to be planted. That includes large shade trees and turfgrass. Be sure, however, that they fit your long-term objectives, because these are also the most difficult plants to move later should you want to change things around. Next will be the large structural shrubs of your gardens, then the smaller shrubs, vines and groundcovers. Annual and perennial color can come at any time, either for short-term impact while the larger plants are maturing, or for color in a mature garden.

53

 Where can I get really good landscape design help?

There are several good ways. You may want to try a combination of them all.

- You can do much of the planning yourself. If you feel comfortable with the various types of plants and how they will perform in your soils and climate, and if you have at least a basic working knowledge of design principles, you can do much of the work yourself. At least you'll be more conversant on the fine-tunings of good design.
- Your local nursery may have a landscape designer on staff. Sometimes they will even do the design for you at a reduced fee if you buy your plants through that nursery.
- Texas is also blessed with a large number of outstanding landscape contractors. These are the men and women who actually do the work of getting the landscapes up and running. In addition to planting the trees and shrubs and building the retaining walls, many of these firms can also do the initial design of those improvements as well. Look for a member of the Texas Association of Landscape Contractors, and ask for references.
- Finally, you may also want to look for a registered landscape architect. These people are degreed, registered planners of fine landscapes. Many work solely on commercial gardens, but some will also do residences. Again, ask for places where you can see their work. Be certain you're comfortable with their design ideas.

54

Q I hear people talking about the "public" and "private" areas of their landscapes, but ours is wide open for all to see. What do those terms mean?

A Generally the "public" area is the "front yard," in Texas terms. It's what the public sees as they approach your house. The "private" area is the back yard, or where your family goes for rest and recreation. There's a third part of any good design, and that's the service or work area. It's where you store tools and power equipment, and it's also where the vegetable garden should be placed, since it's not attractive during the off-seasons. A fine landscape will consist of each of these parts. Sketch them in as you plan your design.

55

 I'd like to do a "foundation planting" for our house. Where do I start?

 That's an old concept of landscape design, stemming back to an era when houses were high off the ground, usually on craggy leveling blocks or old bois d'arc stumps. We had to do something to conceal all those ugly sights, and those tall "foundation plantings" were our answer. Today, though, modern homes are more compact and lower to the ground, and our foundations aren't all that unsightly. Of course, if you're relandscaping an heirloom structure from decades ago, the old concept of straight lines of tall evergreen shrubs might still be in keeping.

56

 I read and hear about "groups" or "clusters" of plants, but what does that mean?

Nature often grows her plants in clumps and groves. As we're trying to achieve that natural look in modern landscapes, we, too, should avoid repeating the straight lines of our houses. By planting in curved lines, or checkerboard-style in little communities of the same species, we can get that natural look. For the record, odd numbers of plants are the most visually restful, especially when you're dealing with comparatively small numbers of plants, for example, up to nine plants of a particular species.

57

How can I lay out my landscape beds so they will look really good?

They need to be in scale with the size of your house. If you're going to plant in curvilinear beds, use a supple garden hose on a warm sunny day. You can move the hose until you get just the configuration you want. Don't let them be too "busy," though. Long, sweeping curves are the most useful. Let them be broader at the corners, and flare them out as they approach the sidewalk. Try to equalize them visually on the two sides of your walk. In other words, if one bed is longer, let it also be narrower. To put it in other terms, the beds should appear to have roughly the same visual square-footage.

58

 How should I prepare the soil for my new planting beds? How can I get rid of the existing turf without harming the soil?

 Once you have the beds marked off, you can kill existing turf with a glyphosate spray. There are several brands on the market, and all can be used without fear of contaminating the soil. They lose their effectiveness the minute they hit the ground. Give them 10 to 12 days to kill the grass, then rototill and mix in all your amendments.

59

 I have a zero-lot-line house, but I still want an attractive landscape. How do I modify my design ideas?

 You don't change a thing, other than to choose plants that stay more compact. Smaller gardens should have the same design elements as their larger cousins. You still want to frame the house, and you still need shade or soundproofing. You still want fragrance, and you're still looking for color. All you have to do is to scale things back to the space you have available, then choose plants that fit within the boundaries. We've been blessed, over the past several decades, with scores of new dwarf shrubs and trees.

60

I'd like to keep our grass and groundcover separated. What type of edging works best?

You need a type that extends 3 to 4 inches into the ground and that doesn't have open cracks or seams. Baked-enamel metal edging works well. It's flexible, yet durable. It can be made to fit almost any type of configuration. There are molded plastic pieces that are similar to the metal edging, and you can also use concrete edging stones, bricks,z or even decay-resistant wood. Your edging should be inserted deeply into the soil, with not more than 1/2-inch extending above grade. If it works up and out of the soil in time, hammer it back in.

61

 How can I keep dogs from ruining my plantings?

You may be able to rely on simple teaching and instruction. You can also use low-voltage shock fences to deter dogs. You can find small boxed kits with all the necessary materials in hardware stores and home centers. There are more elaborate systems with buried cables and with collars the dogs wear anytime they're outdoors. There are pet-repelling products that smell bad, or you might use mothballs or rags dipped in ammonia. Many plantings, especially flowers and vegetables, can even be made in large containers. Not only will it make "featured stars" out of the plants, but it will also keep them out of harm's way.

62

Where should I put my bird feeders so they'll draw the most birds?

Place feeders near trees, but away from dense shrubs which might harbor cats. They should be visible from your house, so you can enjoy watching the birds, being careful not to put them so close the birds might hit your windows. Feeders should be at least 4 feet off the ground, again, to keep the cats away.

63

What type of bird seed will draw the most birds?

Black oil-type sunflower seed seems to attract the widest range of desirable birds. Not only will they flock to the feeders, but the ground-feeding types will keep it picked up off the ground.

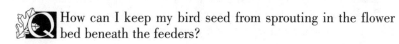

How can I keep my bird seed from sprouting in the flower bed beneath the feeders?

Using the black oil-type sunflower seed will really help, since the birds eat every seed of it. If you have millet and other less desirable seeds germinating, consider heavily mulching the ground beneath the feeders. If you put 1 to 2 inches of bark mulch on the soil it will usually prohibit the germination of the seeds. Any that do sprout can be easily hoed out.

COLOR IN THE LANDSCAPE
••

65

How can I get the very best color for my landscape?

That's a tough question, but there are many great tips. First, have a plan. Know month-by-month which plants will be colorful. Examine all of the plants' parts for color (leaves, stems, fruit, and, of course, flowers). Think about how good or bad the plant may look when it isn't colorful. Some flowering shrubs, for example, and also certain perennials, are almost ugly when they're not blooming. Use those farther out in your garden, so you won't have to look at them in the "off-seasons." Massed colors show up best, and brighter, "hotter" colors advance visually more than the more subdued types.

66

Q What types of plants will give the most color for the least work?

A Strange as it seems, annuals are usually best. They're colorful for 3 to 6 months, while even the best perennials usually flower only a few weeks. Flowering shrubs and trees are the worst, blooming only one to two weeks a year.

Hard Surfaces

67

Q I want to pour concrete near a tree. Will it hurt the tree?

A It could, if it were to cover a major part of the root system and if no provision was made to get excessive water out of the soil. Water accumulates under concrete and asphalt paving. Try not to cover more than 30 to 40 percent of the root area, if possible; and do little if any grade changing or root cutting. Your very best option would be to use interlocking concrete or brick pavers over a bed of washed brick sand. That type of surface would be porous enough to allow water and air to flow into and out of the soil. It also allows you to lift individual pavers as needed for repair or replacement in later years.

68

Q What are our best options at enlarging our patio?

A Often you can use the old patio as the foundation for your improvements. Put a 1-inch layer of washed brick sand over it, then pack it smooth. Use interlocking concrete pavers, bricks, or smooth flagstone as your new surface, making sure they fit together tightly. You can easily expand the surface beyond the old boundaries, but be careful that the added height doesn't interfere with your doors or with the flow of runoff away from your house.

69

 We want to use treated pine in our landscape, both as land-scaping timbers and as a retaining wall. Will the chemicals hurt our plants, our pets, or us? We may have vegetables nearby. Also, what about using that lumber in an airtight greenhouse?

There should be no problem at all. Forestry experts tell us that the chemicals are bound into the wood. There should be no harmful seepage or volatile vapors. Railroad ties, by compar-ison, can be more of a problem, especially if they're leaking the black creosote. It's toxic to plants and probably shouldn't be used next to vegetables or in a greenhouse.

70

 Our patio is hot in the summer and cold in the winter. How can we best control that?

Deciduous shade overhead is an obvious starting point. If you have an arbor over your patio, plant a vine that will be bare in the winter. Wisteria, Lady Banksia rose and Madame Galen trumpetcreeper are all examples. Remove all obstructions to the south breezes during the summer, and erect some type of wind break to the north. To explain, keep all low vegetation from trees and shrubs "limbed up" so that the summer breezes can actually be funneled in underneath. Use dense shrubs such as hollies, ligustrums or elaeag-nus to stop the wind from the north. Be careful, too, how you choose and place fencing near the patio. Use it to block the north winter wind, and leave openings for the south breezes in the summer.

71

I've heard you talk about using rock salt to make pavers at your home. How did you do that?

We used concrete forms that we made in 10-by-16-inch and 10-by-10-inch sizes. As the concrete just began to set we pressed prominent types of leaves such as oaks and ferns into it, then sprinkled rock salt on top. The stones are ready to be removed from their forms within 24 to 36 hours in the summer. Within several days the leaves browned and dried away, leaving their imprint. The rock salt left pock marks which add to the perceived age and beauty of the stones. We also used a rock hammer to knock off the sharp edges to give the stones an even older appearance. We cut the stones with special carbide blades to create a formal round patio.

72

Q What are the best ways to build a retaining wall? What materials work best?

A First, if the wall is going to be more than 12 to 15 inches tall, consider hiring a landscape contractor to do the work for you. They've been trained to deal with the weight and pressure of soil behind such a wall, and they can save you many hours of hard work and frustration by putting the wall up properly the first time. Use timbers, ledgestone rock (many different types) or wall-stone interlocking concrete blocks. Be sure the wall slopes back into the hill, and use long anchoring timbers or stones to hold it in place.

3

TREES

BUYING A TREE

73

 How large a tree should I plan on buying for my home?

 That's a matter of need and budget. For example, if you have a mature landscape that's crying for one tree that will fit in and look like it's been there for years, you may want to buy a larger plant than you would, say, for a brand new landscape where all of the plants were just getting started. Ideally, however, a shade tree should probably be between 1 and 5 inches in trunk diameter at ground line. That would make it large enough to show up and small enough that it should be comparatively easy or inexpensive to transport and transplant.

74

What are the advantages and drawbacks of container-grown trees versus those that have been dug?

Container-grown trees have all of their roots intact, but they're only available in smaller sizes (1 to 2 inches in trunk diameter). Balled-and-burlapped trees are more mature looking, although they'll suffer more setback after they've been moved. Container trees can be planted at any season, as can balled-and-burlapped trees, so long as they were dug during the cold, dormant season. Finally, you may only be able to get the native tree you want as a dug specimen. You'll rarely see clump-form live and red oaks, for example, in containers. They've been dug off hillsides and brought to your nursery. Cedar elms and yaupon holly trees are almost never grown in containers, although you'll occasionally find them dug and then planted into large pots or tubs.

75

 How can I tell if a tree is healthy and vigorous when I buy it?

Look for supple twigs and a normal quantity of leaves during the growing season. Balled-and-burlapped plants should have at least two-thirds their normal number of leaves, and they should be at least two-thirds their normal size. Anything less indicates the tree is suffering excessive transplant shock. Scratch the bark to see if it's green (and moist!). Above all, know your nurseryman, and ask plenty of questions while you're shopping.

76

Should I buy the guarantee with my new shade tree?

That's a coin toss. Most nurserymen will guarantee a large tree only if their crews plant it for you. If you're careful in picking the tree, and if you're sure it's healthy and vigorous when you buy it, it should transplant quite well. It is best if it has been held at the nursery for several months. Your nurseryman calls that "curing," and it gives the tree time to regrow its roots and shed its leaves if it's going to. The guarantee is only as good as your nurseryman. The guarantee will also need to be valid for at least one year, because most shade trees don't die the first few months after they've been transplanted. If the tree was hurt too badly during the digging, the damage usually shows up when it finally gets hot and dry in July and August.

77

What tips will help me get my tree home safely?

Never carry any tree by its trunk. Always lift it by its soil ball. If more than one person is required to lift the tree, cradle it in a large piece of burlap or some other soft sling. Cushion its trunk so it won't rub against the back of a pickup or trailer or on the inside of your trunk lid. Above all, wrap the leaf canopy with an old sheet, discarded nursery shade fabric or some other means of breaking the wind. Just one mile at 30 miles per hour can ruin a tree's leaves. Plant it as soon as you can after you get it home, and be sure it's heavily watered immediately after planting.

78

 I'd like to replace a poor-quality tree that was in our land-scape when we bought our house with a better shade tree, but I hate to give up the shade for those several years. Can I leave the old tree in place until my new tree takes hold? I could cut it down once the new tree is growing quickly.

Bad idea! Remove the old tree before you ever plant your new tree. Invariably, new trees grow contorted and misshapen when they're planted near established trees. Plus, it's difficult to drop an old tree without damaging the new tree growing near it.

SPECIFIC TREE RECOMMENDATIONS

☆79☆

 What is a good fast-growing shade tree? I need shade in a hurry.

 Those terms are mutually exclusive. Fast-growing trees are known for their very short life expectancies and all the asso-ciated problems. Avoid trees such as silver maples, fruitless mulber-ries, sycamores, cottonwoods, willows, catalpas, Arizona ash, mimosas, boxelders and Siberian elms, just because they are so very prone to insects, diseases and other environmental problems. Stick with long-term winners. Given a suitable planting site and good care, trees like oaks, cedar elms, pecans, Chinese pistachios, sweet gums, magnolias, bald cypress and others will grow two-thirds as fast as the others, but they'll live 10 times as long.

80

We need to screen a county road and would like to use trees. What are the best evergreen types for that purpose?

Live oaks, magnolias, including Little Gem, cherry laurels (East Texas primarily), ligustrums (South and Central Texas primarily) and tree-form hollies. You could also use ornamental pears. Although they're deciduous, they do hold their leaves from late winter well into early the next winter. Total down time: probably only 10 weeks or so annually.

Q What tree can you recommend for a wet part of our landscape?

A Best in waterlogged soils would be bald cypress, water oaks or willow oaks. However, unless the soil is almost standing in water days after a heavy rain, almost any tree would do well. If you want to test to see how high the water table is, dig a "post" hole, then cover it to keep anyone from stepping in it. Check each day after a rainstorm, just to see whether water is being retained beneath the soil line for more than 24 to 48 hours, and, if so, at what depth. Gardeners in South and East Texas, where water tables traditionally are higher, may want to plant their new trees "high," that is, 1 or 2 inches higher than they had been growing in the nursery. Save that for extreme cases, however.

☆82☆

Q What are the best small trees for a zero-lot-line landscape?

A There are many small trees or tree-form large shrubs that could be used. Best among them for wide areas of Texas: crape myrtle, yaupon holly, possumhaw holly, ligustrums, cherry laurel, Texas mountain laurel, wax myrtle, smoke tree, ornamental plums, peaches, pears and apples, Mexican plum, golden raintree, redbuds, Lacey oak, dogwoods and Japanese maples.

83

Q What types of trees are least likely to plug my sewer lines with their roots?

A Modern sewer lines don't have the joints that old tile lines had. As a result, it's not very likely that any tree's roots will invade your sewer. That changes, of course, if you're in the country, with lateral lines running out from a septic system. In those situations, you should probably choose a slow- or moderate-growing tree and plant it 15 feet or farther away from the lateral lines. They should be deep enough that the roots won't invade anyway.

☆84☆

 What trees have the best fall color?

 Unfortunately, Texas isn't known for its great fall foliage. Several of our plants, however, do color up fairly reliably. Ask your local nurseryman for specific recommendations, but start with Chinese pistachio, sweet gum, ornamental pears, Chinese tallow, red oak, ginkgo, maples, sumac, persimmon and crape myrtles.

85

I'd like to plant a living Christmas tree. Which types are best? How do I care for it as I take it outdoors after Christmas?

The exact types will vary with different parts of Texas, but the list includes Leyland cypress, eastern redcedar, Arizona cypress, Eldarica pine (for Central and West Texas) or Virginia pine (for East Texas), and deodar cedar in South and Central Texas. Keep your tree indoors no longer than is absolutely essential, preferably not more than 10 or 12 days. Set it into the landscape on a day when temperatures will be moderate. Remember that it has grown accustomed to warm, indoor conditions during its stay inside your house.

86

 I have a little Alberta spruce that I bought as a Christmas tree. How do I care for it after Christmas?

That tree isn't happy with our hot summer temperatures, so it's likely to start pouting once it climbs over 85 degrees. Leave it in its pot, and shuttle it into full sun during spring and fall, and morning sun with afternoon shade during the summer.

PLANTING A NEW TREE
....

87

Q How deeply should I plant my new tree?

A You'll see a spot on the trunk where the old soil line was in the nursery. The tree should be planted so that that line is at exactly that same spot. Planting a tree slightly higher than it grew in the nursery will help in really poorly drained soils, but it can also lead to surface root problems, and the tree may have a hard time getting water in dry spells. Deep planting risks root rot and death of the tree.

88

Q Should I try to remove the burlap when I plant my new tree?

A If it's truly just burlap you should leave it in place. You don't want to take the chance that you might loosen the soil around the roots. The burlap will quickly rot and allow root growth into the adjacent soils. If there is any type of plasticized material involved, however, you should cut slits through it or remove it from the sides of the soil ball. The one thing you do want to do, however, is to cut any twine or wire that is wrapped around the tree's trunk so it won't girdle the tree years later.

89

Q Should I put any fertilizer in the hole when I plant the tree?

A No, but you can use a liquid root-stimulator fertilizer immediately after you get the tree planted, and monthly for the first growing season—if it was balled-and-burlapped or bare-rooted.

90

 Do I need to prune my new balled-and-burlapped trees?

 Yes, to compensate for roots that were lost as they were dug and planted. Generally, you'll want to remove 30 to 40 percent of the top growth, either by cutting the trees back, or by thinning them out. Remove the limbs that have the least to do with the mature shape you want the tree to develop. For the record, bare-rooted trees should be pruned back by 50 percent at planting.

91

 Do I need to stake my new tree?

Probably. Since you'll want its trunk to be perfectly vertical, you should stake it. If you use cables or wires, protect the tree trunk by running them through pieces of old garden hose. Be certain one of your cables is due south, to hold the tree against the prevailing summer breezes. One would then be northeast, the other northwest. Be sure they're tight so the tree can't whip in the wind, but don't let them girdle the limbs or the main trunk. Wooden stakes can also be driven alongside the trunks of smaller trees to hold them upright, but be careful that you don't damage major roots in the process.

92

Should I make a basin to hold water for my new tree?

Usually it's a good idea, unless the tree is in a low, boggy area. It's also not wise if you live along the Gulf Coast, or anywhere else where the water table is quite high in the soil much of the year. You'll want to eliminate the basin after the first year or two.

93

 How important is it that I wrap the trunks of my new trees?

 It is very important for some trees. Shumard red oaks, for example, will almost never develop borers and other trunk problems unless they are exposed to extreme sun the first year or two after they have been transplanted. Because they have no bark at that point, and because they've been protected from the sun while they were growing in the nursery, they're highly vulnerable to problems. Use the paper tree wraps you can find in garden centers, and wrap them from the ground up to the lowest limbs. Remove the wrap after a couple of years, that is, once the tree's canopy shades its trunk sufficiently. Most shade trees will benefit from this wrapping. It can also help ward off rodents and the damage they do to the trunks during the winter.

CARE OF NEW TREES
• •

94

 My new shade tree has browned leaves. What did I do wrong?

There are several possibilities. It would help to know how long you have had it. If it's a brand new tree, you probably didn't protect it from the highway winds as you took it home. Even one mile at 30 miles per hour can ruin foliage. In that case, the tree will usually come back. If you let it get too dry after you planted it, however, you're just going to have to wait and see. Sometimes foliage can be singed by strong, warm winds in the spring, while the leaves are still new and succulent. Of course, it's also possible that a tree that has been dug with some loss of roots in the process could be suffering transplant shock. If that's the case, contact your nurseryman.

95

Q I think I overwatered my new shade tree. It grew very well until August, then suddenly it lost all its leaves. It's about 12 feet tall and has a 3-inch diameter trunk. It was balled-and-burlapped when it was planted last spring. What should I do now?

A If you think about what this tree went through earlier in the year, losing probably 90 percent of its important feeder roots in the transplanting, then encountering three months of scorching Texas summertime, you'd realize it just ran out of gas. It would be quite difficult to overwater any tree in August. Many folks blame themselves for this exact situation, when, in reality, it's just the transplant shock taking its final toll. If you have a guarantee, you should consider talking with your nurseryman.

96

Q We have discovered that our new tree has sunk in its planting hole. It's now 4 inches lower than the surrounding soil. Must we replant it? What will happen if we don't? If we have to, how urgent is it? In other words, can we wait until winter to do it?

A Reset it, if you don't it will be stunted, eventually dying. Its roots will be too deep in the soil to function normally. Do it anytime, except during the hottest part of the summer. Hold its original soil ball together carefully in the process.

☆97☆

Q The bark on my new tree is splitting vertically and the inner tissues seem to be exposed. What causes that? How can I stop it?

A That's usually from sunscald. If it's on the south, east or west sides where the sun is most intense, that's probably the problem. Trees that had been shading one another are suddenly sold and planted alone, generally in full hot sun. Most of the sunscald occurs in winter and early spring, when nights are cold. The early morning sun changes the trunk temperatures very quickly, causing the splitting. Trim away any of the dead wood and seal the wound with a small amount of black pruning sealant. You should always use paper tree wrap for the first year or two if there is any chance of trunk damage from cold or sun.

CARE OF ESTABLISHED TREES
....

(See also chapter 1 for general information on pruning as it relates to trees.)

☆98☆

Q Our yardman cut through the bark of one of our shade trees with the line trimmer. What can we do to save the tree?

A There is probably nothing that you need to do specifically. The tissue that lies just inside the bark is called the phloem, and that's where the manufactured sugars are conducted from the leaves down to the roots. When you cut through the phloem layer, the supply line is closed and the roots will die. That's why this kind of damage is so severe to our important shade trees. Unfortunately, pruning paint and all the other heroic measures you might attempt won't help a bit. Just wait it out and see what happens. Don't apply any high-nitrogen fertilizers around the tree for a season or two. You might also want to invest in some of the hard rubber tree guards that snap in place to protect the trees when you use a trimmer.

99

 Q How good are fertilizer spikes?

A Spikes have the same problem that the old way of punching holes in the ground and inserting fertilizer had: They aren't uniform. They certainly do deliver the fertilizer, and they're easy enough to install. However, they concentrate all of their food in one little area. Surface feedings followed by heavy waterings are probably better in the long run.

100

Q Are the root-watering rods any good?

A They can be wonderful, but you must not stick them full-length into the soil. Any type of tree in any type of soil has 90 percent of its roots in the top foot of soil. If you insert the rods farther than 6 to 8 inches you're going to miss all those important "feeder" roots.

☆101☆

Q My trees are dropping lots of their leaves prematurely this summer. What could be causing that? They're turning yellow before they drop.

A Generally that's a symptom of moisture stress, and usually it's because the leaves haven't gotten the water they need. It can be from dry soils, of course, but it can also be caused by damage to the roots or trunk. It's a very common problem with large-leafed, fast-growing trees such as sycamores, fruitless mulberries, cottonwoods, silver maples, catalpas and varnish trees, among others. Those trees put out large numbers of leaves in cool, moist spring weather, only to run into the "wall" of heat by mid-July. Let the hose run slowly beneath them to supplement the water you give your turf, but be prepared to see a certain amount of the leaf drop anyway.

102

Q I have a tree that has been leaning at an angle for several years. Can I use a cable to pull it back to vertical? How long will I need to leave it staked before I can remove the cable?

A The tree will always go back to its angled habit of growth after the cable is removed, even if you wait for several years before you take it away. The only way you can get your tree back into a vertical plane is to dig and replant it, but this does enough damage to an established tree that you may want to think twice about it.

103

Q We have just discovered that our shade tree has a wire wrapped around its trunk near the ground, probably from an old nursery tag. Now the base of the tree is swollen above the wire, and we can't get the wire out. The tree seems weaker than before. What can we do to help?

A The wire, no matter how fine, has girdled the internal tissues of the trunk, cutting off the movement of manufactured sugars down to the roots through the phloem cells. Until you cut through the wire and allow the phloem to regrow, there will be no way that the tree can survive. If you can make a few cuts straight into the trunk and pull as much of the wire as possible out of the wound, that could very likely help.

GENERAL TREE QUESTIONS

☆104☆

Q I've seen ads in the Sunday papers for fast-growing trees of various types. They always seem too good to be true. Is that a correct assumption?

A Yes. Most times the ads don't even give you scientific names so that you can see that they're talking about some type of cottonwood or willow. All they do is assign a catchy trademarked name to the tree and show you testimonials and unbelievable photos of one year's growth. Stick with proven, quality trees from your local nursery.

☆105☆

Q Several of our trees have mistletoe. How can we eliminate it? What types of trees are most prone to mistletoe?

A To a gardener, there is nothing romantic about mistletoe. Mistletoe is a parasitic plant that actually produces its rooting structures into the limbs of its host trees. There are no effective and "safe" chemical sprays as yet, but you can prune it out before it gets really large. Usually it will start on comparatively small twigs. If you clip it out of the tree at that point it won't get large enough to fruit and reproduce. Use a long-handled pole pruner. Once it's well established, however, you may have to saw out entire limbs, or else console yourself simply to make shallow scalloped cuts to get the worst of it off the tops of the limbs. The sticky seeds are spread by birds onto new limbs. Prime hosts: cedar elms, hackberries and, less commonly, oaks, among others.

106

Q I want to transplant some shrubs and trees to make room for a new driveway. When should I do it, and how can I make sure they survive the move?

A It's always best to transplant woody plants while they're dormant, that being during the winter. You should probably root-prune them with a sharpshooter spade several months before you dig them. Slice through the lateral roots at a point where you'll be making the eventual cut, but don't attempt to sever the tap root. By cutting the lateral roots you'll encourage new root growth within the eventual soil ball. Remember always to prune plants back by 30 to 40 percent after you dig and move them. You can do that either by removing some of their tallest branches, or by thinning them out, or both.

☆107☆

 We have a large tree stump in our front yard. How can we remove it?

 Hire an arborist with a stump grinder. Those machines can fit into even tiny areas. In 20 or 30 minutes they can grind out even a large tree stump. All you have to do then is rake up the shavings, fill the cavity with soil and go on about gardening. If you prefer to do the hard work yourself, cut all the lateral roots with a saw or ax, then hoist the stump with a car jack. The products that claim to dissolve stumps really aren't all that great.

108

 Lightning hit our large tree. How can we tell how much damage it did?

There isn't a good answer for that, because all lightning strikes vary. If it splintered the trunk the tree is obviously badly hurt, but if it just knocked the bark off one side it very likely could recover. You probably should contact a veteran arborist for an on-site consultation. You could also take photos to a Certified Nursery Professional. You can clean up the minor damage by using a utility knife, chisel or pruning knife to cut away all the jagged bark, but cut none that is still firmly attached. Be careful when propping your ladder against a trunk or limb that has been damaged by lightning. It may not support your weight.

109

We have a large tree that suffered damage during a windstorm. The trunk seems to have split, although both main branches are still in place. How can we repair it? Do we wrap something around the trunk, or will that harm it further? Where do we turn?

First be very cautious. The tree has been weakened, and it could split further at any time. You may want to quickly call for the help of an arborist. However, many splits can be handled by home gardeners. You need to secure the trunk temporarily by banding or clamping it tightly together with a padded strap of some sort. Then drill completely through the trunk's split at right angles to the split. Use a comparatively large diameter bit for a large limb. Install all-thread rod through the new hole and put large washers and nuts on each end, then cut the all-thread rod to length. You may want to drill two or three more holes—depending on the size of the trunk and the magnitude of the split. It probably would help to cable the main branches farther up in the tree.

110

 What is the large-leafed tree with the unusual green trunks?

That's varnish tree (*Firmiana simplex*). Lots of folks use it to create a tropical look to their landscapes, although it has many of the same problems as other large-leafed, fast-growing types.

111

I have a tree that has shiny leaves and fruit that look like olives. Do you have any idea what it might be?

You probably have a jujube (*Ziziphus jujuba*). The fruits are about an inch long, green, then tan and brown. They have the consistency of a mealy apple. Two even more identifying features, however: The leaves have parallel veins (running from end-to-end, not side-to-side—almost all other trees have pinnate, or feather-like, vein arrangement), and the limbs have an unusual zigzag growth pattern.

Pruning

112

We have a tree with several limbs that all converge at the same point. They trap water for days after a rain. Should we try to get the water out of the well, or should we fill it with concrete?

Clean it out to see if the wood is still sound. If it is, leave it alone. If one or more of the branches is expendable, and if removing it would allow the water to drain, take it off. Most trees' bark is able to repel water, and it's generally best to do nothing. You might want to have an arborist look at it, however.

113

 We have a cavity in our tree's trunk. Should we fill it? What should we use?

Mortar mix poured into a cavity gives the tree's bark something over which it can cover. However, the mortar adds no strength to the trunk. You should remove all the rotted debris and soft wood, then allow the area to dry for a few days before you pour the mortar in. Trowel it smoothly across the opening, then let the roll of new bark form over it.

114

We have a large tree with limbs that look like they could break in an ice storm. Someone told us to cable them. How do we do that?

You can brace one tree limb against another one on the other side of the tree's center line by installing a heavy cable between the two. You probably should hire a professional to see that the job is done right. The basics, however, are that you would pull the two limbs slightly together with a "come-along" winch. Pad the limbs so the winch doesn't damage their bark. Drill completely through the limbs at least 8 or 10 feet up from their juncture with a long bit in exactly the path the cable will be following. Use all-thread eye bolts and cable clamps (not turnbuckles) to secure the cable. Make it taut, then release the pressure on the winch. You may need more than one cable for very large limbs. Securing the tree in this way allows it all to move as a unit when the wind or ice moves in.

☆115☆

Our tree has large surface roots that are beginning to ruin our driveway and patio. Can they be removed without killing the tree?

Absolutely. You can take one or two roots off each year, preferably totaling not more than 20 percent of the trunk diameter at ground line. Do it in October, so the tree will have the maximum possible time to regrow roots before the following summer's heat. You may also want to trench between the trunk and your concrete, so you can install some type of barricade to stop further root growth there.

116

Q My tree has roots that have become hazards on top of the ground. Can I put soil over them?

A That just won't work. In most cases the trees' roots have actually grown thicker in diameter and have worked their way up and out of the soil. Adding more soil would only buy a little time before you had the problem again. It's better to remove any that are terribly dangerous, then ignore the rest. You could also plant a vining or tall clumping groundcover over them, just to conceal them.

MOST COMMON QUESTIONS ABOUT SPECIFIC TREES

Ashes (*Fraxinus* sp.)

117

Q My Arizona ash tree is thin and appears very weak. What causes that, and can it be saved?

A Borers are the most common threat to Arizona ashes, especially young trees. They'll tunnel through the trunk leaving rather large holes filled with wood pulp. Look closely for signs of their presence. You may be able to insert a flexible wire into the tunnels to eradicate existing worms. Spraying with a borer preventive at 6-week intervals during the summer will help prevent additional invasion. Arizona ashes are also vulnerable to late freezes in the spring. Once they begin to leaf out and grow in early spring they seem to be severely harmed by temperatures in the 20s.

Bald Cypress (*Taxodium distichum*)

118

 My bald cypress tree is constantly yellow. What can I do to correct it?

That's probably iron deficiency. You can use any of the traditional iron and sulfur soil amendments to supply iron and to reduce the alkalinity of your soil. Those steps should help keep the iron "available," but it's going to take a great deal of iron, and you're going to have to add it often. You might also have iron injected directly into the trunk, bypassing the soil and the roots entirely. Bald cypress trees should probably not be grown where soils are shallow and highly alkaline.

119

My bald cypress is turning tan from the base of the tree upward. What should I look for?

That's probably spider mite damage. Cut a twig and thump it over a sheet of pure white paper. If you see small specks start to move, those are the spider mites. Kelthane will control them. Fortunately, they don't show up very often.

Boxelder (*Acer negundo*)

120

What are the black and red insects that are all over my boxelder trees? How can I control them?

Appropriately, they're boxelder bugs. Along with squash bugs and stink bugs, they're identifiable by their shield-shaped backs. This entire group of insects, classed by entomologists as true "bugs," is difficult to control. There are insecticides that are labeled for them, but, unless it's an important part of your landscape, it may be easier simply to remove the boxelder tree. For the record, they do no damage to the trees. There simply are so many of them that they become a nuisance.

Cottonwoods and Poplars (*Populus* sp.)

121

Q My silver poplar has hundreds of sprouts coming up all over our yard. I've mowed them off, but now they're like stubble. How can I eliminate them once and for all?

A You can't. That's the way every one of these cottonwood relatives behaves. The sprouts are part of the original tree, so you can't use a weedkiller. For the record, lots of folks refer to this as "silver maple," but it's easily distinguished by its smaller, very deep green leaves with bright silvery undersides. Silver maples have light green, large leaves with no silver reverse.

122

Q I see large holes in the trunk of my cottonwood tree, but I've seen no insects in them. There is sawdust coming out of the holes. What threat does that pose to the tree?

A It's a very great threat. That's damage of cottonwood borers, nemesis of willows as well. They're the larval form of the large black and white beetle with long antennae extending over its back. You might use a borer-preventive spray at 6-week intervals in the growing season, but that's a lot of work for unpredictable results. If you ever notice a mature cottonwood that is really sparse and lethargic, that's probably the accumulated damage of this insect pest. Trees like that need to be removed before they fall and damage property or hurt people or pets.

123

Q My cottonwood tree loses lots of leaves by mid-summer every year. Is it just the heat, or is there a problem?

 A This is a problem of many large-leafed, fast-growing shade trees, but cottonwoods rank at the top of the list. It is caused by heat and low humidities combined with a lack of rainfall. The tree puts all that new growth on during the cool, moist days of spring. The "wall" of summer heat is quite a surprise to the tree, and that's when the leaf drop begins. Keep the tree moist and the rake handy.

Crabapples (*Malus* sp.)

124

 Our crabapple trees have spots all over their leaves. What disease is it?

Cedar apple rust. Crabapples are one of the two hosts for the fungus, the other being eastern redcedars (junipers). Fungicides applied during the spring may help, but you may eventually just want to switch out to some other type of small tree. If there are native redcedars in your area, you'll end up spraying several times every year.

125

 Our crabapple tree died suddenly. The whole tree died at once. What was the problem?

Usually cotton root rot. The soil-borne fungus has no more favorite host than apples and their kin. Avoid susceptible species when you replant, and stay away from crabapples in your area in the future.

Crape Myrtles (*Lagerstroemia indica*)
(Note: See also chapter 4, Shrubs.)

126

 How can I train my crape myrtle shrub into tree form? Are the trees and shrubs different types?

All crape myrtles are genetically shrubs. Let the plant grow tall enough to establish its normal trunk and branch patterns, usually 6 to 8 feet tall. At that point you can select the several trunks you want to save and remove all the side branches near the ground.

Dogwoods (*Cornus florida*)

127

Q I want to grow dogwoods. What kind of location do they require, and how do I prepare their soil?

A Dogwoods grow best with morning sun and afternoon shade, although they'll tolerate full sun where the soils are perfect (i.e., East Texas). They require an acidic soil, similar to what you would provide for azaleas. You'll need a good bit of it, too, since their root systems will spread 10 feet in each direction.

Elms (*Ulmus* sp.)

128

Q Is the Dutch elm disease a problem for our Texas trees?

A No. The disease hasn't spread this far south, and doesn't appear likely to do so. The insect that is responsible for spreading the disease is not active in Texas, at this time.

129

Q What causes my Chinese elm's leaves to look like lace by mid-summer? The tree is entirely brown when it happens.

A That's the damage of the larvae of elm leaf beetles. If you look closely, you'll see small green worms with brown stripes running front-to-back. Control them with any general-purpose insecticide applied with a power sprayer as soon as you see the damage. You may have to spray two or three times during the season. For the record, you probably have Siberian elms (*Ulmus pumila*), not the true Chinese elms (*U. parvifolia*), which are, by far, the better trees.

130

Q Our cedar elm turns rusty brown in the summer each year. Why?

A If you look closely at the backs of the leaves when you first see this happen, you'll normally see a dusting of powdery mildew fungus. The bottoms of the leaves will take on almost a silvery appearance. Next step: the russeting of the tops of the leaves. To control the problem, apply a fungicide labeled for powdery mildew. The problem isn't life-threatening, however, and you may decide it's too much trouble to try to spray for it. It's primarily cosmetic.

Evergreens (cone-bearing types)

131

Q My evergreens have taken on a pale appearance. I can't see any insects, but the plants seem to be dying from the ground up.

A Several types of evergreens have problems with spider mites. They'll cause the plants to lose their normal green color, often fading to an olive drab, then tan and brown. Thump an affected twig over white paper. If you see very tiny pests start to move, those are probably the mites. Kelthane will help. Potential victims: junipers, bald cypress, leyland cypress, Italian cypress and arborvitae, among others.

Hackberries (*Celtis laevigata*)

132

Q Our hackberry tree has warts all over its leaves. What will stop them?

A That's a particular type of gall that's common only to hackberries. There is no chemical, biological or mechanical control for it. Just ignore them. They are harmless.

Hollies (Tree-form) (*Ilex* sp.)

133

Q How can I make a yaupon holly into a tree? Mine is nothing more than a big shrub.

A All yaupons are, genetically, shrubs. Nurserymen started training them as small trees in the 1950s. Now they're some of our finest small trees for compressed urban sites. Determine which trunks will be the structural framework of your new tree and remove the others. Prune slowly and carefully, one limb at a time. Don't prune the canopy up too high. It's difficult to get new side branches to develop once their predecessors have been removed.

134

Q How can I get rid of the sprouts that come up around my yaupon holly tree? They're a foot or two away from the trunk. Are they seedlings?

A Those are most likely sprouts from the root system. Live oaks and crape myrtles also do that. You'll have to remove them by hand. Chemical sprays would kill the mother tree. You might try putting a barricade of one of the landscape fabrics around the tree, much like a Christmas tree skirt, then covering it with bark mulch or letting a vining groundcover grow across it.

Magnolias (*Magnolia* sp.)

135

Q Our saucer magnolia never finishes blooming. Late freezes always catch it in flower. Is there anything that would slow it down?

A Many folks refer incorrectly to that plant as being a "tulip tree" because its pink or near-white blooms resemble that popular flower. It's actually a deciduous magnolia, suited primarily to the northern half of the state. Unfortunately, it has a very low chilling requirement (not unlike apricots, for example). Once it's had enough cold weather its flower buds will start to open. That usually happens in February along the Red River and in March in the Panhandle. Unfortunately, there's still lots of chance of frost at those times. Learn to enjoy it when it does bloom and don't fret the rest.

136

Q Why do the flowers on my big southern magnolia tree turn brown so quickly?

A Magnolia flowers only last a couple of days, at which time they take on a dusty brown color and shatter to the ground. That's normal. Since they bloom in May, early hot weather can speed up their decline. You will also find thrips on their petals. These very small sliver-like pests rasp at the petals causing premature drop. However, because the trees are so large and the flowers so short-lived, it would be hard to justify spraying for thrips.

137

Q Why are the leaves on my magnolias so ugly every February?

A Those leaves have been on the tree for an entire growing season, also during cold winter weather. That kind of scorch and browning is to be expected.

138

Q Why does my magnolia drop so many leaves in May every year?

 A Like all evergreen plants, magnolias eventually have to release their old leaves. That's normal, particularly if there is also abundant new growth at the ends of the branches. You'll even see leaf drop at other times. Keep the tree well watered to lessen the problem.

139

Why are the leaves of my magnolia cupped downward? It also isn't growing properly.

That usually points to some type of weedkiller damage, most likely from a granular weed-and-feed product. Think back to what has been applied in the past, especially 4 to 6 weeks prior to your first noticing the cupping. Keep the tree moist. Otherwise, there is no antidote that you could add to the soil.

Maples (*Acer* sp.)

140

My Japanese maples lose lots of their red color, and their leaves are browned around the edges by mid-summer every year. What is wrong?

It sounds like they're getting too much sunlight or that you've let them get too dry. Japanese maples need sun no later than mid-morning during the summer, and bright shade after that. The reddish-purple color of new spring growth fades to reddish-green by the first hot days of the summer. Keep them moist and well mulched.

141

My silver maple is yellowish, and it loses so many leaves by mid-summer. What can I do?

Silver maples, by their nature, have lighter green leaves. If they're in alkaline soils they can also show severe iron deficiency. Because they're fast-growing, large-leafed trees, they also will drop as much as one-third of their foliage by late June in hot, dry years.

142

What makes the tiny holes in the trunk of my silver maple? They're scattered all over the trunk.

Red-headed wood borers seem to like silver maples a great deal. They look like yellow jackets with burgundy heads. They're about two-thirds the size of yellow jackets. Control them with a borer preventive spray at 6-week intervals during the growing season, most especially when you see the adults flying near the tree.

143

 My silver maple has root sprouts coming up all over the yard. What can I do to stop it?

That's probably not silver maple, but silver *poplar* instead. Silver maples have medium-green leaves with green backs. Silver poplars have dark-green leaves with white backs. You'll find your answer with the questions on cottonwoods.

Mimosas (*Albizia julibrissin*)

144

Why are the leaves of my mimosa tree all matted together?

That's damage of the mimosa webworm. Control them as they begin to feed with an appropriate insecticide, either contact or systemic. They won't kill the tree, but they can make it look terrible for several months each late summer and fall.

145

 My mimosa tree has mushrooms growing around its base. The tree doesn't appear healthy. What is the problem?

By the time they're 20 or 25 years old, mimosas become quite susceptible to mimosa wilt and mushroom root rot. Both are fatal, and neither can be prevented by actions on the part of the gardener.

146

Q I don't like the looks of the brown seed pods on my mimosas. A neighbor told me that topping the tree would prevent that problem. Is that correct?

A Topping is a terrible act. If a mimosa has seed pods, that means that it also had flowers. If you aren't willing to let the tree flower, why would you want the mimosa in the first place? Don't ruin its best attribute and its natural shape by cutting it back each winter.

Mulberries (*Morus* sp.)

147

Q Is there any way to keep a mulberry from fruiting? We have red stains all over our patio every spring, plus the flies are everywhere!

A You can't change it. Fruitless mulberries are a different type, selected and propagated for their non-fruiting nature. For the record, the fruiting types are probably superior trees with better growth habit and longer life spans. If you can clean up after them those few messy days each year, they can be good neighbors.

Oaks (*Quercus* sp.)

148

Q We have new red oak and live oak trees and wonder: How soon should we start removing the lower limbs to help them develop their trunks?

A As with pecans, oaks' trunks will thicken and grow stronger more quickly if they have limbs close to the ground. That doesn't mean that you should allow them to grow long and rangy, but you should at least leave them in place until the tree gains some height. For example, when the tree is 10 feet tall you'll probably have no limbs below 4 feet, and, by the time it's 20 feet tall, you probably will have removed the lowest limbs up to the final heights of 5 to 6 feet. If in doubt, however, leave the limb in place. You can never get the tree to regrow it later.

149

Q I have a red oak that is constantly yellow. We have rocky soil that tests alkaline. Is that iron deficiency? Why do native red oaks in our neighborhood look dark green?

A The native oaks you're seeing are probably Shumard red oaks (*Quercus shumardii*). It grows all through the central portions of Texas where soils are just as you described. Southern red oak (*Q. falcata*) is native to East Texas and may be sold farther west at times, but the real culprit has been pin oak (*Q. palustris*). It's native in the Northeast, and it's poorly adapted to alkaline soils. It is sometimes dug and transported into Texas from adjoining states, and, unfortunately, it looks very similar to Shumard red oaks, so it's hard for consumers to be sure they're getting what they expect. Limbs on pin oaks hang downward, much like a Christmas tree, while those of Shumard red oaks ascend. For the record, willow oak and water oak, two other common East Texas natives, are also very poor candidates for areas of alkaline soils, again because of iron deficiencies.

150

Q I am originally from the North, and the pin oaks we had there aren't the same as the ones I see here in Texas. What is the difference between these two plants with the same name?

A Texans, especially in East Texas, refer to the true water oaks (*Quercus nigra*) as "pin" oaks. The true pin oak (*Q. palustris*) has leaves that look like a red oak's leaves, while water oaks have smaller tapered and elongated leaves with three rounded lobes.

☆151☆

 What are the growths that are on my oaks?

 Dozens of types of insect galls are common on Texas oaks. Live oaks have woolly oak galls that look like pea-sized tufts of tan fuzz on the backs of the leaves. They also have woody oak galls that cause marble-sized dark brown woody balls to form on the small twigs. You'll see the very large "apple" galls on red oak leaves, and others will occur from time to time. The important thing to remember with galls is that they do no major damage, and there is no way to control them. Move on with your life. Their populations will fluctuate from year to year. Next year may be better.

152

 What can I do to identify and control oak wilt?

 First, the very best way to identify oak wilt is through the Plant Disease Diagnostic Laboratory at Texas A&M. For a small charge they can culture the organism and confirm its involvement. They recommend you send 1½-inch-diameter pieces 6 to 7 inches long. Choose limbs that are in stress, but not yet dead. Send them on ice, via overnight delivery, to preserve the live organism. Contact your county Extension office for the mailing address and other specific directions and charges. Live oaks affected with oak wilt will show yellowing. Leaves will shed freely. On close inspection you'll see that the leaf veins are reddish-brown, light green between the veins. On red oaks the leaves will wilt and die, but they will not fall from the tree. This disease is spread by root grafts and by *nitidulidae* sap-feeding beetles. All pruning of established live oaks and red oaks should be done during the winter dormant season, while the beetles are inactive. Seal all cut surfaces with pruning paint to prevent their entry. You should also trench between afflicted trees and other healthy adjacent trees. The trench should be 100 feet from the dying tree, and it should be 48 inches deep. You can use a propiconazole fungicide such as Alamo so long as you treat it before the disease has affected more than 15 percent of the foliage. One treatment will be sufficient in most preventive programs. The Extension Service has additional information on the subject, as will most professional arborists.

153

Q What causes my red oak and bur oak's leaves to lose all their color? It almost looks like something has bleached out all the tissues except the veins.

A That's probably the work of sawfly larvae. They will skeletonize the entire top surface of each leaf. They work in patches, so you may see their damage scattered randomly over the entire canopy of the tree. If you decide you need to treat, a general-purpose insecticide will help, but they are not life-threatening to the tree.

154

Q My Shumard red oaks' trunks have cracks and sap flowing from them. They were planted a year ago and they seem to be going downhill. What can I do now?

A That's probably sunscald. Young red oak trunks have very little bark to protect them against sudden temperature changes. Perhaps more than any other tree we grow, Shumard red oaks will show this damage on the sunny sides of their trunks—particularly during cold and sunny winter days when the bark heats up very quickly. The solution is to wrap every new Shumard red oak's trunk with paper tree wrap up to the lowest limbs for the first year or two you have it in your landscape. At this point you'll have to use a utility knife very carefully to clean up any decayed wood along the edges of the cracks. It's possible there will be little or none to cut, in which case you'll merely need to clean the wound with turpentine, let it air-dry for a day or two, and wrap the trunk. A day or two prior to wrapping the trunk, spraying with a borer preventive would be a good idea.

155

We have native post oaks around our house. Suddenly one of them has died. Are there any diseases or insects we should be worried about?

Probably not. Post oaks are notorious for having "people problems." They simply resent human invasion into their lives. If your house is fairly new, the damage done during construction is probably the reason they died. If the house has been there for five or more years, you might analyze recent changes that might have occurred within the tree's vicinity. Be especially careful when changing the grade, cutting roots, or doing extensive planting beneath the tree. If you can rule all of those things out, it may just have been its time. It would be wise to consult a local arborist concerning the health of your remaining trees.

156

We want a clump of live oaks in our yard, but we've only been able to find really expensive ones in the nurseries. They're much larger than our budget will allow. Can we plant several together and let them develop into a clump?

That probably won't work. The clumps of trees you see in nurseries grew that way in nature, then were transplanted as a unit. When you plant new trees they're all perfect, and they all grow straight. You lose that natural twisting and gnarling you get with the old trees. Either stick with a single-trunk tree or save until you can afford the clump. Keep looking; you may find a smaller clump for less money.

157

My live oak has rows of holes in its trunk. Is it borers?

 No. It's the work of woodpecker relatives, sapsuckers. They feed on the sap flow and, essentially, do no real damage to the tree. Put some type of sticky repellent on the trunk to discourage their activity.

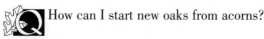

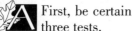 How can I start new oaks from acorns?

 First, be certain each acorn is healthy. It will need to pass three tests.
1. If it has a hole in it, discard it. That means a larval insect has eaten its embryo.
2. If it rattles, discard it. That means it has dried up.
3. If it floats, that means it's no good.

Those that pass the tests should be planted immediately into 1 gallon containers filled with well-prepared potting soil. Plant them in the fall, as soon as they hit the ground, for the best chance of germination. Next, cluster the pots together and pile shredded tree leaves around the pots to protect the plants from extreme cold.

159

 Is there any way to keep my oaks from producing acorns?

 No, but to easily pick them up use a lawn vacuum. You can rent a vacuum, or some power blowers can be reversed and attached to bags and used as vacuums.

☆160☆

My live oak has sprouts or seedlings coming up all through my groundcover. Can I stop them?

Those are probably root sprouts, and they're a real nuisance because you can't spray them. They're a part of the mother plant, and any weedkillers you might use would be carried back to it. Use a dandelion digger to remove them annually. Sorry that there's no better answer. Luckily, only a small percentage of live oaks have the genetic potential to produce the sprouts.

161

How important is it that I prune limbs within the center of my live oak?

If you're in an area that is prone to ice storms, pruning would reduce the weight of ice pulling down on the major limbs. It also gives the trees a clean, attractive look. It isn't especially critical, however, for the long-term health of the tree.

Pears, Ornamental (*Pyrus* sp.)

☆162☆

 My Bradford pear tree branches are yellowed and slow growing. Why?

Bradford pears, along with a few other varieties of these popular spring-flowering trees, have ultimately poor branch angles. You'll notice that the major limbs are clustered together like flowers in a bouquet. The problem is that they trap moisture and debris within those angles as they grow larger over the years. The unions are very weak, and the conducting tissues aren't very efficient at carrying nutrients such as iron and nitrogen. You need to train the tree to its strongest possible branch angles. Bradford pears often develop serious structural problems within 8 to 10 years, if the poor branching isn't corrected early in the trees' lives. Varieties like Aristocrat have stronger branch angles and are probably better investments.

163

What might have caused my Bradford pear to die very suddenly this summer?

 We've seen a great deal of cotton root rot damage to ornamental pears in recent years. There is no chemical control for this soil-borne fungus—other than to apply a sulfur soil acidifier. Cotton root rot is not a problem in acidic soils.

164

My young ornamental pear has black leaves from mid-summer on. They don't seem to be out where the new growth is occurring. Is this a major problem?

That's normal for young pears. Those are old leaves, the first produced in the spring, and that's just the way they turn as the trees hit summer's stressful heat. This phenomenon happens for several years while the trees are young, but they seem to outgrow it eventually. Keep it moist and it should abate.

165

My ornamental pear doesn't bloom very well. Why?

Usually, that happens to new trees that are strongly vegetative. Until the branches start to hang downward more, it seems that the hormone balance is directing increased leaf and stem growth at the expense of the flowers. Usually, by the time the tree is 3 or 4 years old, it starts blooming normally.

Pecans (*Carya illinoensis*)

166

Our pecan tree is constantly dropping limbs. They look like they've been cut off with a knife. What can we do?

That's damage caused by twig girdlers. They're fairly large insects. The female lays her eggs near the ends of the twigs, then cuts almost all the way through the limb. Several months later the dried twigs will break and fall to the ground. The developing larvae are in the twigs, so raking and removing them is the best control. There is no chemical spray that will work, since the adult is there such a short time, and since the larvae are in dead wood.

167

 Why are there "warts" all over the leaves of my pecan every spring?

 Those are pecan phylloxera galls. They crack open to release small gnat-like insects. Fortunately, they won't do serious harm to the tree, but they can disfigure many of the leaves and cause them to fall in May and early June. You can lessen their populations with dormant oil sprays applied in late winter. There is no effective control during the growing season.

168

Q I have moss growing on the trunk of my pecan tree. Is it damaging?

A In no way. Just ignore it. It's a lichen, a growth of algae and funguses living together. It does no harm to the tree. It uses the tree's trunk only as its support.

169

Q I've seen holes in rows around the trunk of my pecan. Is that borers?

A No. It's "damage" done by a sapsucker. That's a relative of woodpeckers. Its activity does not indicate any particular insect problem within the tree. It normally comes back later to feed on the sap that flows from the holes. Rarely, if ever, will you see any serious damage done to a tree by this interesting bird. You can use a sticky product such as Tree Tanglefoot to discourage its activity.

170

 What can I do to stop the sticky drip from my pecan late each summer? It coats our patio furniture and car.

 That's honeydew from pecan aphids. You can use a general-purpose insecticide labeled for aphids, but you're going to need power equipment to be able to reach to the top of the tree. It might make better sense just to park somewhere else for a few weeks and to move the patio furniture.

171

 Should I spray for the webworms in our pecan?

 Many general-purpose insecticides will control webworms. Include one or two drops of a liquid household detergent with the spray to help it penetrate into the webs. You'll need a power sprayer to reach the tops of the tree. You might find it easier to buy a pole pruner and merely nip the webs off the tips of the branches as they get started. They will not kill the tree or even the individual limbs. You'll see tent caterpillars in late spring and fall webworms in late August and September. Walnut caterpillars will do similar damage, but they won't form the webs. You'll sometimes see them *en masse* on bare branches.

172

Is it true that pecans will keep other plants from growing underneath them? Is there anything I can do to counteract that?

That's a physiological process known as allelopathy. Some plants do retard the growth of other plants nearby, although much remains to be learned about this phenomenon. To the point, it needn't be much of a problem with your pecans. If you amend the planting soil carefully prior to putting shrubs, groundcovers and flowers under the pecans, they should do fine. The amount of shade a large pecan casts is actually much more damaging to the plants underneath, unless, of course, they're shade-loving plants.

173

Our pecan tree loses big hunks of bark, but the tree still seems fine. Should we be worried?

No. It's mentioned elsewhere in the book, but bark is a dead tissue that lacks the capability of expanding as the trunk grows thicker. Unless you see some type of problem underneath it, don't worry. It's quite normal.

Pines (*Pinus* sp.)

174

Q I'm trying to grow East Texas pines west of their native habitat, but they look terrible. They're 15 years old and 25 feet tall, but they've gotten yellow and ugly. What can I do to turn them around?

A To give you the merciful, simple answer, get rid of them. What you're seeing is iron deficiency. You might be tempted to try adding an iron/sulfur-soil-acidifier material, but you'd be kidding yourself. Their roots are so extensive and the area you'd have to cover is so great that you'd probably never be able to get enough iron into the trees. You could try having iron injected directly into the trunks by an arborist. All of these, however, are only temporary solutions to a decades-old problem. They're just not suited outside of their native regions.

175

Q My pines seem to be branching more than they should. It looks like some type of worm has eaten their buds.

A That's damage of the shoot tip moth larvae. Control them with general-purpose insecticide sprays, during the spring and early summer.

176

Q Why do my pines look so bad late in the summer and into the fall? They're losing lots of needles.

A Those are usually old needles, down within the foliage. As with other evergreens, pines shed their leaves all through the growing season. It seems to be more pronounced after a hot, dry summer and just before the winter. Japanese black pines seem even more prone than others. It's not a big concern, however.

Pistachios, Chinese (*Pistacia chinensis*)

177

 My Chinese pistachio tree doesn't seem to be branching very well. It's tall and gangly. Should I cut it back?

That's fairly normal for them until they're several years old. Once they establish a strong trunk they seem to start branching out and filling in better. Usually you wouldn't want to prune it, other than to remove branches that are obviously growing out of bounds.

Plums, Purple (*Prunus* sp.)

178

My purpleleaf plum is great looking in the spring, but, by summer, it isn't very purple. Is there some fertilizer I should add?

No. That's what happens to almost all red- and purple-leafed plants when it gets bright and hot in our Texas climate. They fade to reddish-green. It is definitely not a nutritional problem. Just bear with it and it will be handsome the following spring.

179

 My purple plum blew over in a windstorm. Can I reset it vertically, and will it survive?

Purple plums are notorious for having the worst root systems of any shade tree we grow. They're shallow, weak, and the trees are quite vulnerable to wind damage. Reset and stake it if you wish, but it probably won't survive too many more years. Average life expectancy: probably less than 8 years.

180

Q My purple plum looks like something ate holes through all of its leaves. What kind of an insect causes that damage?

A In most cases it's not an insect but a disease. It's usually the result of bacterial leaf spot that hits in the spring, as the new growth is developing. Use Bordeaux mixture or other copper fungicide in early winter, just after the leaves have fallen, to stop the overwintering phase of the disease. Spraying in the growing season could cause leaf burn.

181

Q What is the waxy sap I see on the trunk down near the soil line of my purple plum and flowering peach?

A That's work of the peach tree borer. Spray with a borer preventive the last week of August to prevent its invasion. It's extremely difficult to cure an established outbreak because the worms are in their tunnels, safely behind the congealed sap. Perhaps the damage isn't too severe already.

182

Q What causes waxy sap all along the twigs of my plum and peach trees in the landscape?

A Bacterial stem canker. Spray in early November with Bordeaux mixture. If it doesn't turn around in one season, you'll probably not be able to stop its spread from within the tree.

Redbuds (*Cercis canadensis*)

183

Q What would cause my redbud to die over a period of months? It's just gotten weaker and weaker. I see small holes in the trunk.

The holes are probably from the redheaded wood borer. The adults look like small yellowjackets, with burgundy heads. Redbuds' life expectancies are usually in the 25- to 35-year range, so time alone will take its toll. The borers can be either a primary problem, or they can move in after old age drags the trees down. You can slow their spread by spraying with a borer preventive every several weeks in the summer.

Sweetgums (*Liquidambar styraciflua*)

184

 Is there any way to keep my sweetgum from making those spiny balls that litter the ground?

 Unfortunately, no. If the tree is healthy, it will flower; if it flowers, it will produce the fruit.

185

 Can sweet gums be grown in alkaline soils?

 Sweet gums are native to East Texas for a reason. Soils there are acidic, meaning the trees will be able to get as much iron as they need. Their worst problems arise in alkaline soils that are underlain by shallow caliche bedrock. Best advice: Have your soil tested to determine its pH (acidity or alkalinity), ask your local nurseryman for precise recommendations for your area, and look around to see how other sweet gums are doing.

186

My sweet gum has some kind of bad growth on its twigs. There are two rows on every branch. Is that some kind of scale?

Those are the corky wings that several of our good landscape plants happen to have. It's a normal part of the bark growth.

It's absolutely natural for sweet gums, burning bush (or "winged") euonymus, winged elms and others.

Sycamores (*Platanus occidentalis*)

187

Q Big limbs in my sycamore tree began suddenly dying in the summer. Can I save the tree?

A That's almost assuredly anthracnose. It's been a curse of sycamores for decades. Affected leaves turn copper, then brown in irregular patterns, then hang on the limbs for weeks. You need to prune it out of the tree, so it won't spread through the conducting tissues. Disinfect your pruning tools between cuts with a 10-percent solution of chlorine bleach. Spray as the leaves are about half their normal size in the spring with Bordeaux mixture or a comparable fungicide.

188

Q My sycamore's leaves have turned straw color. Help!

A Look closely at the backs of the leaves. You'll probably find small black waxy balls, proof that lace bugs have visited the plant. They won't kill the tree, and you won't be able to get those leaves to green back up again. In future years, however, you can protect the tree by spraying with a general-purpose insecticide just as the tan discoloration starts to appear.

Willows (*Salix* sp.)

189

Q Our weeping willow appears to be slowly dying. I can see no visible insects, but there are holes in the trunk with sawdust pouring out of them. Is that borers? What can I use to stop them?

A That's damage of cottonwood borers, to be specific. Unfortunately, they're very large beetles (black and white, with long antennae over their backs) that move through the neighborhood. There isn't much hope of controlling the adults. You can use a borer preventive spray to stop the entry of as many of the larvae as possible, but you're fighting a tough battle. Cottonwood borers probably account for the death of 90 percent of all types of willow trees, usually within 5 to 10 years of infestation.

SHRUBS

PLANTING SHRUBS ....

190

Q What time of year is best to plant shrubs?

A You can plant container-grown shrubs at any season, although cold-sensitive types should be set out in the spring, so they can establish themselves over the entire growing season. If you plant shrubs in the summer you'll need to be vigilant about watering them. The soil in their original root balls will dry out much more quickly than adjacent soils, so normal sprinkler irrigation won't be adequate.

191

Q How important is it that shrubs be planted into dedicated beds?

A It's really helpful in their care and management. You can amend the soils exactly as needed. The defined beds will showcase the shrubs—plus you'll be able to sculpt naturally curved lines to your design, rather than simply planting into long rows.

192

Q How much peat moss and compost do I need to add to the soil in my shrubs beds, as I'm getting ready to plant them?

A That depends on the types of plants you're going to be using. Azaleas, for example, will need much more peat moss and compost than hollies or nandinas. It helps to know what kind of plants will go where, prior to working the ground. If you're going to use annual flowers or groundcovers in front of your shrubs, you may want to save part of the soil amendments for that part of the bed.

193

Q We don't have gutters and downspouts, so it stays fairly wet around our house. Do I need to do anything special to make sure my shrubs don't "drown"?

A Gutters and downspouts also would help your house's foundation, so you might want to consider them anyway. However, if you garden without them, raise the planting beds by several inches. That way much of the incident rainfall will run off into the turf. You will need to be careful that your raised beds don't cover the weep holes in the bottom course of your bricks.

194

Q How do I install a French drain?

A These are subsurface drainage systems designed to remove excess water from a low area. The process is fairly simple, but you need to do it carefully. It involves trenching one foot under or very near the waterlogged area. Put 1 to 2 inches of coarse gravel at the bottom of the trench, then an inch of pea gravel. Place 4-inch PVC perforated pipe on top of this gravel, with the two rows of holes running the length of the pipe placed down (at the 5 o'clock and 7 o'clock positions). Be sure the pipe has at least 1/4-inch of fall per 10 feet of length from its high end to the low end. Place more gravel up and around the pipe, then sand, then loam garden soil. You'll need to continue the piping to a spot where it can empty out into a ditch or onto the lawn. As the water seeps into the pipe it will be carried out away from the bed.

195

 What sizes of shrubs are best to buy?

 That depends on how carefully you'll maintain them, also on your budget and your patience. Larger plants have deeper roots, so they won't dry out as rapidly as smaller 1-gallon shrubs. You'll also have a better initial impact from the larger plants, so you'll be less likely to overcrowd them. If you need a really stunning large shrub for an especially important spot in your garden you can even find shrubs in very large 100- and 200-gallon containers. Selection, of course, will be more limited, but big hollies, crape myrtles, wax myrtles and others give an instantly mature look to your plantings.

196

 Q Do I need to do anything to my shrubs' root systems as I take them out of their containers?

A If the roots wrap around and around inside the pots cut through them once on each side. That encourages them to get out of the spiral mode of growth, so they'll more quickly start growing out into the adjacent soil.

☆197☆

Q I have some shrubs that need to be moved. When should I do it, and how can I tell how well they'll survive?

A If the shrubs have been in place more than 4 or 5 years it may be difficult. Factors to consider: speed with which new shrubs could attain the same size, the prices for those new shrubs, and the shapes of the old shrubs. Many times shrubs grow together and can actually ruin one another. Finally, you must consider whether, if you were going out to buy new shrubs, you would buy this kind anyway. There's no point in transplanting a loser to another part of your landscape. As for timing, it's best done during the winter dormant season, and you'll have the best chances of their surviving if you can carry a large soil ball and a good bit of the root system with each shrub.

198

 Q What kind of fertilizer do I use on my new shrubs?

 A Since you're probably going to be buying most of your new shrubs, not transplanting them, they're probably going to come to you in containers with all of their roots intact. That means you could use a high-phosphate root stimulator when you plant them. Soon thereafter, however, you should switch over to a regular lawn-type food to promote new stem and leaf growth.

199

 What is the best way to water my shrubs?

Slowly and deeply, then wait until they begin to dry out to water them again. Truth is, that advice goes for almost any plant you're trying to grow. With shrubs, however, there are some added considerations.

- Most of our shrubs are near our foundations, so we need to keep a fairly uniform moisture level in the soil.

- Since shrubs will grow taller and denser—if you're using automatic sprinklers to water them from overhead—you need to watch them regularly to see that the heads properly aligned and that they're not blocked by new growth.

- You can also use drip irrigation or soaker hoses.

- Mulching the shrub beds will help keep the soil uniformly moist.

☆ 200 ☆

I have lost two shrubs in the same location in my landscape. The shrubs to the left and right are doing great. I found no diseases or insects. They just dried up. What happened?

If you have a sprinkler system, remember that it's quite common for shrubs to grow tall and cover sprinkler heads. The water is then deflected down into one plant and shielded totally away from the other. You may need either to trim the shrubs back to expose the old head, or you can install a short extender to lift the head above the foliage. Make certain, too, that it's not partially plugged, and that it is angled the proper direction. If it isn't a difference in irrigation, look for subtle differences in lighting, soil type, and depth, as well as the possibility of a gas leak in the vicinity of the dead plants.

201

Q Do I need to fear having shrubs near my foundation? The foundation repair people have told me that the shrubs are causing a big part of my problem by robbing the moisture.

A There may be some specific situations where shrubs actually do directly cause foundation problems, but usually you can add any water that the shrubs are removing. A home landscape without shrubs would be a pretty bleak affair. Keep the front sides of the shrub beds properly watered to encourage vigorous root growth out into the landscape and away from the house and you should have nothing to worry about. You could also cut a trench against the house and install some type of root barrier.

202

Q The foundation company took out all of our shrubs as they re-leveled the house. Shall we put them back, or should we just get new plants?

A That depends on the time of year and their condition. If it's during the growing season, especially the summer, their chances of surviving are far poorer than in the winter. If it's in the winter you need to evaluate the way they look. If they've grown together and "travel as a group," it may be hard to reset them with any good results. If you do try to save them, however, you'll need to trim them back drastically, since foundation repair people usually don't take time to do a very careful job of digging the plants.

203

Q What is the best way to fertilize our shrubs?

A You can usually do it at the same time that you're feeding the grass, since both groups of plants will be actively growing at those times. If it's convenient, and if the bed is fairly narrow, enough of the lawn food may actually carry into the shrub beds that you won't need anything else. Otherwise, distribute 1 to 2 pounds of a quality lawn food per 100 square feet of bed space. You can use a handheld spreader, or you can sprinkle it by hand. Just try to apply it evenly across the entire area. If any catches on the foliage, shake the plants vigorously to cause it to tumble to the soil. Water deeply, immediately after you fertilize.

204

When should I fertilize shrubs that bloom in the spring, such as flowering quince, forsythia, bridal wreath, weigela and azaleas, among others? What should I use?

It's usually best to apply a lawn-type (high-nitrogen) fertilizer immediately after the shrubs finish blooming. You do that in conjunction with pruning and reshaping, to stimulate vigorous new growth over the ensuing several months. You might make a second application in very early summer. By fall you'll want to switch over to a complete-and-balanced analysis or even a high-phosphate fertilizer to promote good flower bud set before winter. A soil test will give you the best answer for your specific needs.

205

When do I fertilize shrubs that bloom later in the season, such as crape myrtles, pomegranates, gardenias, oleanders, hydrangeas, althaeas and Texas sage?

Again, it's best to start the year with a high-nitrogen fertilizer applied in very early spring. These plants generally bloom on their new growth, so you need to keep them active to produce the most buds. A soil test will tell whether you will ever need to apply anything different.

206

 How do I feed my evergreen shrubs, and when?

 These are the simplest. Fertilize them with a high-nitrogen lawn-type fertilizer any time that they're actively growing.

Obviously, that's going to be in early spring, again in late spring, and in very early fall.

When should I prune my shrubs?

This is a 3-step answer.

- If they bloom in the spring, prune them immediately after they finish flowering.

- If they bloom in the summer or fall, or if they don't bloom at all, prune them in January or February.

- Minor reshaping can be done at any time of the year.

208

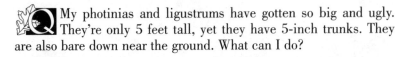My photinias and ligustrums have gotten so big and ugly. They're only 5 feet tall, yet they have 5-inch trunks. They are also bare down near the ground. What can I do?

Those are obviously old plants, and it may be time to replace them. Truth is, those are varieties that should have been allowed to get 10 or 15 feet tall. They're essentially just "running out of gas." They probably don't have the vigor to regrow new branches down low, even if you were to prune them way back.

209

In pruning my evergreen shrubs (junipers and arborvitae), I find that I can't cut them back more than a few inches before I'm into dried stems and stubble. What can I do?

Maybe nothing. Unfortunately, evergreens lack the ability to sprout out from their old dormant buds. If you cut back into that stubble it will probably kill the plants. Move them, discard them, or learn to love them.

☆210☆

 How much can I prune shrubs like hollies, photinias, boxwood and waxleaf ligustrums back without killing them? I really need to trim them back.

 Again, that depends on their vigor. Generally, you can prune them back by 30 to 40 percent. They'll look very leggy for a couple of months after you do that, however, so time it for very late winter—just before the flush of spring growth. Try not to do this time and time again, or the plants will fairly quickly go downhill.

211

 I have dead branches in several of my shrubs. Do I need to wait until winter to remove them?

 No. Any dead wood can always be pruned out at any season.

212

 I need to get a hedge to thicken up better. Will pruning help?

 Usually. Every place that you cut a stem you should get three or four branches back in its place. You can also change an upright pattern of growth into a more rounded shape by careful trimming. Be cautious when you're pruning screening hedges that you don't cut them back too many times at exactly the same heights. Hedge shears can be a big foe of healthy plant growth. It's always better to let them grow fairly naturally, then gently "sculpt" them with your shears.

Note: See also pruning guidelines for specific plants.

213

How can I protect my tender shrubs from extreme winter cold?

The actual plants will vary with Texas' various regions, but the techniques will be the same. Don't do anything to promote vigorous growth late in the season, including pruning and feeding with nitrogen. Keep them moist as cold weather approaches. Mulch the soil as a general rule, not just for the winter. However, winter mulching can actually reduce the stress of extreme cold. If you have old sheets, and if ice or snow are not factors, cover the plants. Commercial landscapers use lightweight fabric covers with great success.

214

How can I tell, during the winter, if a shrub has frozen and needs to be removed?

You usually can't tell. You need to leave them in place until early spring. If they fail to start growing, you'll know it's time to make some changes. If you must prune earlier, indications that the plant may have frozen are brown and dry twigs and bark that has peeled away from the trunk.

☆215☆

What are the best tall screening shrubs I can use for privacy?

Your nurseryman will need to answer that for your specific needs and conditions, but some of the best include tall hollies such as Nellie R. Stevens, burford, willowleaf (needlepoint), Mary Nell, Foster's, Wilson's, Savannah and yaupon: also ligustrums, wax myrtle, cherry laurel, oleanders, elaeagnus and viburnums. Redtip photinias might be included in the list were it not for their disease and insect problems.

216

 What are the best low shrubs I can grow under my windows?

 Again, get professional help for the most precise answer, but choose from any of the dwarf hollies (dwarfs of burford, yaupon, Chinese, or Carissa, the several low nandinas (nana, Harbour dwarf, Gulfstream and Moonbay), compact Oregon grape holly, trailing junipers, dwarf barberries, dwarf crape myrtles, and, where winters are mild, dwarf pittosporums.

217

 What types of shrubs have berries that either are colorful or that might attract birds, or both?

Hollies, especially yaupon, possumhaw, burford, Nellie R. Stevens and willowleaf; also mahonias, pyracanthas, Indian hawthornes, Chinese photinias, bush honeysuckles, ligustrums and nandinas.

218

Is it true that hollies and oleanders are poisonous? How is it that they can be sold?

To eliminate all species that could cause problems would be to turn our backs on many of our really great plants. Obviously, we need to teach our kids not to "graze" in our landscapes. Among the plants that have some degree of human toxicity, you could include both holly berries and the oleanders, along with oak acorns, most spring-flowering bulbs, tomato leaves, Carolina jessamine flowers, moonflowers, castor beans, dieffenbachia stems, azaleas and many others, but not including poinsettias.

MOST COMMON QUESTIONS ABOUT SPECIFIC SHRUBS

Abelias (*Abelia grandiflora*)

219

 Does abelia develop an iron deficiency problem?

Yes, and that's about the only problem this long-proven plant will have. It can be identified by the yellow leaves with dark green veins, most prominently displayed first on the newest growth. Use an iron/sulfur-soil-acidifier product.

220

My dwarf abelia seems to be lopsided. Is that normal? What can I do?

That's normal for that plant, and about all you can do is to keep trimming it to keep it properly shaped. Although the large original is a great and stout shrub, the dwarf seems to develop a lean through the years until it finally just lays down.

Agaves (*Agave americana*)

221

I have an agave (century plant) that bloomed last year. Now the mother plant looks bad and there are dozens of new plants around it. What do I do now?

You start digging. The mother plant dies after it finishes flowering. What you're seeing is rootsprouts, or "pups," that come up around the old plant's crown. You need to dig the mother plant out and discard it. It will never bloom again. Save one or a few of the new plants to fill the void. Be very careful working around century plants. Their leaves can inflict serious puncture wounds. Be careful, in fact, in giving plants to friends, that they don't have pets or small children that could be hurt by the leaves.

Aucubas (*Aucuba japonica*)

222

Q My aucuba plant has black leaves. Is that a disease?

A No. That's almost always some form of sun scorch. Aucubas can't take any direct sunlight. If you look closely, you'll probably see the leaves that poke out into the most light are more blackened.

Azaleas (*Rhododendron* sp.)

223

Q What kind of soil mix do I need to grow azaleas? I hear they're difficult to grow.

A Plant azaleas in a highly organic acidic mixture. In East Texas that can mean little more than adding some peat moss or compost at planting time, but in the rest of the state you're probably going to need to plant them in 16-inch-deep beds of half peat and half finely ground pine bark mulch. You'll have to topdress each spring immediately after they finish blooming with another 1 to 2 inches of the same mix. Part of the bed should be above the surrounding grade to ensure perfect drainage.

224

Q How do I prune my azaleas?

A As with our basic information for other spring-flowering shrubs, azaleas should be pruned immediately after they finish blooming. You'll do a lot of hand work with azaleas. Don't even reach for the hedge shears. You want to remove the leggy shoots that extend out beyond the plants' canopies, plus any stems that are dead or dying. Try to maintain a natural, unsheared appearance to the plants. You'll also have some minor tune-ups during the growing season, again to remove the shoots that grow vigorously away from the rest of the plants' canopies.

225

Q What kind of fertilizer should I use on my azaleas, and when must it be applied?

A There are several plant foods that will benefit azaleas. Use a high-nitrogen lawn-type fertilizer to stimulate new stem growth after you prune them following their blooming period. Repeat that application in early summer. Use 1 pound per 100 square feet of bed space, and water it into the soil thoroughly. In early fall, you'll want to switch over to a high-phosphate azalea/camellia/gardenia fertilizer. Should iron chlorosis be a problem during the growing season, you may also want to use an iron/sulfur material.

226

Q What is the life expectancy of azaleas in my garden? I've planted them in the recommended mix, but now they're looking old and tired. They've been in the bed for eight years.

A You need to prune, dig and reset your azaleas after that length of time. As the organic matter wears out and compacts, their root growth slows down and the plants quit growing. Prune them back by 30 to 40 percent, reset them into well-prepared soil, and water them thoroughly. Apply a high-phosphate root stimulator soon after you replant them.

227

Q My azaleas are losing a branch here and there. I see absolutely no signs of insects, and it doesn't look like any kind of leaf spot. What might cause that?

A There is a stem dieback that sometimes (rarely) kills an isolated branch in an established azalea. Spraying is seldom justified. Merely prune the dead branches out of the plants.

Barberries (*Berberis* sp.)

228

My barberry isn't very colorful. It starts out bright coppery red, but, by the summer, it's more of a rusty green. Is there some kind of fertilizer I should be adding?

That's not a nutritional problem. As it gets hotter the pigments that give the red color take a back seat to the chlorophyll. Farther north, where summers are cooler, the colors hold better. You also should check the amount of sunlight they receive. If they're tucked back under deciduous shade trees, that could account for their being brightly colored in early spring, before the trees fully leaf out, then losing their reddish color once they're plunged into shade. They need at least full morning sun.

Boxwoods (*Buxus* sp.)

229

My boxwood plants are dying, one at a time. I'm afraid I'm going to lose the whole row. What could cause that?

If you see one plant die, then the ones adjacent to it, that's probably root knot nematodes. They're microscopic soil-borne worms that love boxwoods more than almost any other plant. There is no chemical control for nematodes. If you eventually have to remove and replace the boxwood, use dwarf yaupon hollies. They're resistant to nematodes, yet they have about the same texture and form as a boxwood. They can also handle the shade far better than boxwood.

230

 My boxwoods' leaves are tan every winter. Is there some way to prevent that? Should I prune it out?

 Boxwoods always seem to lose 1 to 2 inches of their tip growth after the first hard freeze. The original Japanese boxwoods aren't reliably winter-hardy here in Texas. Switch over to varieties such as Wintergreen or Green Beauty, which hold their color better in the cold. Prune your plants lightly to remove any dead tissue.

231

Q My entire boxwood planting has turned a pale tan color this summer. I see no insects, but lots of black specks on the backs of the leaves. What caused it?

A Lace bugs. The adult is a smallish insect with transparent wings, hence the name. However, you'll seldom see the insects themselves, just the black globs they leave behind. They won't kill the boxwood, but they can make it look really ugly for the rest of the growing season and through the winter. Control them at the first signs of their tiny tan mottling by spraying with any general-purpose insecticide. Their early damage looks somewhat like that of spider mites, which rarely visit boxwoods.

Camellias (*Camellia* sp.)

232

 Q My camellia's flowers never develop. The plant grows well. Why don't I ever get any full flowers?

A The answer depends on where the camellia plant is growing. In North Texas they're probably freezing, especially if you're growing a variety of *Camellia japonica*. Their prime blooming time is January and February, and the cold at that time catches them in tight bud. Moisture within the buds freezes and ruptures the floral tissues, hence no flowers. Varieties of *C. sasanqua*, by comparison, bloom in late November and December, so they get most of their flowering over with by the first hard freeze. The plants are also several degrees more winter-hardy, which is an added advantage. For South Texas, on the other hand, you're probably dealing with a disease called botrytis (if the buds turn wet and mushy), or with thrips (if they're dried to a crisp and fail to open properly). Use a fungicide for botrytis and a systemic insecticide for thrips.

233

 If camellias bloom in the winter, when should I feed them, and with what?

 Camellias should be fertilized in very late summer with an azalea/camellia specialty fertilizer. Not only will it have the acidifying effects you need for these two plants, but it also will be high in phosphate and promote good bud set in the fall. You can add a high-nitrogen lawn-type fertilizer in early spring, as the plants start to grow; and, you may need to add an iron/sulfur material to supply iron and acidify the planting medium.

234

 My camellias are covered with an ashen-looking material. What is it, and how do I control it?

That's tea scale, and it's a scourge where camellias are common. You'll need to spray the plants with a horticultural oil spray during the late winter, just after they finish blooming and before they start growing. You can also use a systemic insecticide spray such as Orthene, or a summer-weight oil if you find the scale insects during the growing season, but carefully read and follow label directions to avoid damage to the plants.

Cherry Laurels (*Prunus caroliniana*)

235

My cherry laurel is very yellow. Yet, others nearby look fine. What is the likely cause?

That's probably iron deficiency, particularly if you have alkaline soils. Adjacent plants can be either green or yellow. It's odd how even short distances can spell big differences in iron deficiency. Given time, the other plants will probably also show the problem. Keep iron products off masonry surfaces.

236

Q The trunk of my cherry laurel has rows of holes all over it. Is that something that will kill it?

A No. Those are holes drilled by sapsuckers. They're woodpecker relatives, and they do no damage to the plant, nor do they indicate the presence of insects that might harm the plant. Use a sticky repellent such as Tree Tanglefoot to discourage them, and seal the holes with black pruning paint to stop their sap flow.

Cotoneasters (*Cotoneaster* sp.)

237

Q I have several cotoneaster plants that have suddenly developed dead branches. What causes that? I find no insects, and the branches have not been broken.

A That's probably fire blight, a very serious disease of all cotoneasters. These plants are in the rose family, and this disease on that group of plants will make isolated limbs look like they have been burned with a blow torch. Prune them out, cutting back into healthy wood. Disinfect your pruning tools with a 10-percent chlorine bleach solution between each cut. Spray while the plants are in full bloom in the spring with agricultural streptomycin.

238

Q The leaves of my cotoneaster are stuck together in clumps. There seems to be a worm inside each cluster. What is it, and how do I stop it?

A That's a leaf-tying insect, and you'll need to use a systemic insecticide next year. Make note of when you first saw the damage this year, then treat a couple of weeks earlier next year. It's not life-threatening to the plant.

Crape Myrtles (*Lagerstroemia indica*)

239

Q My crape myrtle's flowers don't open properly. They have a white mold on their buds. What will stop it?

A That's powdery mildew, the only common problem with crape myrtles. Researchers who are evaluating mildew resistance between varieties will look first at the flower buds, even though the disease is more obvious on the leaves. Control it with a systemic fungicide. Plant crape myrtles where they will receive good air circulation, and try to keep irrigation water off their leaves.

240

Q My crape myrtles look like they have been varnished. The leaves are shiny and sticky. Is there a spray to stop it? Can I wash it off?

A That's honeydew that drips from areas of aphid activity, usually beginning in late July or early August. Control the aphids with a general-purpose insecticide and you'll control the honeydew. Left unchecked, the honeydew will give rise to a fungus known as sooty mold. It will turn the leaves black and cause premature shedding as early as late August and September. You could use a hard stream of soapy water to try to wash the honeydew off the leaves and stems.

241

Q I am getting new sprouts near where I removed an old crape myrtle. The old plant was damaged and really ugly, but I wouldn't mind transplanting these plants. Will they be the same color when they bloom?

A Yes. Crape myrtles are not budded or grafted onto other types of rootstocks. Any sprouts that emerge will be the same genetically as the mother plant. Be sure, however, that you prune these sprouts back as you move them. They will probably have poorly developed root systems initially, until they're forced to grow on their own.

242

 My white crape myrtles have a bunch of lavender flowers. Why does that happen?

One of the older dwarf crape myrtles called Snow Baby (because of its white flowers) tends to revert to a lavender form. Merely trim out the lavender stems, if you don't care for the mix.

243

When do I fertilize crape myrtles, and with what?

Apply a high-nitrogen lawn-type fertilizer in early spring, to stimulate new growth, and again in late spring, to keep them actively growing into the summer. Flower sprays are produced on the current season's new growth.

☆244☆

Is it necessary that I prune my crape myrtles each year? How much do I cut off?

You really don't have to prune crape myrtles, other than to remove branches that are growing where you don't want them (basal sprouts that ruin the plants' tree forms, for example). Crape myrtles often will have very minor dieback of 8 to 10 inches of the tips of their branches each winter. However, you should never remove anything larger than a pencil in diameter from the tops of the plants. Avoid "topping" crape myrtles at all costs. You may also want to remove the spent flower heads as soon as all the petals have fallen, to promote additional bud formation during the summer.

245

 My crape myrtles bloom later than anyone else's. What can I do to get more and earlier color from them?

That's usually a genetic difference between varieties. Some types bloom 4 to 6 weeks earlier than others. It also can be a function of mid-winter pruning. Excessive winter pruning can delay those pruned plants' first flowers by 4 to 6 weeks compared to unpruned plants.

Elaeagnus (*Elaeagnus* sp.)

246

 My elaeagnus has grown too fast. In fact, it's grown in a really odd way. How do I trim those long branches off?

Those long, arching branches can be trimmed back into the canopy of the shrub at any time during the growing season. If you do it carefully you won't even be able to tell you've done any pruning at all. However, because the plant does grow rather vigorously, don't try to keep it too short (allow 5 to 6 feet in height and 6 to 8 feet in width), and avoid formal shaping. It just isn't a formal kind of a plant.

247

What are the red specks on the backs of my elaeagnus leaves? Is that spider mites? The plants always seem to have that dusty look I'm used to seeing with mites.

Those are normal parts of the leaves, but they do scare lots of gardeners. No cause for concern at all.

Euonymus (*Euonymus* sp.)

248

 My euonymus plants are dying. I looked closely and found some type of crust on their leaves. It looks like cigarette ashes stuck all over the leaves and stems. Is that responsible for the dieback, and what can I do?

That's euonymus scale, an insect. No plant that we grow is any more susceptible to scale than euonymus, and that scale is responsible for the eventual death of probably 90 percent of the euonymus shrubs planted in Texas. Control it before it gets out of hand, either with a horticultural oil spray (a late-winter application is the very best control), or with a systemic insecticide such as Orthene applied during the growing season. For the record, dead scales won't fall off. You can tell if they're alive by rubbing them with your thumb. If they're dry and flaky, they're dead. If they're moist and yellow several weeks after you treat, then you will need to treat again.

249

 My euonymus plants have a dusting of powder on their leaves. How threatening is that? What is it?

 It's not life-threatening, especially compared to the scale insects. It's powdery mildew, and several fungicides will control it. Plant euonymus in well-ventilated areas to lessen its severity.

250

My goldspot euonymus has green stems mixed in with the yellow ones. Should I prune them out?

Yes. If you don't they'll quickly overtake the less assertive variegated branches. Within a couple of years you'll have an all-green planting.

251

My golden euonymus looks like it froze. It went into the winter in good shape, but now all its leaves are brown. Will it come back in the spring?

Golden euonymus seems rather prone to freeze dieback in the northern parts of Texas. As with all other plants that are hurt by unusual cold, you need to wait until spring to determine the magnitude of the dieback, then prune to reshape the plants. Your plant will probably come back just fine.

Gardenias (*Gardenia jasminoides*)

252

Q My gardenia plants are yellow. Someone told me that was iron deficiency. What should I add?

A Gardenias are very prone to iron chlorosis, and yet we continue to grow them along and west of I-35, the general line of shift from acidic East Texas soils to the alkaline soils of West Texas. Iron deficiency in gardenias can be recognized by yellowed leaves with dark green veins, which appears most prominent on the newest growth first. In fact, the yellowing can become so severe in Austin, San Antonio, and westward into Kerrville and Uvalde that the plants will turn pure white, which means there is no chlorophyll at all left in their leaves. You can add an iron/sulfur material to supply the needed iron and to keep it relatively "available" by acidifying the soil, but you also need to start out with a planting mix that is all organic matter, including peat moss and bark mulch. Truth is, you probably should grow your gardenia in a container in those alkaline-soil areas. If you do opt for the container route, remember to set it in the garage any time the temperature will drop into the low 20s.

253

Q My gardenia flowers only last a day or two before they turn yellow. Why, and what can I do to prolong their lives?

A That's fairly normal for gardenias. Usually by the second or third day the flowers will begin to shatter. Gardenia flowers are notorious for being filled with thrips. Look closely down within the petals. If you see very small sliver-shaped insects where the petals all attach, you might prolong the flower life by a bit by spraying with a systemic insecticide while the buds are forming. Once the flowers open, the thrips have done their damage.

Hydrangeas (*Hydrangea macrophylla* sp.)

254

Q How can I get my hydrangea to change its flower colors?

A Florists' hydrangeas are botanical oddities, in that their flower color changes with changes in the acidity or alkalinity of their soil. They bloom rich blue in acid soils and bright pink in alkaline. Truth is, it's probably best to accept the color you already have, rather than trying to change it. If you miss in your attempt you'll have floral bracts with very muddy brownish colors. For the record, however, you would add agricultural lime to turn an acidic soil to alkaline, and you'd use aluminum sulfate to get plants to bloom blue in alkaline soils. If you're going to attempt the latter, you should also plant them in pure organic matter—including peat moss and bark mulch. For the record, other hydrangeas such as oakleaf and pee gee have white bracts that are not affected by the soil's acidity or alkalinity.

255

Q My hydrangea didn't bloom at all this year. What went wrong?

A Usually that's either because you've had really cold weather, which killed the plant back significantly, or because you pruned it during the winter. Hydrangeas bloom on the stems they produced the year before, so protect that growth during the winter. Any pruning you do should be done after they finish flowering in late spring.

Hollies (*Ilex* sp.)

256

Q Why don't my hollies have berries?

A Many hollies have male and female flowers on separate plants, so half of the population of that species or variety will never have any fruit. Yaupon and possumhaw hollies are two classic examples. If you look at their flowers very closely with a hand lens in the spring, you'll see that each plant has only one type of flower. Either the flowers will have pollen (male), or each (female) flower will have a primordial fruit that will look like a tiny bowling pin in the bottom of each flower. Other hollies, such as burford, willowleaf (needlepoint) and Nellie R. Stevens, have both male and female flowers on each plant. Every plant of these types should have fruit. There are other reasons that a holly doesn't have berries, however. It may be that you have poor bee activity in your neighborhood at the time the plants are blooming. Unless the pollen is transferred to the female flowers, there will be no fruit. It's also possible that you don't have any male plants blooming at the same time in the general vicinity (within a block or two). Sometimes, late freezes will catch the plants in flower or fruit, ruining that year's crop of berries. Finally, if the plants grow really vigorously they may conceal their berries.

257

Q Which of the hollies don't have spines? I don't want a stickery plant around my house, but I know that they're great shrubs and small trees.

A Yaupon hollies and all of its selections (dwarf, weeping, Will Fleming, and others) and possumhaw hollies have no spines at all. Some that do have spines aren't especially piercing, including willowleaf (needlepoint), burford, dwarf burford, Nellie R. Stevens, East Palatka, Savannah, Wilson's, Mary Nell and Fosters. The *most* prickly types include Chinese and dwarf Chinese, Dazzler, Berries Jubilee and Carissa. However, if you use these in the backs of your beds, they needn't be a problem. They're all among our most useful landscaping plants.

258

Q My yaupon tree keeps sending up seedlings or sprouts. I don't want them in the groundcover bed where the plant is growing. What will stop them?

A Those are root sprouts. Unfortunately, no chemical spray can be used, since they're attached to the mother plant. You'll either have to dig and remove them, or you could try a roll-type mulch around the crown of the plant. If you have a vining ground-cover, it will sprawl back over the mulch. If you're using something like mondograss or ajuga, however, you'll either have to bury the fiber mulch 4 or 5 inches in the soil, or simply use bark mulch to cover it up around the holly's trunk.

259

Q I understand that hollies are some of the best screens. How far apart should I plant them to secure good privacy? How long will it take?

A The best types include Nellie R. Stevens, yaupon, burford and willowleaf (needlepoint) hollies. Each should be planted 5 to 6 feet apart to allow them to reach full height and width. If you crowd them closer together, you'll pay the price later as they shade themselves out and begin losing their lower limbs. Be sure they're dense and full when you plant them, then keep their growing shoots pruned back lightly to encourage side branching.

260

Q I have some Japanese hollies, also blue hollies, that just don't grow very well. What can I do to speed them along?

A Those aren't adapted very well to Texas conditions. While they'll hold their own in Northeast Texas, elsewhere they will be very slow. Since they're better adapted to the North, all of these varieties will need sun in early morning, then shade the rest of the day. If you ever replace them, try some of the other, better-adapted hollies. For the record, American holly varieties (also Savannah holly) will have trouble west of the favorable soils of East Texas.

Indian Hawthornes (*Raphiolepis indica*)

261

 Q Our Indian hawthornes have maroon spots on their leaves. If it's a disease, what kind of spray should we use?

That's a fungal leaf spot. It can be controlled with regular sprayings of a general-purpose fungicide. Left unchecked, it can ruin the plants. Be especially mindful to spray in the spring, since that's when new growth becomes infected.

262

My Indian hawthornes didn't bloom well this spring. What can I do differently in the future?

There are several causes. For one thing, late winter and early spring freezes often ruin their bud clusters. If your plants are in the shade they won't bloom as well as you might expect. Also, if you prune them very much in late winter you'll be cutting off their flowering buds with the foliage. Apply a high-phosphate flower-promoting fertilizer in the fall, so they can set more buds over the winter. Keep in perspective, however, that Indian hawthornes only bloom for a couple of weeks each spring. The rest of the year you have quality evergreen landscaping shrubs. That should be the real reason you grow them.

Junipers (*Juniperus* sp.)

263

My junipers are dying from the inside out. They're just turning brown, yet I can't see any specific problem. What's happening?

That's an increasingly common question, and the culprits are usually spider mites. If you thump one of the affected (dying, but not dead) twigs over white paper, you'll see the nearly microscopic mites start to walk on the paper. Control them with Kelthane. For the record, this particular mite shows up very early in the growing season, often in February, so keep an early lookout.

264

 What will kill bagworms on my junipers, and when do I need to use it?

 Almost any general-purpose insecticide will control bag-worms if you apply it before they seal themselves in their fibrous bags. If you watch in late spring you may be able to see the very early stages of their feeding. All of a sudden you'll notice that the plants' branches aren't as full as normal. On closer inspection you'll see the very small worms working their way over the branches, carrying their bags on their backs. That's the time to treat. Once they have quit feeding you must hand-pick the bags to get rid of the over-wintering insects. They can strip plants entirely, in which cases they rarely come back.

265

 Isolated branches keep dying in my shrub junipers. I don't see any insects. What might cause it?

Check closely at the point to which they die back. If it looks like it's been ringed and girdled, that's probably left over from an old bagworm tying fiber. As the branch has grown larger, the fiber eventually cuts through the tissues. On the other hand, there is also a bacterial stem canker that causes that kind of branch die-out. Prune to remove the dead twigs. Disinfect your pruning tools in a 10-percent solution of chlorine bleach between cuts; also, spray with Bordeaux mixture in spring and early summer to slow the spread of the disease.

266

I have some old, overgrown shrubby junipers. Is it possible to trim them back, and, if so, how and when?

You have to be careful when you start pruning junipers because they're very reluctant to send out new shoots from old wood. It's best to remove entire branches clear back into the crowns of the plants. Leave some of the existing branches to conceal your cuts and from which the new growth can develop.

Ligustrums, Privet (*Ligustrum* sp.)

267

 I'd like to use privet as a hedge. How far apart should I plant it?

There are much better hedges. Its main problem is that it gets too tall and eventually will grow stemmy and ugly with repeated prunings. If you want to use it you should plant it on 4- or 5-foot centers and allow it to grow to 6 feet or taller. Hollies are better choices, particularly if shade is a factor.

268

My waxleaf ligustrums have gray sunken spots all over their leaves. They look like somebody walked on them with hot golf cleats this winter. What caused that? Is it a disease?

That's winter damage, and you can expect to see it in North Central Texas (the plant's northern extreme) following extreme winter weather. It's not a disease, and the new growth will usually conceal it by April 1. Record winters in recent years have reduced waxleaf ligustrum, once our most popular shrub, to an "also-ran" in the northern half of the state. Again, hollies perform better with no risk of cold injury.

269

 My variegated privet is turning green. How can I stop it?

Those are reversions to the original form. As with other variegated plants, the green stems will be much more vigorous. Keep them pruned out as soon as you see them.

Lilacs (*Syringa vulgaris*)

270

 Why don't my lilacs grow better? They were my favorite shrubs when we lived in the Midwest.

They're not in Kansas anymore. When you cross the Red River you quickly begin to see lilacs in distress. By the time you pass south of the Dallas/Fort Worth Metroplex you can pretty well kiss them good-bye entirely. Our problem is that lilacs can't handle our high summer temperatures. They run out of gas just coping with the heat.

Nandinas (*Nandina domestica*)

☆271☆

 How do I prune my nandinas? They're far too tall, but, more than that, they're also very leggy down near the ground.

Nandinas are pruned in an uncommon way. If you cut a given stem back almost to the soil line, it will regrow from its base. If you do that to the tallest one-third of the canes every year, you'll have a constant supply of fresh and new growth coming up from the ground line each spring. In severe cases, for example, where extreme cold has "burned" most of the foliage, you may even want to prune half or more of the canes back to the ground. Do it with hand shears, so you can leave any new growth that is already forming in place. This works with any of the standard types, but you probably wouldn't want to do it to nana nandinas. Do this pruning in very late winter, before the new spring growth starts to emerge, and follow it up with an early spring feeding of a high-nitrogen, lawn-type fertilizer.

272

My nana nandinas are yellow. They seem to look sickly all through the year. What do they need?

Probably iron. While all nandinas can show chlorosis in very alkaline, rocky soils, nana seems most likely to do so. Add an iron/sulfur soil acidifier to their planting beds several times during the growing season. Keep it off adjacent concrete and bricks. If you're planting new nanas, prepare their soil carefully.

273

My nandinas never develop really good winter color. Why?

Winter color with nandinas is a function of:

• cold weather,

• full sunlight,

• vigorous plants with healthy foliage, and

• diminishing amounts of nitrogen fertilizers in their root zones going into the winter.

Oleanders (*Nerium oleander*)

274

My oleanders never flower very well. Is there anything I can do to help them bloom better? They come back well after the winter, although they do die down fairly often because of the cold.

You've answered your own question. When oleanders freeze back, they spend much of the next growing season producing new stems and leaves. Where they normally would flower in late May, through June and into late summer, they're busy re-establishing themselves as shrubs during that prime time. Any flowers they are able to produce later in the summer will be less prominent than that first burst of June would have been. For the record, reds are the most cold-hardy color, followed by pink, white and the creamy yellow form. Answering it mercifully, you really can't count on oleanders for regular blooms each summer in the central third of the state. In far North Texas they may not even survive the winters, and in South Texas they should be fine most seasons.

Palms

275

 Which types of palms are the most winter-hardy?

The best of the common types include windmill palm, California fan palm and the sabal palmettos. Each of these will be winter-hardy to Zone 7, which means they should survive most winters to the Red River. Palm hardiness also depends on satisfactory "hardening," or prior conditioning, as well as the length and severity of the cold spell. Your local nurseryman can give you more precise information.

Photinias (*Photinia* sp.)

☆276☆

 What is killing my redtip photinias? Their leaves have purple spots all over them.

Anytime we grow too much of any one type of plant, we need to watch out for insect or disease problems that move through entire neighborhoods. Such is the case with *Entomosporium* fungal leaf spot. This disease was comparatively uncommon until we planted wall-to-wall photinias. Now it has reduced them to third-class plants. The toxins it puts into their wood seem to stop all of their growth and development. Soon the plants are sickly yellow, then dead. Control it with a suitable fungicide. If they're too far gone, replace them with large types of hollies or other suitable shrubs.

277

My photinias seem stunted. Their green color is acceptable, but they just aren't growing. What gives?

Check for those maroon spots as mentioned in the previous question, but look, too, for signs of scale insects. They form a crusty mass on the twigs of photinias, and, given many months or even a year or two, they can take away all the photinias' native vigor. Dormant oil sprays applied during the winter work well on scales, or you can use a systemic insecticide such as Orthene during the growing season. The dead scales will remain attached to the twigs for many months after treatment. Watch each season's new twig growth to see if the photinias are spreading.

278

 My photinias are too tall. Can I cut them back by half, and when should I do it?

If you're trying to maintain photinias at less than 6 feet of mature height, you're really just waiting for failure. These are very large plants, and they need to be used where they can grow to a full 8 to 12 feet of height and 6 to 8 feet of width. If you do decide to try pruning them back severely, do it in late winter just before the new coppery growth comes out in the spring. Trim them one limb at a time using only hand shears and loppers to maintain a natural shape.

279

My photinias don't have very good red color. Why?

You may be pruning them in late winter, in which case you're cutting off all the buds that would produce the new red growth. It's even more likely that they're in shade part or all of the day. It's still more likely that they're not vigorous, because of one of the pest problems we've mentioned.

280

 I have some of the old-fashioned Chinese photinias. I like them even better than redtip, but their new leaves seem to roll badly in the spring. What causes that? Is it a mold? I see white dust on the leaves.

Yes. That's powdery mildew. Control it with a fungicide, and do what you can to improve air circulation around the plants.

281

 Isolated branches of my photinias have suddenly died. What should I do to keep the problem from spreading?

That sounds like fire blight, the bacterial problem of the rose family. Affected leaves will remain attached to the stems for many months. Prune to remove the dead wood, cutting back into healthy tissues by several inches. Disinfect your pruning tools by dipping them in a 10-percent chlorine bleach solution between each cut. Spray while the plants are in full flower with agricultural streptomycin.

282

 My photinia has suddenly died. It looked fine just a few weeks ago, and now there is nothing green. What hit it?

Probably cotton root rot, particularly if you live in an area with alkaline soils. You'll have to replace it with a resistant plant such as the various large junipers or hollies. This is a soil-borne disease for which we have no reliable chemical control. If your photinia was part of a row, apply a sulfur soil-acidifier to the other plants, 4 to 8 ounces per square foot. That's a heavy application of sulfur, but it's intended to lower the soil pH, thereby lessening the probability of the disease's spreading.

Pittosporums (*Pittosporum tobira*)

283

 How can I prune my pittosporums that have grown too tall?

If you look closely at a given branch of pittosporum, you'll see that the new growth emerges from a cluster, or whorl, of branches. One of the new twigs will become dominant and shoot out several inches. When it comes time to prune you need to trace those dominant branches back into the plant and trim flush with the rest of one of the whorls. One of the other somewhat dormant twigs will take over and fill in the area. This is a process intended only for hand shears. Electric or gas hedge trimmers will ruin pittosporums.

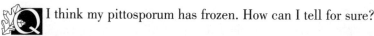

I think my pittosporum has frozen. How can I tell for sure?

 Look at its trunk. If the bark is falling away, that's freeze injury. It will show up within just a couple of days of extreme cold. Green pittosporums are the least likely to have winter damage, followed by variegated, then Wheeler's dwarf, and, finally, the variegated form of Wheeler's dwarf, which really only adapts along the Gulf Coast and in deep South Texas.

Pomegranates (*Punica granatum*)

Why don't my pomegranates set fruit? They bloom very well.

You probably have the ornamental type. These generally have fuller, more double flowers (more petals). The most common fruiting type ('Wonderful') has just a single row of petals around its swollen base.

Purple (Texas) Sage, or Ceniza (*Leucophyllum frutescens*)

My Texas sage isn't growing very well. I've had it several years, and it's thinner than ever this year.

Along the Red River that can be caused by severe winter cold that has damaged the stems. Anywhere in the state it can be caused by growing the plant in excessive shade or in a poorly drained location.

Pyracanthas (*Pyracantha coccinea*)

287

Q My pyracanthas have turned tan. I see no insects, but lots of black specks on the backs of the leaves. What can I use?

A That's lace bug damage, and pyracanthas are their favorite host. You'll rarely see the adult insects, but you will see the excrement that you mentioned. Lacebugs won't kill the plants, but they do make them unsightly. Once you spray and control them with a general-purpose insecticide you may see some bright green new growth before the season is over. Watch for early signs of them the next year, so you won't get the two-toned effect.

288

Q My pyracantha has clusters of chocolate-brown leaves. They seem to be matted together. What insect causes that, and can it be controlled?

A Leaf-tying insects do that damage, and they can be controlled with a systemic insecticide applied a week or two before you traditionally see their damage. You might want to trim off the clusters to reduce future populations.

289

Q Some of my pyracantha's branches have suddenly died. It seems to affect 10- to 12-inch parts of the plant, and the damage is scattered all over the plant. Is it an insect or disease?

A It's probably fire blight. Pyracanthas, like other members of the rose family, are susceptible to it. It enters the plants carried by bees as they pollinate the flowers. Spray with agricultural streptomycin while they're in full flower. Prune out the dead tissues during the growing season, cutting back into healthy wood. Disinfect your pruning tools by dipping them in a 10-percent solution of chlorine bleach between each cut.

290

Q My pyracantha plant suddenly died. I see no signs of insects or diseases. Last week it was fine, now it's dead. What causes that?

A Cotton root rot. Pyracanthas are quite susceptible. It's a soil-borne fungus that waits for just the right weather conditions, then kills susceptible plants in a matter of days. There is no control for it once it's evident. It is a problem only in alkaline soils, so work lots of organic matter into the ground if you're planting in a part of Texas where cotton root rot has been a problem. However, you should not replant another pyracantha in the exact same place, if one has been already lost to the disease.

291

Q How and when do we prune pyracanthas? I don't want to cut off any berries.

A Pruning a plant that holds its fruit almost completely through the winter is always a challenge. If you prune it while it has its fruit, you'll diminish the show. If you prune it just before spring you'll be cutting off some of that season's flowers, so you'll cut into the fruit count. If you prune it during the growing season you'll be cutting off green fruit. All things considered, major pruning should be done at the end of the winter, before the spring growth begins. If you lose some of the fruit, so be it. However, try to keep ahead of the problem by doing minor reshaping of the plants' strong growth all through the growing season.

Roses-of-Sharon (Althaea) (*Hibiscus syriacus*)

292

Q My rose-of-sharon drops almost all of its buds before they ever open. Do I need to water it better, or is it some kind of pest problem?

A That's a common problem for all of the hibiscus clan, tropical and hardy alike. They seem to overproduce flower buds, only to be at the point of having to support that reproductive growth just as it's getting hotter and drier. Their prevalent reaction is to abort half or more of their buds just before or just as they begin to show color. Check the buds for signs of thrips (small, nearly microscopic insects that sometimes will be inside buds). You probably won't find them, so plan on mulching your plants and keeping them uniformly moist during the heat. Avoid high-nitrogen fertilizers around althaeas as they begin setting buds.

293

Q My rose-of-sharon died very suddenly. I can see absolutely no signs of leaf diseases or insects. It's just as dead as dead can be. What can I replant there?

A That's cotton root rot. Like so many other plants, althaeas are susceptible. Stands only to reason, too, since they're closely related to cotton. Replant with hollies, junipers, nandinas or other resistant types.

294

Q My rose-of-sharon plant isn't as dark green as I remember from growing it elsewhere. In fact, it looks pretty anemic. What can I add to darken it up?

A That's iron deficiency. With althaeas, it seems to give the plants an overall pallid appearance. Add an iron/sulfur supplement, but also use a granular lawn-type fertilizer.

Spiraeas (*Spiraea* sp.)

295

Q I have several kinds of spiraeas, but they never get very dark green. I've tried my standard lawn fertilizer, but it hasn't helped. What do they need?

A Probably iron. The variety Anthony Waterer commonly shows iron deficiency in the western ⅔ of Texas, most especially when we try to grow it in shallow, chalky soils. Whenever possible plant them in a rich, organic soil. As needed, apply iron and sulfur to correct the chlorosis.

Texas Mountain Laurels (*Sophora secundiflora*)

296

Q What can I do to make my Texas mountain laurel grow faster? I know they get 10 feet tall, but mine just isn't making progress.

A You can apply a high-nitrogen lawn-type fertilizer to encourage more rapid growth, but, even with the feeding, they're going to be among our most deliberate shrubs. Buy larger plants whenever possible.

5

VINES

GENERAL QUESTIONS RELATING TO VINES

297

 Will vines pull the mortar out of my brick wall?

 No. However, there are several other concerns you need to address.

- Don't plant dense vines against a wooden wall. You can still plant some type of vine near the wood, but use a twining vine on a hinged trellis, so there will be good air movement behind the vine.

- Don't plant clinging vines against really light-colored brick, since it can trap dust and debris and leave the surface stained.

- Beware of Boston ivy and other vines with clinging "roots" as they start to grow across window screen, siding and other surfaces that cannot be scraped with a wire brush. Remember: They are tenacious and still will be in place years after you decide to remove the vines.

☆ 298 ☆

 What vines are best against the walls of my house?

In sun, Boston ivy is excellent in most of Texas. If you want a smaller version, plant Lowi Boston ivy. Purple wintercreeper euonymus would be an interesting option for sun or part sun. If you need something to cover a really large wall surface, Virginia creeper will do the job. In South Texas climbing fig ivy is the vine of choice for sunny sites, and in shade anywhere in the state you'll probably want to use English ivy or one of its selections.

☆ 299 ☆

 What are the best flowering vines for Texas gardens?

Climbing roses rate high, of course. The antique types are the most refined, as well as being durable over many years of growth. Other popular woody vines include Madame Galen trumpetcreeper, clematis, Carolina jessamine, coral and Hall's honeysuckles, passionvine (some types are tropical), Confederate star jasmine and wisterias.

300

 I need a really quick vine. I don't mind if it is only an annual. Which types are the best?

 If you're looking for showy color in a real hurry, plant morning glories, moonvine, cypress vine or clock vine. You can also use tropical perennial vines such as mandevilla and bougainvilleas as annuals, although they won't be as fast as the seed-grown annual types.

☆301☆

 What are the best vines to use over my patio? I want shade, but I don't have room for a tree.

 You need something that is rather aggressive. Best choices for wide areas of Texas: wisteria, Madame Galen trumpetcreeper, and Lady Banksia and the many other fine antique roses. Wisteria and trumpetcreepers are deciduous, so you'll get almost full winter sun. Roses are semi-evergreen in most of the state. Grapes would be an option, but use a white-fruiting type to avoid stains. If you want an evergreen vine, consider Carolina jessamine. It's smaller than the others listed, but it's a proven favorite from the Red River southward. Confederate star jasmine is outstanding along the Gulf Coast. Queen's wreath dies to the ground each year, but it certainly is beautiful in South Texas. It would, however, tend to shroud your patio cover. Sweet autumn clematis would be pretty in East or Central Texas, although it, too, dies to the ground most winters and wouldn't cover the entire patio roof in one growing season.

302

 How can I get my vine to start climbing my brick wall?

Make certain that your vine has the genetic potential to cling to that wall. Some vines, you'll remember, have tendrils, and other types twine. Neither of these will attach itself to a solid flat surface. Vines that have appendages that let them climb walls should be planted slightly off-vertical, with their nursery stakes touching the wall. Don't try to remove the stake. It will decay within the first year, and by that time the vine will have firmly attached to the wall.

MOST COMMON QUESTIONS ABOUT SPECIFIC VINES

Boston Ivy (*Parthenocissus tricuspidata*)

303

Why are the leaves of my Boston ivy tan? What can I do to get them to green up again?

That's usually damage done by lace bugs. These are pinhead-sized insects with clear wings. You may not actually see the adult insects, but you'll see their black droppings on the backs of the leaves. Once the leaves are tan there isn't much you can do to get those leaves to green back again, but you can protect new foliage by using a systemic insecticide. Watch closely, then spray when you see the very first tan specks start to develop.

Bougainvilleas (*Bougainvillea* sp.)

304

 I have had my bougainvillea vine in a large patio pot all summer. Now I need to bring it indoors. Can I trim it?

Absolutely. In fact, you'll need to do so. Bougainvilleas get really leggy and they'll take up entirely too much space indoors. Prune and reshape it. It will regrow and fill in handsomely if you'll give it really bright light.

305

How much cold will my bougainvilleas tolerate?

Almost no freezing weather. In fact, if it's going to drop much below 40 degrees, you probably need to get them into a protected environment. Bougainvilleas are useful as landscaping vines only from Houston to San Antonio and southward. Even there they may freeze in extreme winters.

Carolina Jessamine (*Gelsemium sempervirens*)

306

How do I prune my Carolina jessamine? It's become bare and ugly at the bottom of the plant. All I see are stems from the top of the fence downward.

There will usually be strong new canes that will sprout out around the base of the plant in the spring and early summer. Let those develop, "pinching" out their growing tips to make them branch and stay more compact. You can also prune all the really lanky canes back near the ground immediately after the plant finishes blooming in March. Apply a high-nitrogen fertilizer, 1 pound per 100 square feet of bed space, to encourage new growth.

307

 My Carolina jessamine isn't as dark green as it used to be. What will get it better looking?

 Several things done in unison will help.

- Apply iron and a sulfur soil-acidifier during the growing season, especially if your soils are highly alkaline.

- Nitrogen usually will also help; in fact, it seems that the plants utilize the iron better once you have applied nitrogen.

- Make sure you're watering it regularly. Extremes of winter weather can also leave part or all of a Carolina jessamine plant yellowed and weak, in which case you'll need to prune out the dead wood and encourage regrowth.

Clematis (*Clematis* sp.)

Will clematis grow well in Texas? We grew it up north.

The showy northern types of clematis, which bloom in late spring and into the summer with their large white, pink and royal purple blooms, aren't as strong here in Texas. It is simply too warm too long. The vines will be less vigorous and the flower count will be less than what you saw in the North. However, sweet autumn clematis (*C. paniculata*) is superior. It blooms in late summer and early fall, with creamy white flowers atop small green leaves. It's fragrant, and it's a refined grower. Grow it and all the other clematis in part afternoon shade. Evergreen clematis (*C. armandii*) is a beautiful, reasonably winter-hardy (Zone 7) vine with handsome foliage.

English Ivy (*Hedera helix*)

☆319☆

Will English ivy climbing a tree trunk hurt the tree?

It can in two specific cases:

- If you let it grow out over the limbs so that it forms a dense canopy over the tree's foliage, it can literally "shade the plant to death."

- If you have a severe ice storm, the ice on the added leaf surface can add enough weight that the limbs end up breaking.

Otherwise, the ivy stems and roots will not rob any nutrients or moisture from the tree's trunk, as some will tell you. All things considered, it's probably best to keep the stems of the ivy pruned off before they get into the main part of the tree's canopy.

310

Q I've tried to start new English ivy plants by putting runners from my old planting into a new bed. They don't do very well. Why would that be?

A We all have tried that at one time or another, and it never does work. There simply aren't enough roots on the runners to sustain all the leaf and stem tissues of the old vine. If you want to start new English ivy plants you'll want to take those same runners and cut them into pieces so that each piece will have one leaf, one leaf stem (petiole) and a part of the real stem, the runner. Plant several of those into a 4-inch flower pot filled with loose potting soil. Keep them moist and in a shady location until they root. At that point you can either pot them up and let them get larger before you plant them, or you can try setting them directly into really well-prepared garden soil.

311

Q My English ivy has dark spots all over its leaves. It eventually seems to kill the entire stem, and it's scattered all over the planting. What can I do?

A That's a fungal leaf spot, and you'll need to treat it each time you see it with a general-purpose fungicide. Overhead watering certainly doesn't help the problem, nor will frequent spring rains and high humidity in the shady areas where we normally grow English ivy. There may be some differences in susceptibility between the species and its many cultivars. Some seem less likely to develop the disease.

312

Q Why are the leaves of my English ivy so very different up in the trees?

A Those are the mature "adult" leaves that English ivy makes when it has vertical support. It's only among those large rounded leaves that English ivy will ever flower. As long as it's growing along the ground you'll see the traditional triangular foliage.

Fig Ivy, or Climbing Fig (*Ficus pumila*)

313

 Q I'd like to use fig ivy vine in topiary. How do I get it started?

A Start with a wire form that you either made yourself around a supporting frame, or you bought at a specialty shop. Pack it with sphagnum moss and fill the inside with potting soil. Plant the small plants or cuttings through the moss and into the soil, then keep it moist at all times until they form good roots and start growing. Don't leave it outdoors when temperatures will be below 40 degrees. Frost and freezes can ruin fig ivy.

Honeysuckles (*Lonicera* sp.)

314

 Q Which of the various honeysuckles makes the prettiest vine?

A Beauty is in the eyes of the gardener, but most would agree that coral honeysuckle is the best landscaping vine. It's more refined than the others, plus its coral-red flowers are more appealing. Hall's honeysuckle is a better vine than purple Japanese honeysuckle, which is best suited as a tall groundcover.

315

 What is the white dusting that's all over my coral honey-suckle?

That's powdery mildew, a fungal disease. You can use a labeled fungicide to control it, but you'll also want to avoid wetting its foliage, especially at night. Plant honeysuckle where there is good air circulation.

Roses, Climbing (*Rosa* sp.)

316

 My climbing roses never bloom. I've had them three years, but no flowers to date.

That usually results from late winter pruning. While bush roses are properly pruned in February each year, climbing roses bloom on wood they produced the previous year. You must wait until they finish the spring burst of flowers to prune them. Late winter pruning removes all their developing flower buds. Remember, too, that climbing roses won't usually bloom their first year in the garden for the very same reason—they must produce long canes for one season before they will set buds. It's also noted that climbing roses bloom better and quicker when their branches are somewhat horizontal, rather than just vertical.

 ☆317☆

How do I prune climbing roses?

Immediately after their biggest spring floral display has finished you should remove all the weak, internal stalks and cut the main stems back to 4 to 6 feet from the ground. That generally means you'd be removing some 50 percent of the top growth.

Always prune just above a bud that faces out from the center of the plant. Pruning during other seasons should be primarily to restore the plant's shape. For example, if you have canes leaning out into an alley you use to get to your driveway, you don't want to wait until May to remove them. Prune them as needed.

318

 How and when do I prune my climbing Lady Banksia rose?

 As with other climbing roses, Lady Banksia should be pruned immediately after it finishes flowering in the spring. However, one thing is different. You'll notice that Lady Banksia roses produce two distinctly different types of growth. Some of their shoots are normal, zigging and zagging their way skyward, while others zoom bolt upright like rockets. Those "rockets" are slow to bloom and can be removed whenever necessary to keep the plants attractive. If you prefer to tip-prune them to keep them from growing so tall they'll probably send out more normal side branches.

319

How do I train my climbing roses to climb?

Climbing roses are actually leaning plants. You have to provide them some type of sturdy support, then tie them to it until they grow to their mature height and form. Use elastic plant ties to hold them in place. Once they cover the support they will need less, but regular, attention to keep them in place.

Note: See Roses in Chapter 9, Perennials, for answers of questions of thrips, black spot and other general rose questions.

Trumpetcreeper (*Campsis radicans*)

320

My Madame Galen trumpetcreeper doesn't flower very heavily. Others in the neighborhood are beautiful every summer.

That can be caused by several factors. Foremost, it may be getting too much nitrogen fertilizer, particularly if it's adjacent to turf. Morning glories and trumpetcreepers are notorious for staying vegetative when they receive lawn-type fertilizers. It also needs to be in full or nearly full sunlight, and you shouldn't be pruning it very heavily. If you cut it way back during the winter, you can expect really strong vegetative regrowth the following spring and summer.

☆321☆

I have trumpetvine coming up all over my yard. How can I stop it, or must I kill the entire plant?

That's the problem with trumpetcreepers (more commonly called trumpetvines). The native form is extremely invasive. It will send up root sprouts as much as 20 to 30 feet from the mother plant. The dilemma is that the chemicals you use to kill the sprouts will also harm the mother plant. If you could sever their connecting roots that tie them to Mama, then treat just the leafy sprouts, you could eliminate them without harming the original plant. Use a broadleafed weed-killer spray to kill any part of the trumpetcreeper that you wish to eliminate. For the record, the larger-flowering selection called Madame Galen is less invasive and more attractive than the native one.

Virginia Creeper vs. Poison Ivy

322

How can I tell whether I have Virginia creeper or poison ivy?

Virginia creeper, as indicated by its botanical name (*Parthenocissus quinquefolia*) has five leaflets per leaf. Poison ivy will always have three. Although it's not a good way of confirming which plant you have, Virginia creeper does not cause an allergic reaction, while poison ivy certainly does.

Wisteria (*Wisteria sinensis*)

 My wisterias don't bloom. They were blooming when I bought them, but no flowers since. What is the problem?

This is the most common vine question of all time. Unfortunately, there are several possible explanations, none of them definitive. For example,

- If you have your wisteria in the shade, it won't bloom very well.

- If you prune it in the winter, you're going to be removing most or all of its buds.

- If you have it in a turf area, you may be using too much high-nitrogen fertilizer near it.

- If you keep it really moist, it may be staying vegetative all fall, when it should be setting its flower buds for the following spring.

324

My wisteria's leaves are almost pure white. What are they lacking?

Iron. Your soils are probably extremely alkaline, and the first signs of iron chlorosis would be yellowed leaves with dark green veins on the newest growth first. With wisterias the veins aren't very prominent, so the plant's newest leaves take on an overall yellowed appearance. Very quickly the deficiency becomes so bad that the leaves have no chlorophyll at all. Use an iron/sulfur-soil-acidifier material to correct the problem. Several applications may be necessary, during each growing season.

325

My wisteria blooms in the summer and fall. Is it abnormal? Will it affect the next spring's flowering?

Anytime a wisteria comes out of a prolonged dormant period, its natural tendency will be to set buds and then flower. That, of course, happens as it makes ready for spring blooms, but it also can happen to a lesser degree after the summer. Pears and apples will often do the same thing.

GROUNDCOVERS

GENERAL QUESTIONS RELATING TO GROUNDCOVERS

☆326☆

 What groundcover would be less maintenance than my lawn-grass? I'm tired of mowing, feeding, weeding and watering.

That may not be the way the question is usually worded, but the implications are the same. The lowest-maintenance way to cover bare ground is with turfgrass. True, you'll have to mow it, but you also have to periodically trim groundcovers. You shouldn't walk in your groundcovers, and you also have to hand-pull the weeds, since weedkillers would damage the groundcover. Neither of these is a problem with turfgrass. Turf probably requires less attention to watering and feeding than any groundcover you might like. Use groundcovers where it's difficult to maintain turf, for example, in long, narrow beds, on steep slopes and in really shady areas. You can also use them as transitions between shrubs and turf.

☆327☆

 What are the best groundcovers for shade?

Mondograss and dwarf mondo, liriope, English ivy and its cultivars, Persian ivy, Algerian ivy (South Texas only), pachysandra (North Texas only), ajuga, strawberry geranium, vincas and ferns are all good.

328

 What groundcover can I use to cover my tree's roots? They extend above the soil surface and they're really ugly.

 Use either a tall groundcover such as liriope or ferns, or a vining type that would sprawl over the exposed roots. Your choices include English ivy and its many cultivars, Persian ivy, Algerian ivy (South Texas only), and the several vincas.

329

Q How can I prepare the soil around my tree's roots without harming the tree? Do I have to till the soil?

A Groundcovers won't thrive unless you prepare their soil carefully. Use a small rototiller and try to work it in between the major roots. You may be cutting many of the smaller roots, but the tree will recover. You can add organic matter into the soil, even though it means you'll be raising the grade by a couple of inches. Organic matter doesn't compact and drive out the available oxygen like a layer of new soil would do. If you're going to install spray heads for the groundcover bed, run them into the bed from its perimeter (like spokes on a wheel) so you can parallel the major roots without having to cut them.

330

Q What types of groundcovers hold the soil best on a slope?

A You need something that is aggressive and dense. It should have good and deep roots. Best choices for the sun probably would be purple honeysuckle or wintercreeper euonymus; or, for the shade, liriope or mondograss.

331

Q What kind of a groundcover can I use between patio stones in my walk? It needs to be low and non-invasive.

A Best choice of groundcover for shady sites in most of Texas would be dwarf mondograss planted slightly below the grade, so its top leaves extend up to the surface of the stones. Many of the sedums also work well in the sun, as could the low-growing Peruvian verbena. In certain circumstances, one of the really dwarf bermudas or zoysias might be attractive.

332

 Are there any groundcovers that flower?

There are several, although you probably should choose your groundcover based on how it looks when it isn't flowering, not just on how it looks when it flowers. Some to consider: Peruvian verbena and the other perennial types of verbenas, mock strawberry, potentilla and the several vincas, liriopes, honeysuckles and ajugas.

333

 What is the best time of year to plant a new groundcover?

You can actually plant groundcover at any time. The plants will establish most quickly (and spread and fill in the shortest amount of time) if you plant them before their burst of new growth in the spring. Many of our most popular groundcovers, including Asian jasmine and English ivy, do most of their growing before summer's extremely hot weather.

334

What size of groundcover plants would be best to buy at the nursery?

It depends on time of year and budget. The later you plant in the fall, or if you plant during the summer, the greater margin of error you'll build in by using larger plants. You'll find groundcovers in 4-inch and even 1 gallon containers, for example. They have deeper roots, so they're better protected against frozen soil or heat. Otherwise, you can use the smaller plants for most types of groundcovers.

I want to kill all the grass where I'm going to be putting my groundcover bed. What do I use?

 There are several outstanding grass killers. Ask your nurseryman for a recommendation for your specific situation. The various glyphosates and similar products would be excellent. They need only a few days to do their work, and there is no leftover residue to damage your new groundcover plants.

How do I fertilize my groundcover bed? How often, and with what?

You can use a complete and balanced water-soluble plant food, initially. Apply it with a siphoning proportioner on your garden hose; and, apply it each time you water for the first month or two, just to get the new groundcover off to a quicker start. Use the same fertilizer you use on your lawngrass and at the same intervals. That would have you using a 3-1-2 ratio lawn food every two months starting April 1. Use a handheld rotary spreader to distribute it over the bed. Water thoroughly after each application.

☆337☆

How can I keep weeds out of my groundcover bed?

 That may be difficult. Until the ground is fully covered there may be incidental weeds. You may have to hand-dig them, or you can spot-treat them with a foam-rubber paintbrush dipped in an appropriate herbicide and spread carefully over the leaves. Dandelion diggers are great tools for this.

MOST COMMON QUESTIONS
ABOUT SPECIFIC GROUNDCOVERS

Ajuga (*Ajuga reptans*)

338

Q My ajuga is dying out very quickly in large patches. It just seems to be melting away before my eyes. What can I do to stop it?

A Look for very visible signs of a fungal disease. You may see dramatic white spore masses around the crowns of the ajuga plants. If so, apply a general-purpose fungicide as a soil drench. You'll probably need to repeat the application a couple of times every year. If the plants get any amount of sunlight, they may, indeed, be burning up from the heat. Ajuga isn't totally satisfied with our Texas summers. Ajugas are also very susceptible to nematodes, so check their roots for signs of knots or galls. You'll have to change over to some other type of groundcover if nematodes are involved, since we have no chemical control available. Planting Elbon cereal rye would be a help if you could plant it in the fall and leave it until spring, but it might be too unsightly for a formal part of your landscape. It's also not terribly likely that nematodes would show up over an entire bed all at once. That would be more typical of the fungal organism.

339

Q My ajuga seems to lose its leaves in the winter. Is there anything I can do to keep it more "evergreen"? The bed looks bare when it's cold.

 A That's pretty much the genetic nature of ajuga. It usually comes roaring back the following spring.

Asian, Confederate Jasmine (*Trachaelospermum* sp.)

☆340☆

Q I have bermudagrass in my Asian jasmine. How can I get rid of it without killing the jasmine?

A Although it hasn't been listed on the product's label, many commercial landscapers and home gardeners alike have used one of the glyphosate sprays to kill the bermuda, but only in Asian jasmine. As long as you wait until the jasmine has taken on its leathery summer dark green color, the spray doesn't seem to bother it. Try a small area first, however, to be certain you like the results, because you accept all responsibility when you use a product in a way that is not prescribed on its label. Use a hand applicator so you can accurately position the spray. Keep it away from areas that do not have any bermudagrass.

341

Q My Asian jasmine has frozen. All of its leaves are brown and crisp. Should I prune it back?

A Let the stems be your guide. If they're dried and brittle, then the plants will have to form new stems from below ground. In that case you might as well mow the entire bed and tidy things up. If, on the other hand, the stems are still green and supple, just trim across the top of the planting to even its height. New leaves will come with the first warm days of spring.

342

Q How can I get my Asian jasmine to cover more quickly? It's been in my landscape for more than a year now, and I can still see bare ground.

 Asian jasmine does almost all of its vigorous growing in April, May and early June. You need to capitalize on that by feeding it in March and again in May. In fact, many gardeners use water-soluble complete and balanced analyses to promote the quickest possible cover. Apply this diluted material with every watering.

343

 What size Asian jasmine plants should I set out?

 Commercial landscapers like the smaller plants set closer together in the groundcover bed. They feel that the cover is smoother that way than if they initially start with tufts of mature plants. However, if there is any chance that occasionally you might let the bed get too dry, the larger plants have deeper roots for a better margin of error until they are established.

344

 How do I trim Confederate jasmine that I'm using as a groundcover? Its limbs are so tall and wavy.

Confederate jasmine does get much taller than Asian jasmine, but that's part of its beauty. Trim it lightly immediately after its spring bloom, and as needed the rest of the season.

English Ivy and other Ivies (*Hedera helix*)
(Note: See also Ivy questions in Chapter 5, Vines)

345

How winter-hardy is Algerian ivy? I've seen it in nurseries, and I know it's popular as a groundcover in California.

It's listed as hardy to Zone 9, meaning you'd better confine its use along the Gulf Coast. It freezes in severe winters in College Station and Austin, to be certain. Persian ivy (*Hedera colchica*) has similarly large leaves, but far superior winter durability.

Honeysuckles (*Lonicera* sp.)

346

Q Which honeysuckle would make a good groundcover for a steep slope along a road? I don't want anything that is expensive or hard to maintain, but it needs to hold the soil well.

A Best of the bunch would be purple honeysuckle. It's aggressive, drought-tolerant, and reasonably handsome. It will grow to 18 to 24 inches tall, although you can shear it back somewhat in late winter to keep it more compact. It tolerates full sun very well.

347

Q I have the green Hall's honeysuckle coming up in my purple honeysuckle bed. What should I do?

A You'll have to dig it out. That's probably from random seedlings that have sprouted among the plants you set out. They'll have their own individual root systems, so they should be reasonably easy to remove.

Junipers, Trailing (*Juniperus* sp.)

348

Q My trailing junipers are dying out from their centers. What might be the cause?

A Generally that's spider mites. Interestingly, this particular mite also is an early one, with the damage starting even in late winter. You can confirm its presence by thumping a suspect twig (dying but not dead) over a sheet of white paper. The mites will be more visible on the plain, light-colored background. If they're there, spray with Kelthane. Be certain, too, that the plants are getting full or nearly full sunlight and excellent drainage—a lack of either can lead to trailing juniper failure.

349

 I have bermudagrass in my trailing juniper groundcover bed. How can I get rid of it without hurting the junipers?

Probably the best way would be to pull and hoe as much of it out as is possible, then put a layer of roll-type mulch in place around the plants. Juniper groundcovers don't root into the ground as they trail, so you can snug that type of covering up around the plants' stems. Overlap it by several inches so the grass can't grow up through the seams, and cover it with 1 to 2 inches of ground pine bark mulch. You will have to hand-treat any grass that comes up near the stems with a glyphosate or a similar herbicide. Apply it with a foam rubber paintbrush, to keep it away from the junipers' stems.

Mock Strawberry (*Duchesnea indica*)

350

 I planted mock strawberry, and now I can't beat it back out of my beds. What can I do?

That is one of the raps on this attractive groundcover. It's so very fast to cover that it instantly becomes invasive. Hoe it out where it is near shrubs, perennials and other broadleafed plants. Use a broadleaf weedkiller where it has invaded turf.

Mondograss, or Monkeygrass (*Ophiopogon*) and Liriope (*Liriope*)

351

 I have nutsedge in my liriope and mondograss. How can I eliminate it? It grows taller than the groundcovers.

Use Image. Read and follow label directions for the best results. Your treatments will need to be made while the nutsedge is active, meaning mid-May into mid-September. Image is slow-acting, so be patient.

352

Q My mondograss is invading my turf. Is there anything I can spray that will stop it?

A Not without killing the grass, too. What you need is a better edging at the boundary. Use one of the quality metal or plastic edging materials, and insert it a full 4 inches into the soil. It's highly unlikely that mondograss will grow under that, but if it should, just pound it in deeper and put another strip above it.

☆353☆

Q Do I need to trim my mondograss and liriope groundcovers?

A You can do that if they're coming out of the winter unsightly. Sometimes they will scorch from prolonged or extreme cold. You can use a quality power hedge trimmer (well-sharpened!), or perhaps your mower. Their leaves are quite fibrous and can be difficult to cut. Finish the trimming before any of the new growth "candles" start to emerge from the crowns of the plants, usually by early to mid-February. Try not to trim at other times.

354

Q How much sunlight can liriope and mondograss take?

A If they're out in open lawn areas, away from hot, reflective surfaces, and in really well-prepared beds, they will do well with full morning and perhaps some afternoon sun in the summer. Winter sun under deciduous shade trees does them no harm. If you notice the plants are losing their rich, deep green color where they're exposed to the sun, and if you're giving them the best possible care, you need to move them to a shadier spot.

355

 Do I have to dig and separate mondograss and liriope like I do my perennials?

 No. Both will be well content to stay in place for many years so long as you continue to give them good care and attention.

356

 When can I dig and share my mondograss with a friend?

 It can actually be dug and divided just about anytime, but fall is ideal.

Purple Wintercreeper Euonymus
(*Euonymus fortunei* 'Colorata')

357

 My wintercreeper euonymus loses lots of its leaves in the winter, enough so that the branches look almost bare. Why?

While purple wintercreeper euonymus gets its name from its winter color, it does lose many of its leaves. Enjoy the ones that stay. It's one of our unsung plant heroes for Texas. It looks so good the rest of the growing season that we need to overlook this small blemish.

358

Will purple wintercreeper get the same scale insects that bother the shrub forms?

Yes, but it's not nearly as common. One spraying will usually eliminate the insects. Use a systemic insecticide during the growing season, or a horticultural oil spray in the winter, or, at more diluted rates, during the growing season.

Vinca, or Trailing Myrtle (*Vinca major, V. minor*)

359

Q My vinca groundcover turns brown every August. What will stop that?

A That's the damage of a leaf-rolling insect, and it will happen to both *Vinca minor* and *V. major*. If you look closely, those browned leaves are cemented together. Use a systemic insecticide one to two weeks prior to the time when you normally have seen the pest. Even with that help, however, vincas do run out of steam by the end of the summer.

LAWNS

TURF SELECTION
···

☆*360*☆

Q What is the best lawngrass for my part of Texas?

A That's a very common question, and its answer is quite long. First, promise yourself that you'll become familiar with any type of grass you might be considering. Walk on it. Look at it. Ask questions about it as it relates to your specific locale. From a standpoint of popularity, bermuda is king in the northern half of the state, while St. Augustine remains quite popular in South and Southeast Texas up into Central Texas. The questions that follow will identify some of the other problems you'll want to consider before making your choice.

☆*361*☆

Q We have shade. What type of grass will grow best there?

A We have two shade-tolerant turfgrasses for Texas landscapes. St. Augustine and fescue each must have 4 hours of direct sunlight during the summer if they're to hold their own. Fescue produces no runners, so it won't spread anyway, but you'll need more like 6 hours of sunlight if you expect St. Augustine to spread vigorously. If you have less sunlight than those prescribed limits you can remove guilty limbs, or switch to a shade-tolerant groundcover that needs no direct sunlight.

362

Q We have frequent water curtailments in the summer. Which grasses are most drought tolerant?

A Buffalograss and bermudagrass. Fact is, both will survive almost any summer drought, although both will go brown and dormant during the dry period. Of the two, bermuda is the more aggressive. If you plant buffalograss, and if you intend to water at all during the summer, you need to be very cautious about keeping bermuda out of a buffalograss lawn. Given even that minimal level of care, bermuda will invade the buffalograss and take over the area.

363

Q What are the advantages and drawbacks of bermuda?

A It can be planted from seed, sod, by plugs or by hydro-mulching, so you have many options of varying costs. You can use more weedkillers on it than on any other type of lawngrass, so it is easier to keep it free of invaders. It's drought- and heat-tolerant, and it's durable to traffic. It's winter-hardy, and it can be grown from the Gulf Coast to the Panhandle. It does invade flower and vegetable gardens aggressively, and it may give some folks more allergic problems than other lawngrasses. It also isn't quite as crisp and green by late summer as some of our other grasses. Still, it's the most popular lawngrass choice for Texas today, particularly in the northern half of the state.

364

Q If I'd like a really pretty lawn, should I consider Tif bermuda?

A The term *Tif* refers to the origin of that particular type of grass from the U.S.D.A. breeding program in Tifton, Georgia, several decades ago. These dwarf hybrid bermudas (the more proper term for them as a group) were bred to be used on golf courses and athletic fields. They're the ultimate in picture-perfect turf, but only if you give them the frequent maintenance they require. Tifgreen (more commonly known as "328") requires almost daily mowing with a golf green mower. You'll need to maintain it at less than 1/4-inch height. Tifway ("419") is a more manageable grass that can be kept at 3/4- to 1-inch height. There are other dwarf hybrids as well, but be certain you don't mind that added maintenance.

365

Q What are the advantages and drawbacks of St. Augustine?

A Although it grows best in full sun, St. Augustine tolerates shade (as little as 4 hours of direct summer sunlight) better than any of our other warm-season grasses. It's quick to cover, crowding out all other turfgrasses, even bermuda, if it's given average or better care. It holds its crisp, green look all summer and into the fall. However, it can be damaged by temperatures of 10 degrees or lower, depending on its prior hardening. You cannot use sprays to control dallisgrass, crabgrass and other existing grassy weeds in it, and it has more problems with diseases and insects than bermuda. It can only be started from sod or plugs, so it will be more expensive to plant than any grass that could be seeded. You may occasionally see St. Augustine seed on the market, but be certain it's guaranteed to be winter-hardy in your part of the state—usually, it is not.

☆366☆

Q I saw an ad in the Sunday paper for a grass called zoysia. How well will it do here?

A Zoysias are attractive grasses that are intermediate in many respects (texture and shade tolerance, for two examples) to St. Augustine and bermuda. However, the Sunday supplement ads, which have been running every spring for forty or more years, overstate its virtues. If you do decide you want to consider zoysia, buy a type that is recommended for your part of Texas, not some variety from the East Coast where those ads usually originate. Your local sod dealer can get Meyer Z-52 or other adapted type in for you, but ask him to refer you to a yard where you can see it before you buy it. Don't buy your lawn from an out-of-state mail-order house. If you do, it's unlikely you'll end up with the lawn of your dreams.

☆367☆

 I hear more about buffalograss, and I'd like to consider it. What is its record in Texas?

 Buffalograss is the only native North American grass that is suitable as a Texas turfgrass. It grows all across the Great Plains, and in Texas as well. In wetter parts of Central Texas you'll see it growing in ditches along the roads, where it crowds out all invaders, even really aggressive weeds. However, for all its durability, buffalograss isn't as luxuriant as some folks expect a turfgrass to be. It has a rather wiry look, and, if you don't water it during the summer, it will turn brown. As soon as you try to irrigate it (even infrequently) to keep it green and attractive, you can expect bermuda to start moving in. There are improved all-female forms of buffalograss on the market today, including Prairie and one that is called by its university research number, "609." They don't have the flower stalks, which extend above the blades like the seed-grown male plants have, so they make a more uniform, attractive turf. However, since they are female, you're likely to get pollination from adjacent buffalograss in the neighborhood. As those seeds sprout and grow, half will develop into male plants, so you're back where you started. Buffalograss is a good Texas turfgrass, but it's not the final answer to our prayers. As we've said before, go see the grass before you decide on it. Make sure you'll be satisfied.

368

I hear... Some of our neighbors have fescue turf. They seem happy with it. Any tips?

Fescue is a cool-season grass that is at its prime from mid-fall until very early summer. In the hottest part of a Texas summer it may go completely dormant and stop growing. Like St. Augustine, it's shade tolerant. It needs at least 4 hours of direct summer sunlight daily, however, if it's to hold its own. With less light it will gradually fade away 4 to 6 weeks after the trees leaf out. It requires more water than any of our other Texas turfgrasses.

Fescue is best adapted in North Central and Northwest Texas, and it is best planted in September or early October. You can also plant it in late February, although it may not establish adequately before the hot summer weather. There are dwarf types of fescue, and many varieties of "tall" fescue. You need to stick within the same category ("dwarf" or "regular"), but, having done that, it's probably best if you use a new variety with each fall's overseeding, just to get a mix of types.

☆369☆

 I want a green lawn in the winter. Isn't that why folks use ryegrass? When should it be planted? I have a mix of St. Augustine and bermuda.

 Ryegrass is the choice, and you'll probably want to use "perennial" rye. It's a finer-bladed grass than annual rye, so it's much easier to maintain in the spring. Annual rye will need to be mowed every couple of days, while perennial rye can hold out for 5- to 7-day intervals. Its seed does cost more than annual rye, but it's worth every penny. Sow it in September and keep the lawn moist until it germinates. Rye works better in overseeding bermuda than it will in St. Augustine, owing primarily to the density of the St. Augustine turf. Beware using rye to overseed St. Augustine in really shady areas. The added competition may seriously weaken the St. Augustine as it tries to green back up in the spring. Added to that, perennial rye will actually live far into the summer in the shade, an added competition problem for the St. Augustine.

370

Can I use a pre-emergent weedkiller in September and still overseed my lawn with ryegrass?

No. What works to kill the seedlings of grassy weeds will also kill the seedlings of your desirable ryegrass.

371

 Where is centipede best adapted? We had it in another southern state.

Centipede has to have sandy soils. For that reason, it's used almost exclusively in East Texas. It requires less fertilizer than most of the other grasses we're discussing.

PLANTING AND EARLY CARE
....

372

 How do I prepare the soil for my new lawn?

You do exactly the same soil preparation for any type of lawn, regardless of how it will be planted, be it from seed, sod, plugs or by hydromulching. Use a total-kill herbicide such as a glyphosate or similar product to eliminate all existing weeds. Allow the weedkiller 10 days to do its work, then rototill to a depth of 4 to 5 inches—deeper if you're going to be doing significant grade changing. A rear-tine tiller does the best job of pulverizing the soil to the consistency of flour, with no clumps larger than marbles. Use the back of a garden rake to establish the grade. Be sure the soil slopes away from your house to ensure good drainage. At that point you'll be ready to plant the new grass.

373

 Do I need to add peat moss or compost to the soil as I work it?

No. Your grass is going to have to grow in the native soil that you have. Rototilling alone should be sufficient. If your soil is too shallow and rocky, consider bringing in additional sandy loam topsoil. Be certain, however, that it contains no difficult weeds; and, be sure you're not changing the water-flow patterns on your lot in some harmful way.

☆374☆

Q When can I plant my new turf?

A Warm-season grasses (bermuda, St. Augustine, zoysia, buf-falograss) are all planted from mid-spring into very early fall. Cool-season grasses (fescue, rye) are planted in mid-September. Planting outside these time windows greatly endangers the survival of the turf.

375

Q We're going to move into our new house in December. What kind of grass can I plant then so I won't be tracking mud all winter?

A If you're in the southern half of the state you might get annu-al ryegrass to germinate. It will give you a quick cover, if it does sprout, but it will die out come spring. For the rest of the state, you're going to have trouble getting anything to germinate while the soils are that cold. If you can gain access to your new home's grounds by late October you could probably still get something up and grow-ing. Otherwise, wait until spring. Don't rototill until you're ready to plant in the spring. Weeds and compacted soil are far better than soft, eroding mud all winter.

376

Q How soon should I mow my new lawn?

Mow it as soon as it's tall enough to need mowing. That will usually be within the first couple of weeks after planting seed, even sooner for sod. Letting the grass get tall does nothing to help its vigor. Closer mowing keeps it spreading and dense.

When do I feed my new lawn?

Apply a 3-1-2 ratio lawn-type fertilizer after the second mowing. Use half the recommended rate at that time, and follow that up one month later *at* the recommended rate.

378

My new bermuda is reddish-purple. I sowed the seed one month ago. It came up within 10 days, but it's not growing well at all. Why isn't it growing?

That sounds like a deficiency of phosphorus. Its shortage causes purple, stunted growth. You could add a high-phosphate flowering houseplant or root-stimulator fertilizer one time to turn it around, but you're probably also keeping the ground too wet. It usually helps simply to cut back somewhat on the watering to give the grass roots a chance to develop.

379

I need to get grass going on about one acre near our house. I want to use bermuda, but that's a lot of space to water so carefully at the outset. What tips do you have?

Consider planting blocks of sod on 4- or 5-foot centers. Granted, it may take one entire season for them to cover, but it's so much easier to do that than it would be to rototill the entire acre, rake it, sow the seed and then water it twice daily until it's established. If you use the sod, you can use a rear-tine tiller to create the planting holes (assuming the grade is the way you want it already). Rear-tine types move forward because of their powered wheels (where front-tine tillers are propelled by the tines pulling through the ground). You can walk alongside your rear-tine tiller and merely drop the tines to the ground every 4 or 5 feet, and then only for the length of each piece of sod. That way you won't have to rerake the entire acre, but only to scoop the soil out of each planting hole. Rake the soft soil around the edges of each piece of sod. Hand-water the pieces for the first week using a water breaker at the end of your hose. By then they'll be well rooted and ready to grow.

Watering

380

 How can I tell when it's time to water my lawn?

Each grass will have its own subtle signs. The blades may roll or fold, and patches will turn a dull metallic green. As you walk across the dry grass you'll leave foot impressions that won't bounce back. Certain parts of your yard will dry out first, so water when those spots become dry.

381

 How much should I be watering my grass, and how often?

Those are unanswerable questions. You need to water the grass when it's dry, whether that's after 3 days or 3 weeks. When you do water it, soak it deeply to encourage deep root growth.

382

 I want an automatic sprinkling system. What things should I look for to be sure I'm getting my money's worth?

You want durability first and foremost. Whether you're deal-ing with the heads, the valves, the time clock or the wiring, you want materials that will last for many years with little or no ser-vice. Bargain equipment will end up costing you more in the long run, not to mention the frustration. If you're doing the installation yourself, make sure you have asked all the appropriate questions and that you know every step. If you're having the work done for you, closely check references and compare bids. The pipes, for example, need to be 8 to 12 inches in the ground. It takes a lot more labor to fill those deep trenches, and that's where some companies will cut their costs. Be sure the types and numbers of heads compare from one bid to the next, and feel comfortable with the installer you're hir-ing. Be sure they're using wiring that is intended for burial in the soil. Some companies cut costs by using doorbell wire to activate the valves, which breaks down within one or two years. There are plenty of good companies. Don't make a bad mistake.

☆383☆

I have an automatic sprinkling system. What intervals should I plan for watering my landscape and turf, and how long per station?

The answer is the same with a sprinkler system as it is for hand watering. You need to watch for signs of drought, then turn the sprinkler system "on." Leave your time clock in the "manu-al" mode all the time you're in town. That way you can determine when the best time for watering is. If you leave town, you can always program it for automatic watering. Again, look for indicator plants that tip you off when things are getting dry. They may be parts of your lawn, or they may be a bed of hydrangeas, but you're always going to have plants that are the first to wilt. Adjust and re-adjust the stations on your clock until all areas of your landscape dry out at approxi-mately the same time intervals. Some stations may run only 8 or 10 minutes, while others could run for up to an hour. It depends on the plants you're growing, the sprinkler heads and their delivery rate, and a lot of other variables.

384

Q When should I water my lawn, in the evening or in the morning?

A If the grass is really dry, water it. Month in and month out, it's usually best to water early in the morning. The grass won't stay wet for prolonged periods of time that way, plus water pressure will be at its highest. You'll have less wind to blow the water droplets, so coverage will be more uniform. Evening and night watering can lead to disease problems, especially with St. Augustine, and especially in the fall.

385

Q What kinds of sprinkler heads are best for my lawn and shrub beds?

A All you ask of any sprinkler system is that it deliver its water uniformly over the entire area being irrigated. You can accomplish that with large-area turf heads, and you can also do it with spray heads placed closer together. Of course, you'll have to leave the station running longer if the heads are covering larger areas. Either hire a competent landscape irrigation contractor, or ask plenty of questions at the supply house where you buy your equipment.

386

Q Several of my heads are down in foliage now, both in the shrub beds and in the lawn as well. Is there something I can use to elevate the heads without having to do major work on the system?

A Indeed. There are elongated extensions for the risers in the shrub beds, or you can easily unscrew the entire riser and install one that is 6 or 12 inches taller. As for the ground heads in your lawn, there are special extenders that can be cut to length. They're approximately 6 inches long when you buy them, but you can trim them with your hacksaw to exactly the length you need to elevate the various heads.

387

 The head at the bottom end of my sprinkler system is always oozing water. So much so, that I now have a really boggy area there. The system is not running, and I don't know what the problem might be. Do you?

Usually, that indicates a valve that is stuck open. Locate the valve. If it's not in an easily found valve box, consult your installation drawings. If you don't have any drawings, have someone turn that station on and off several times at a very quiet time of the day. Listen closely in the area where you expect the valve to be until you hear it clicking on and off. Open the valve up and clean all of its parts. Soil or small stones may have collected against the gasket, or the gasket may need to be replaced. In some cases you may even have to replace the entire valve, but these are all things you can do yourself.

388

 Do I have to worry about my sprinkler system freezing in the winter?

 Not if it was installed properly. The only lines that will freeze are those that are under constant pressure, which are the supply lines to the valves. The risers and other heads and the lines that supply them directly won't freeze, since most of the water should drain out of them after they shut off. Do be careful, however, that your system doesn't come on during freezing weather. Not only can it cause an ice hazard on paved surfaces, but it can also weight your plants down and cause them to break.

389

 Can I add a few more heads to one station of my sprinkler system?

You can always add heads. The bigger question is whether there will be enough pressure to drive them all. Talk with an expert at your local hardware store or pipe supplier. You'll need to know things like your average water pressure, the sizes of valves and supply lines that feed that station, the numbers of heads on the station and the water flow that each of those heads can deliver. Once all those variables are mixed into the equation, you can start to determine if there will be sufficient pressure. All of which explains why it's good business to hire a veteran contractor for anything other than simple tasks.

390

Several of my sprinkler heads don't seem to be spraying straight. How do I get them back into better working order?

It's not at all difficult. Most will have some type of plastic strainer to catch debris that creeps into the system. Take the head apart and remove the strainer. If it's full of chaff and other debris, clean it thoroughly, then put it back into the head. Most heads have small arrows embossed onto their tops to indicate the direction of the spray pattern. Make sure they're properly aligned.

391

Some of my large in-ground heads that lift and spray ground-cover beds don't come out all the way. It also seems like there isn't as much pressure as before. What might be the problem?

Usually, a gasket is worn out. Generally, you can take those heads apart and get the old gasket out. Take it to a local supplier and buy extra gaskets for future needs. When one loses its seal, watch for the rest to follow suit.

Fertilizing

What type of fertilizer is best for my lawn?

If you're asking about a specific brand, there are many good fertilizers on the market. The important thing is that it have the proper ratio of its nutrients, and that half of its nitrogen be in a slow-release form. For much of Texas, research has shown that our soils are already quite high in phosphorus, the middle number of the three-number analysis. Excessive phosphorus can actually cause problems of toxicity. That buildup is especially true for Texas's clays, and that's why you'll see suggestions of a 3-1-2 or 4-1-2 ratio fertilizer for those soils. You should have your soil tested every two or three years to monitor the levels of all three elements.

 Which is better, 21-7-14 or 15-5-10? I see both at the nursery.

 Both are 3-1-2 ratio fertilizers. Check the fine print to see how much of the nitrogen (first number of the analysis) is in a slow-release encapsulated form. If those percentages are equal you should expect to pay approximately 50 percent more for the 21-7-14 than you do for the 15-5-10, simply because it has that much more nutrient content. If the prices don't follow that pattern, select the better value.

☆394☆

 When do I need to fertilize my lawn?

 There are lots of variables to fertilizing, including type of grass, amount of rainfall, and location within Texas. If your grass is pale and sluggish at a time of year when it should be growing more vigorously, that's when you should think about feeding it. If bermuda or St. Augustine are producing seed heads, you probably need to fertilize. Most of the quality fertilizers will last for 8 to 12 weeks, some even longer. For most warm-season grasses (St. Augustine, bermuda, zoysia, etc.), you could fertilize April 1, June 1, August 1, and October 1 in most of the state. In far North

Texas you could probably get by with three feedings: April 15, June 15 and September 15. If you have had a problem with gray leaf spot in St. Augustine you should probably not feed the grass during the middle of the summer. The September or very early October feeding is one of the really critical elements of good lawn management for any type of turf, so don't forget it. Cool-season grasses, by comparison, such as fescue and ryegrass, are fertilized in September, November, late February, and early April.

395

 We live in an area with really sandy soil. What changes do we need to make in feeding our lawn?

Fertilize it more often, but with less at each feeding. Sandy soils don't have as much surface area, so they can't retain as many nutrients as long as their clay counterparts.

396

We fertilized our lawn last week, and now we've had a really heavy rain. Do we need to feed again?

No. If you used a quality slow-release fertilizer most of it should stay in place. In any event, it takes longer than one week to assess the impact a fertilizer would have on your turf. Watch it closely over the next month or two and fertilize when its growth slows and color pales. Water departments suggest that we try to time our feedings in dry times, not just ahead of expected big rains. That will lessen the nutrient runoff into lakes and rivers. Be sure, too, that you sweep the walk and drive after you fertilize. Not only will you prevent staining of the concrete or brick pavers, but you'll also prevent all that fertilizer from washing into the storm sewers.

☆397☆

 What do you think about the "weed-and-feed" fertilizers?

On the surface they sound like terrific ideas—just one pass over your lawn and all of your problems are solved. However, it's more complex than that. It's not all that common that your grass needs to be fertilized at the same time that you need to put a weed-killer out. Make the two decisions separately and you'll be satisfied with your results, whether you choose the combination product, or whether you decide on two applications at different times. Be especially careful, too, about weedkillers that you apply near the roots of trees and shrubs. Some types can damage the rest of your landscape.

398

 I have stripes in my lawn after I fertilize it. How can I prevent that?

 Use a rotary spreader instead of your drop type. Rotary spreaders throw the fertilizer pellets out at right angles to your path, so they cover a much wider area. If you really want to get uniform coverage, you could apply half of the fertilizer going east-to-west, the other half going north-to-south.

399

 Can I save my bags of fertilizer from one year to the next?

 You bet, just as long as you don't let them get wet and turn hard.

400

 How can I identify iron deficiency in my lawn?

 Iron deficiency is characterized by yellowed leaves with dark green veins, and that's true of grasses, too. However, their veins run the length of the leaves. They actually look striped if iron is lacking. Other things can cause the grass to turn yellow, but only iron will give the stripes. Sometimes this will show up within a week or two after you have used a high-nitrogen, quick-release plant food such as ammonium sulfate (21-0-0). Go back to your quality, slow-release nitrogen source. St. Augustine is most commonly affected. Bermuda almost never is. When you apply products with iron to your turfgrass quickly sweep away any granules that land on your drive or walk before they collect moisture and cause rusty stains on your concrete.

Mowing

☆401☆

Q What mowing heights are best? My grass doesn't look good after I mow it.

A For spreading grasses with stolons ("runners"), closer mowing encourages thicker turf. With that in mind, optimum heights for season-long mowing would be: bermuda (1 to 1¼ inch); hybrid bermudas (less than 1 inch, some less than ½-inch); St. Augustine (2 to 3 inches); zoysias (1 to 1-½ inch); fescue (2 to 3 inches); buffalograss (2 to 3 inches); and centipede (1-½ to 2 inches).

402

Q My bermuda lawn always looks really bad for a day or two after I mow it. It's brown in large areas. What am I doing wrong?

A You're mowing into stem stubble. Either you need to set your mower up one notch, or you need to mow more often. Try cutting the grass on 4- or 5-day intervals for two months to see if it looks better. Be certain, too, that the blade is sharp.

403

Q How often should I mow my grass?

A That varies with the type of grass, time of year and how aggressively you have been feeding the grass. In the summer, however, it's conceivable that you'd be mowing bermuda or St. Augustine on 4- or 5-day intervals. Aim never to remove more than 1/3 of the grass blades' length at any one mowing.

404

 I still catch all my clippings. I like the way the lawn looks when I do. Can I work them into the garden?

 It would be much better if you would compost them for 6 to 12 months, so they're dried and unrecognizable. That's true whether you intend to till them into the garden soil or just use them as a mulch. Fresh clippings pack together and prohibit good flow of water and fertilizers, plus they can actually rob the soil of available nitrogen as bacteria break them down.

405

 The ends of my grass blades are visibly browned. What does that tell me?

 It suggests you need to sharpen your lawn mower blade. Remove the spark plug wire so the engine can't crank while you're taking the blade off. Remove equal amounts from each side of the blade to keep it balanced. Re-sharpen the blade after every 20 to 30 hours of use, more often if it's been used in extreme conditions.

406

 What do we do when we have consecutive days of rainy weather and the grass grows far too tall? How can we get it back to its normal mowing height without causing it to be yellowed?

Mow it in two steps. Set your mower up one notch and mow it. Drop it back down one or two days later and mow the second time.

407

I notice at the ballparks that the grass seems to have a grain. How does that happen?

It's all determined by the direction of the mowers. Curiously, there are some important messages to be learned from their turf examples. Mow in different directions every time that you mow so that your grass won't develop its own grain, or "lean" of the blades. If you mow consistently in the same direction, the grass will lay down and your mower eventually won't cut the grass at the proper height. Also, the ballpark professionals mow twice each time that they mow. They make their cuts at right angles to each other, giving that checkerboard appearance. That can really make your lawn look nice, and it will grind up every clipping.

Insects

☆408☆

Q My St. Augustine is turning yellow, then tan along my sidewalk and out in the middle of our front yard. What causes that?

A If it's in the hottest, sunniest part of your yard, it's probably from chinch bugs. The grass will first appear dry, but watering won't bring it back. Get on your hands and knees in the hot part of the day and look at the interface between healthy grass and dying grass (not in the dead areas) for pinhead-sized black insects with white diamonds on their backs. You may also see the immature red forms. Control them with a recommended insecticide.

☆409☆

Q My lawngrass pulls loose easily from the soil. Both bermuda and St. Augustine seem to be equally affected. It's like an old, dead rug out there now. Before I lose it all, help! What can I do?

A It sounds like grub worm damage. Dig at the edge of one of the affected areas. If you find more than 3 to 4 of the fat white C-shaped worms per square foot (3/4-inch long) with legs and brown heads, then they are your problem. Treat with a listed insecticide, and water the insecticide deeply into the soil. It will take it 3 to 4 weeks to take effect. Next year, treat 6 weeks after the major flight of the adult of that pest, the June beetle, with the same insecticide. You'll use less, plus it will be much more effective because it will be addressing the grub worms while they're still small and quite near the soil surface. Mid- and late-summer treatments are most effective. You will gain very little by treating existing problems in late fall.

Don't make winter and spring treatments, which waste money and introduce chemicals that aren't going to be effective anyway.

410

Q Grub worms have ruined my lawn. Should I leave the old dead grass in place, or should I rake it up?

A You might as well remove it. It's not going to re-root. The grubs will have done all of their current damage by the time spring planting season rolls around, so you won't have to treat immediately after planting your new grass in April or May, even if you do still see some signs of the grubs. By mid-spring they'll be preparing to pupate (change to adult June beetles), so they won't be feeding any longer.

411

Q My bermuda looks sick in odd patches. The runners, such as they are, don't appear vigorous, and the grass is dying. What are the possible causes?

A It's very likely that bermuda mites are involved. They're even smaller than red spider mites, their more common cousins, so you won't be able to see them at all. You can see their damage, however. They cause the runners to be very shortened, almost clubby, and eventually look almost like an old-fashioned shaving brush with very small leaves attached in clumps. Control them by spraying with a listed insecticide directly down into the affected patches. Since they're an inch or two off the ground, sprays are better than granules.

412

Q I have swarms of tiny gnats that fly up while I'm walking across my lawn. Do they do any harm? Should I worry about spraying them?

A They do no damage to the turf or to you. Although general-purpose insecticides will eliminate them easily, it would be hard to justify using an insecticide.

Diseases

☆413☆

Q My St. Augustine seems to be hungry. It appears yellowed from a distance, yet fertilizer seems to make it worse. Iron hasn't helped. It seems to be dying. What is wrong?

A That has become one of the most common sets of symptoms in turf care. It's probably gray leaf spot, a fungal disease. Look closely at the blades and the runners. If you see pinhead-sized gray-brown lesions that are diamond-shaped, that's the disease. You'll have to look closely to be certain it's present. This has become a very serious threat to our St. Augustine, and it's hard to recognize. It does, indeed, get worse after you feed it during the summer. Control it with Daconil, and avoid any high-nitrogen fertilizer in the affected area between mid-June and early September.

☆414☆

Q My St. Augustine has almost circular yellow spots. It's happened in the same areas in previous autumns. The grass does seem to come back, but I lost one of the spots in a cold spell a couple of years ago. What causes that?

A That's probably brown patch. If you pull on the leaf blades, and if they come loose easily from the runners, that's the problem. You'll notice that the blades are browned and deteriorated where they attach to the runners. Control it with a listed fungicide.

415

Q My fescue is dying, clear down to the soil. It's in 2- and 3-foot round patches, and it doesn't look like there will be anything left to come back. It looked fine coming out of the winter a couple of months ago, but I don't think there will be anything left by the time it gets really hot this summer. What is its problem?

Fescue can develop brown patch in late spring. It attacks the blades near the soil line. Fescue does not produce runners, so, unlike St. Augustine, fescue can actually be killed by the disease. Treat with a fungicide at first confirmation of the problem.

☆416☆

I have dead spots in my bermuda. They're about 18 inches in diameter (more or less), and they're almost completely round. They came on very quickly. What is it, and what can I do to stop it?

It sounds like fading out, a disease that often hits in late summer and fall. The grass takes on a greasy dark green look for a couple of days, then turns tan in those circles. Control it by spraying with a listed fungicide such as Daconil.

417

My St. Augustine pulls loose easily, runners and all, yet I can't find even one grub worm. It's definitely dying, however. Is that some disease?

Yes, and it's one that only in recent years has been diagnosed. It's called "take-all patch," and it works exactly like grub worms, just without the grubs. Control it with a fungicide treatment. Repeat as needed.

Weeds

☆418☆

I'm confused by weedkillers. There are so many types. Can you make some sense of them for me?

You're right. There are many different types of weedkillers. That's because there are many different categories of weeds. The interesting thing is: You don't really have to know exactly what weed you have, so long as you can put it into the right categories. To explain:

- Is it an annual weed, or does it come back as a perennial, year after year, from its old root system?

- Is it a grassy type of weed, or is it a non-grassy ("broadleafed") plant?

- Does it do most of its growing in the late spring and summer ("warm-season" weed), or is it most evident from late winter into mid-spring ("cool-season" weed)?

If you can answer those three questions, you can pick the right weedkiller.

To illustrate further:

- For annual weeds you can use a *pre-emergent* weedkiller before its seeds start to sprout. These are generally granular materials, and prime times of application would be in late winter, again in late spring, with both of those treatments aimed at the summer weeds, then in early to mid-September for the cool-season annual weeds.

- You will need to use *post-emergent* granules or sprays to eliminate existing weeds that you can see in your landscape.

- There are broadleafed post-emergent sprays and granules, and there are post-emergent sprays for grassy weeds.

Your local nurseryman can show you several options.

419

Q The weedkiller I used seemed to be a fertilizer for the weeds. They didn't even know they had been sprayed. What could I have done wrong?

A Usually, when that happens, it's because of an error in our application. Weedkillers require as much leaf area as possible for the best results. For that reason you don't want to mow for several days before or after you spray. You don't want to spray while there is dew on the leaves, and you should not spray before a rain. If the weeds were especially woody, toward the end of their growing season, for example, the weedkiller might not be effective. Some weedkillers take longer than others to do their work, and it may be that you were simply using the wrong category of weedkiller for the problem you faced. Show your nurseryman the product you used and the weed you were trying to control, just to make sure you were properly directed.

420

 Can I use pre-emergent weedkillers around my trees and shrubs? How about in my flower beds?

In theory, pre-emergent weedkillers attack only the seeds as they start to sprout. As a result, they should be safe around any existing trees and shrubs. Nonetheless, you always want to read the directions very carefully before applying them. As for the flower beds, your nurseryman can recommend two or three pre-emergents whose prime use is in perennial gardens to stop the growth of crabgrass and other annual grassy weeds.

421

I have misused a weedkiller and now my trees are suffering. Can I do anything to reverse the effects?

Keep the plants moist, and avoid any high-nitrogen fertilizer that might cause them to grow too rapidly. There are probably no heroic measures for you to use, but you might contact the manufacturer for specific suggestions.

422

 I put a weedkiller on my lawn and two days later it rained. Do I need to spray again?

Probably not. Most weedkillers would have been absorbed into the leaf tissues by that time. Wait a week or two to see the result, then treat again if it looks like it's not going to do its job.

423

Q I have weeds coming up under my bird feeders. I'm sure they're coming from the seed that was dropped by the birds. How can I prevent that?

A Try black oil-type sunflower seed. It's a favorite with all kinds of desirable birds. Any seeds that fall to the ground are quickly eaten by ground-feeding species, and, should any germinate, you can easily cultivate and remove them. What you're probably seeing is millet that the birds have kicked out of the feeder as they looked for seed they preferred. You could also place your feeders over a bed of bark mulch, so you could spray or cultivate to remove any seedlings that showed up.

CONTROL OF SPECIFIC WEEDS

☆424☆

Q How do I stop the spread of crabgrass and grassburs?

A They are both warm-season annual weeds, so pre-emergent weedkillers will work well. Make your first treatment March 1-20 and repeat June 1-20 and you should have no further problem. You can eliminate existing crabgrass from bermuda turf with MSMA or DSMA applied in late spring or early summer. By August there is no justification for treating, as the weed will be dying away soon. Use MSMA and DSMA only in bermuda—both will kill St. Augustine.

425

Q How can I eliminate St. Augustine that is invading my bermuda lawn? Both of my neighbors have St. Augustine, and now it has almost covered my bermuda.

Use either MSMA or DSMA in late May or June. Either will kill the St. Augustine without doing anything worse than temporarily yellowing the bermuda. Freed of the competition of the St. Augustine, your bermuda will fill back in fairly quickly.

426

What is the little grass with all those seed heads in March and April?

That's annual bluegrass. You'll also see it listed as *Poa annua*. Your only reliable way of controlling it is prevention with a pre-emergent weedkiller applied in early to mid-September. That same schedule will also eliminate rye, rescuegrass and other cool-season grassy weeds from your lawn.

☆427☆

How do I eliminate dallisgrass from my lawn? How can I be sure that's what I have?

Dallisgrass forms thick clumps that are 12 to 15 inches in diameter. It is deep green, and its flower heads form within days of mowing. Some folks confuse it with Johnsongrass, which is much taller and light green. Johnsongrass is seldom a problem in lawns that are regularly mowed. It produces large white roots with red overtones at their joints. Use MSMA or DSMA for either grass, but in bermuda turf only. It will yellow the bermuda, but it will kill the dallisgrass. In St. Augustine you'll either have to spot-treat with one of the glyphosates or hand-dig this one weed. Dallisgrass is the only weed (and only in St. Augustine) for which we have no chemical control for use in an existing lawn. Once you have eliminated it from your lawn, you might benefit by using a pre-emergent weedkiller. Its seeds are all viable, and they're also persistent in the soil for several years after the mother plants have been eliminated. Times for those applications: March, May, and July.

☆428☆

 What will kill things like clover, dandelions and that ugly little weed with the purple flowers that I have every spring?

 That weed is henbit, and simply mowing your lawn will usually get rid of it. It's a weak grower that doesn't have the energy to form new stems and leaves once it's been cut down. You can use any of the many broadleafed weedkiller sprays to control all three of these non-grassy weeds. Read and follow label directions carefully, for the best results. Treat prior to Thanksgiving, if at all possible. These weeds will be small and just getting started at that point. If you wait until they're big and unsightly, it will be too cool for the spray to work and you'll have to look at them until it warms up in the spring. Best answer of all: Prevent them from germinating with a pre-emergent named Gallery. Unlike all of our older pre-emergents, Gallery attacks broadleafed plants' seeds as they sprout. Time your application for early to mid-September.

429

How can I kill poison ivy?

If it's out in the open, where you can easily spray it, use a broadleafed weedkiller applied while it's really actively growing in late spring. Keep that type of weedkiller off any trees or shrubs that might be damaged. If it's growing against tree trunks, and if it has made very large trunks of its own as it ascended the trees, carefully cut those poison ivy stems near the ground. Leave the tops of the vines to die in the trees, then spray the regrowth that comes up from the base of the old poison ivy stumps. You could even pour the broadleafed weedkiller at full strength directly onto the freshly cut stump, but don't let it run off and into the soil. In a year or two those stems you have left hanging in the tree will relax their hold and fall to the ground, at which time you can gather and discard them. Remember that all parts of poison ivy can cause an allergic reaction, including leaves, stems and even roots. It's the oil that is in all parts of the plant that causes us to break out, and that oil can splatter as you're cutting the stems. Remember, too, that every human being is, at some point or another, very susceptible to poison ivy. Don't ever assume you're a super-human, because that's when you'll have your outbreak. Wear protective clothing and washable gloves. Take a hot soapy bath immediately after you work around it, and wash your clothes in hot water. If you are one of the unlucky folks who are always being bothered by poison ivy, perhaps you'd better find some other person to do any and all work around it. Finally, should poison ivy come up in a groundcover or shrub bed, use a foam rubber paintbrush to apply weedkiller directly to the poison ivy foliage. You could also use a disposable glove on one hand and insert a dandelion digger with the other to cut and pull young poison ivy seedlings as they start to grow.

430

 I have two really difficult weeds, wild violets and wild onions. What will kill them?

Both can be killed with a broadleafed weedkiller, even though only the wild violets have what you would call "broad" leaves. Neither is a grass, so the broadleafed herbicides are appropriate. Use a fine spray pattern to coat the leaves without runoff, and, if necessary, mix one or two drops of a liquid dishwashing detergent to help the spray stick on the leaves. Spring is the time to treat.

431

What is the little flat milkweed-like plant that's in my lawn and flower beds? How can I deal with it?

That's spurge, and it should be no trouble for your turfgrass. You can apply a broadleafed weedkiller in the lawn, but you also need to take better care of your turf. Spurge doesn't show up unless there is some major problem. In shrub bed areas you can spot-treat with one of the glyphosate sprays. Mulching also discourages it, and you could apply Gallery broadleafed pre-emergent weedkiller in March and again in June.

432

 Q What is the low spreading weed with the kidney-shaped leaves? It's really quite pretty, but it's taking over my lawn.

 A That's dichondra. It is pretty enough that it's used as a lawn substitute in California. You can eliminate it with any of the broadleafed weedkillers. In fact, Californians are specifically warned not to use them on dichondra lawns.

☆433☆

Q What will kill nutgrass in my lawn and in my flower beds?

A The product that will do the best job is called Image. The manufacturer recommends two treatments 30 days apart, with both of them being made between May 15 and September 15 in most of Texas. That's the time period the nutsedge (sedges have triangular stems, while true grasses have round stems) is most active. Image will retard the growth of your permanent lawn grass, but it won't harm it. Fact is, Image was originally tested as a means of slowing the growth of turf, to reduce the number of times it had to be mowed. The fact that they found a reliable way of eliminating our most tenacious weed was like drilling for water and discovering oil. Give it 3 to 4 weeks to cause a reduction in the population of nutsedge.

☆434☆

Q What is the stemmy little weed that has light orchid flowers in August and September, and how can I eliminate it?

 A That's roadside aster, and it should be the easiest weed of all to eliminate if you take just minimal care of your turf. Fertilize the grass and mow frequently, and the aster seeds will never germinate next year. They simply can't compete. You can use a broadleafed weedkiller to eliminate any that are visible. It's an annual weed that germinates in the spring, so again Gallery applied in early April could stop its sprouting. Truly, though, you'd be better served spending the same money on good lawn food.

☆435☆

I have briars coming up all over my yard. How can I eliminate them? We're about to move into the new house, and I don't want to have to contend with these forever.

Those are smilax briars. Mowing alone will eliminate 95 percent of them. The plants have few leaves, and those that are there are quite glossy, so they shed any weedkillers that you might spray on them. The best way to get rid of them is to mow them, then hand-dig the tubers of those few that do return. It only takes 20 to 30 seconds to dig each tuber, and those plants will never sprout again.

MULCHING, DETHATCHING AND AERATING

436

Is mulching grass clippings back into the lawn a good idea? Doesn't that lead to thatch?

If you're using that quality, slow-release fertilizer, and if you're mowing on 4- or 5-day intervals during the active part of the growing season, mulching the clippings back into the lawn will not lead to thatch formation at all. That's the essential principle behind the "Don't Bag It" lawn-management program that has been designed to conserve Texas's landfill space.

437

Is "scalping" my lawn a good idea? When is it done?

That's a term to describe cutting dead stubble back in very late winter, so the new spring growth can freely develop. It involves dropping your lawn mower down one or two notches, then bagging or raking and collecting the clippings to tidy up your lawn. To a degree, scalping is an aesthetic project that merely lets you see the bright green new growth more quickly. However, it also eliminates many of the early spring weeds, plus it lets the sun's warming rays hit the soil more efficiently. It's not the most critical job you'll ever do for your lawn, but it certainly doesn't hurt. What it can hurt, however, is you. Wear a quality respirator and goggles to prevent a serious allergic reaction to the dust and mold it stirs up.

438

Q I think I have thatch in my lawn. Should I use a dethatcher, and when? Why does thatch form?

A Thatch is the layer of undecomposed organic matter that develops on top of the ground and under grass runners. Given time it can become impenetrable to water and nutrients, almost like a piece of thick canvas. Don't confuse thatch, however, with the dried stubble that a lawn has after a cold winter. Those are just old grass blades that are standing in place. Bermuda is most likely to have a layer of thatch, and your first evidence will be random areas that just don't seem to respond to fertilizer and water. They'll often be in sunny spots, where the grass has grown very actively in the past. You may even detect a spongy feeling when you walk on those areas. If you suspect thatch, take a square-bladed shovel and dig a piece of sod. If there is thatch, you'll be able to see it beneath the runners. Use an aerifier that actually pulls plugs through the thatch and out onto the top of the lawn to help eliminate the thatch. Dethatchers work, but they also tear away at the runners, which is not good for the vigor of the grass. Dethatching is a spring job, but aerifying can be done at any time. St. Augustine is less likely to form thatch. Hybrid bermudas seem to be the worst for thatch. Avoid high-nitrogen, quick-release fertilizers, and mow your lawn frequently so the grass clippings will be comparatively small—two practices that will lessen the potential of thatch.

439

Q I saw a product that claimed it would "eat the thatch" organically. Would that help?

That's probably an extravagant claim made for a product with limited or no *bona fide* testing and proof. Ask a trained horticulturist at the store where you saw it for his or her advice.

GENERAL PROBLEM SOLVING

440

My bermuda has black seed heads all over it. When I walk though the lawn my white sneakers turn dark. What will stop it?

That's smut, a fungal disease. However, instead of trying to control it with some type of fungicide, use a high-nitrogen fertilizer to promote vegetative growth in the grass.

441

My St. Augustine has seed heads. Will they produce good seeds, and, if not, how can I stop them? They're very unsightly.

Same answer as with the bermuda. Stop them by applying a high-nitrogen fertilizer. They will not produce viable seeds.

442

My St. Augustine has runners that arch out over the lawn. What causes that, and do I need to be concerned?

That's a very common situation with St. Augustine. It usually seems to develop when the grass needs to be fertilized. However, if you don't need or want to fertilize, just lift them up with your foot as you're mowing, then let the blade shred them on the next pass around the lawn. They are basically a non-issue.

443

We have low spots in our lawn and need to fill them. What time of year is best to do that? What kind of soil should we use?

Do it when the grass is growing aggressively. Late spring is ideal. Use dry washed brick sand for shallow depressions (1 inch or less). Either use a leaf rake to "comb" the fill through the grass, or wash it in gently with a spray head on your garden hose. For deeper ruts, dig the sod and fill the low area with topsoil, then put the sod back in place.

444

I have noticed that my grass stays green longer if I leave tree leaves on top of it. Is that a satisfactory process?

No. It encourages disease by creating moist, dark conditions. Also, should a January cold front blow those leaves away, suddenly your grass could be exposed to severe cold for the first time and damage could be equally severe. Plus, your landscape would look untidy. It's better just to keep the leaves picked up and let the grass go naturally dormant.

445

Do mushrooms do any damage to my lawn? How can I stop them?

Mushrooms do no long-term damage to turf. They live off the dead organic matter from old building debris or rotting tree roots, forming their toadstools and mushrooms as a part of their life process. They tie up the available nitrogen in the soil for a short period of time, then they release it back to the grass. That's why you may see streaks of dark green in otherwise average turf. To eliminate them just drag the hose over them and break off their caps. No spray is especially dependable on mushrooms.

ANNUALS

GENERAL QUESTIONS ABOUT ANNUALS

446

Q I don't like to replant my flowers every year. Aren't annuals a lot more trouble than perennial flowers?

A Not if you consider the great display they'll make and the length of time they flower. That's why all the amusement parks and other major commercial landscapes that feature lavish color always use annuals. Granted, you have to replant two or three times each year, but the rewards are worth the extra effort. Periodically, you must dig and divide perennials, too.

447

Q What kind of soil preparation will I need to make for my annuals?

A Think about preparing a sort of potting soil. Annual flowers need loose, well-drained, highly organic planting soils, which means you'll want to include 4 to 5 inches of organic matter. If you're dealing with a tight clay soil you might also mix in as much as 1 inch of washed brick sand or a similar product—but only in combination with the organic matter. Rototill all of this 4 to 5 inches into the original topsoil. Not only will you have an excellent planting mix, but also you will have automatically prepared a raised flower bed. That will ensure adequate drainage.

448

Q Will I need to redo my annual beds every year? How long will the soil improvement last?

You should probably add one new inch of organic matter between each crop of annuals. That may actually mean that you'll be adding organic matter two or three times every calendar year. Always re-till the soil to blend it all together.

449

What kinds of annuals can I start from seeds sown directly into the garden?

That's really risky, primarily due to the cost of seed and the insects and diseases that are waiting to take their toll on the young plants. However, some of the fast-growing, large-seeded plants can be sown directly into the ground. These include: zinnias, marigolds, cleome, celosia, sweet peas, larkspur, hollyhocks, amaranthus, gomphrenas, sunflowers, morning glories, California poppies, nasturtiums, moss rose, and, of course, wildflowers.

450

If I want to start my own seedlings indoors, how do I do it?

You'll need a highly organic, porous and sterile potting mix (with no native soil). Thoroughly moisten the planting mix, then sow the seeds in rows in very shallow furrows. Sow them thinly, with enough space between seeds that they won't crowd one another. You can crease the seed packet to make a line along which you can tap the seeds. Smaller seeds will not need to be covered, but BB-sized seeds can be covered one to two times their thickness with the same mix. Remoisten the surface of the planting medium, then place it in a bright and warm location until the seeds start to sprout. Once you can see seedlings you'll need to move the seed flats to very bright light, so the young seedlings won't get lanky and spindly. Once they're tall enough to handle by their true leaves (never touch the stem itself), replant them individually into small pots filled with the same good potting mix. Fertilize them with a root-stimulator liquid fertilizer after planting, then use a complete-and-balanced analysis with each subsequent feeding.

451

 Can I save seeds from my annual flowers?

For some, yes, and, for others, it wouldn't be a good idea. If you're growing hybrid flowers, remember they won't come back true to their original looks and habits. If you want the same type of flowers, you'll need to buy new seeds. For inbred types, however, you can collect the seeds, dry them and store them in a cool, dry spot until the next planting season. Unfortunately, there is no way you can distinguish between hybrids and inbreds unless you know from the start.

452

 My flower and vegetable transplants died within a few days of being planted into the garden. What went wrong?

Usually that's either because you let them get too dry, or else they weren't acclimatized to the sun, wind and temperatures to which they were suddenly exposed. Make sure your transplants are always tough, or "hardened," before you set them out.

453

What size of transplant works best for annual flowers?

There has been a shift toward larger 4-inch and even 6-inch potted transplants. These are plants that are half-grown or more and that look good the day they're set out. That's the whole principle behind the "change-out" at amusement parks and botanic gardens, where the beds look almost as good the day after the new plants are planted as they will when they mature. However, if your budget is tight, consider smaller potted transplants. You'll have to be careful that they don't dry out on hot or windy days until they are sufficiently rooted.

454

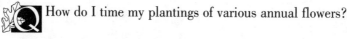 How do I time my plantings of various annual flowers?

There are types that grow best in cooler weather, including pansies, pinks, petunias, snapdragons, calendulas, nasturtiums, sweet peas, flowering cabbage and kale, alyssum, English daisies, poppies and wallflowers. Depending on where you live in Texas, you may be able to plant some or all of these in the fall for flowering through the winter and into mid- or late spring. The farther north you are, the fewer of these plants you'll be able to set out in the fall, and the more that you will need to plant in late winter. Ask your nurseryman for precise information for your area. As those finish you can replace them with plants that endure maximum heat, including lantanas, moss rose, purslane, dahlberg daisies, marigolds, zinnias, cosmos, celosias, gomphrenas, fire bush, copper plants, coleus, caladiums, and cleome.

455

 Do I need to pick the seeds off my annuals as they finish blooming?

That's not practical in most cases. However, for large-flowering plants such as zinnias and marigolds, you may want to "dead head" the old flowers, not so much to remove the seeds, but to keep the plants looking tidy.

456

 How do I pick the best combination for my annual flowers? I want something that is really showy.

Use just one or two types and colors of flowers per bed. That way you'll be able to mass colors together for the greatest impact. Beds of mixed colors, pansies, for example, don't show up very well from a distance. Remember that brighter, "warmer" colors advance visually, so passersby will see them first. If you want to have an area look larger, use pastels and "cooler" colors.

457

What kind of a weedkiller can I use to get my flower bed ready?

Use one of the glyphosates or similar herbicides to kill all existing vegetation prior to working the soil. These materials do not contaminate the soil, so you can use them within a week or two of your planting date. They'll need that long to kill the existing bermudagrass and other weeds.

458

How can I keep weeds out of my flower beds once I get things planted?

Use a 1- to 2-inch layer of shredded pine bark or other mulch. That will discourage most weeds enough so that you'll be able to cultivate the survivors with a small garden hoe. There are pre-emergent weedkillers that are labeled for use in annual gardens, but be certain that you'll not be sowing seed any-time within 3 to 5 months after the treatment. You can also spot-treat with the same glyphosate by using either a small squirt bottle sprayer or a foam rubber paintbrush to apply the herbicide direct-ly and only to the weeds.

459

Many times my transplants just sit there. They fail to grow or bloom after I get them planted. What might I be doing wrong?

It may be that they were rootbound and stunted. If that's the case, buy younger, more vigorous plants the next time. With some plants, such as celosias, marigolds and zinnias, among others, it's better to buy transplants that are budded, but not show-ing color to their flowers. Buy plants that are growing in approximately the same amount of light they will receive in their new spots. If you take a plant out of a shady nursery and set it into full sun, it will usually stop growing. It sometimes helps to break the soil ball apart ever so slightly, so the roots get out of that circular growth pattern. Be careful not to let the plants become too dry the first week or two they're in your garden. Use a water-soluble fertilizer to keep them active. Once transplants are stunted they rarely recover and reach full potential.

460

 What kind of fertilizer is best for my annual garden?

 There are many good options. Water-soluble complete-and-balanced fertilizers work well for young plants, and you can continue using them for the whole life of the crop. However, you can also use quality, slow-release lawn foods for most flowers in most Texas soils. A soil test will be the best indication of the precise needs. There also are timed-release fertilizers that could be worked into the top 1/2-inch of soil, to release their nutrients over the entire season.

461

I'd like to grow flowers in pots. I have very little ground space, but a nice deck and patio. How successful will that be?

Depending on the size of the pot, your choice of potting soil and the care program you practice, it can be really successful. Use a lightweight commercial potting soil (no native soils to be sure). Each pot must have a drainage hole, and they should be 12 inches or more in diameter, just to give the annuals enough root room to grow. Keep them moist at all times, and fertilize them regularly with a water-soluble, complete-and-balanced fertilizer. Include a few hanging baskets, too.

TROPICAL ANNUALS

Bananas

☆462☆

Q I'd like to save my banana trees for another year. What do I need to do for the winter?

A That question depends on where you live. If the bananas are along the Gulf Coast, they'll come back just fine, even if their tops do freeze in extreme cold. In Central and North Central Texas bananas usually come back from their roots, even though their tops freeze to the ground. In the northernmost parts of Texas you're going to have to bring them into a greenhouse or heated, bright garage. If you decide to leave your plants outdoors, mulch over them with 1 to 2 feet of shredded leaves. Secure them in place with a "tent" of old burlap. Remove the covering when things begin to warm up in March.

Bougainvillea

☆463☆

Q Why won't my bougainvillea flower? What does it need to do its best?

A Unlike hibiscus, which flower all through the hot months, bougainvilleas are much more cyclical. They bloom best when they're somewhat rootbound, and they seem to flower well coming out of dormancies brought on by cool winter greenhouse temperatures (55° F to 60° F minimum) and summer's heat. Use a diluted solution of a complete-and-balanced fertilizer analysis with each watering.

Tropical Hibiscus

464

Q Why don't my tropical hibiscus plants bloom? They have grown beautifully, but have had no major numbers of flowers since the day we bought them.

Hibiscus plants produce their flower buds on new growth, so plants that are lethargic growers will follow suit with their flowers. Specialty hibiscus fertilizers have comparatively high nitrogen contents. It's also important that the plants receive really bright light, preferably full sunlight, at least into mid-afternoon. If you're growing them in pots that means you'll have to redouble your efforts of keeping them properly watered. With all that watering, you're also going to have to use the water-soluble hibiscus fertilizer fairly often. One last reason: Hibiscus plants seem sluggish to bloom if they have been over-wintered in cool, dark conditions, such as a garage or even a cool room in your house. It really seems to stop their growth and subsequent blooming for many weeks in the spring and into the summer.

Mandevilla

465

I'm in love with mandevilla. What special needs does it have?

This tropical vine has really caught the hearts of Texas gardeners. Give it morning sun and shade from mid-afternoon on in the summer. It requires warm temperatures, so it won't grow and bloom as well in early spring and late fall. It needs a complete-and-balanced fertilizer with each watering. The biggest specific problem it's likely to encounter is mealybugs. Use a tender house-plant insecticide to eliminate them as they show up.

Wildflowers

☆466☆

I want to plant wildflowers. When do I sow the seed?

You need to follow nature's lead, at least in general. That means that spring-flowering types that would have been wild-sown in nature as the seeds matured in early summer, should at least be planted by late August or September. They germinate with the first fall rains, establishing their deep roots over late fall and winter, for the early spring bloom. Planting after mid-October is probably a waste of time and seeds. By comparison, summer- and fall-flowering types can be planted in the spring.

467

 What kind of soil preparation do I need to make for my wild-flower plantings?

 Believe it or not, they will benefit from a little extra help. That doesn't mean that you have to add in 4 inches of organic matter like you might do for pansies and petunias, but you should at least kill the existing turfgrass and rototill or cultivate the soil lightly. Give them their own dedicated planting sites. Most important of all: Don't plant them into existing turf. They need the entire spring to grow, bloom and set seed, and, by that time, the turf will completely choke them out. Think about where you see the best wildflowers in Texas, and it's never where there is abundant bermudagrass. Usually they're in the forsaken, eroded soils on slopes and in draws.

468

Do the mixtures of wildflower seeds work very well, or will one type eventually overtake all the others?

If you buy a mix that has been blended for, or collected in, your area, it should establish well. Some of the species may do better than others, but that's the way it is in nature, too. Avoid mixes from out-of-state sources that are selling species you don't know and that won't grow in your area. There are in-state specialty houses that feature Texas' best-adapted wildflower seeds.

469

When should I plant my bluebonnet seeds? Will transplants that I see in the nurseries work? When should they be set out?

Bluebonnets have extremely hard seed coats, which means that native bluebonnet seeds will germinate over a period of many years. If you want really good germination for a specific planting area, and if you're going to be able to water them as they sprout, plant acid-scarified seed. These have been bathed in a special acid solution to break through their seed coats. They germinate uniformly. As for the transplants, they're a good way of getting a few plants started, perhaps to act as seed sources for subsequent years. However, for large-scale plantings, they're not nearly as practical as the seed.

470

 I want to plant Indian paintbrushes. How do I do that?

 This second most-popular of our Texas wildflowers is much more difficult to establish. Where it grows natively there are microorganisms that are part and parcel to its vigor. In virgin soils it will be much weaker. It's probably a lot less frustrating just to let this one stay in its native homes.

471

How long must I leave the dead stubble where my wildflowers were? It's getting unsightly.

If you hope for the wildflowers to reseed and bloom again next year, you need to leave that stubble until all of their seed capsules and pods have ruptured and distributed their seeds. For spring-flowering types, that may mean that you don't mow clear into June.

MOST COMMON
QUESTIONS ABOUT SPECIFIC ANNUALS

Alyssum

472

I planted sweet alyssum when I found them in the nursery. Now that it's summer, the plants are still growing. Should I leave them in until the fall?

No. Remove them and replant in the fall or next spring. Alyssum isn't equipped for the summer in the South. Treat them only as cool-season annual flowers.

Begonias

473

Q My young begonia plants are toppling over. Their stems seem to have been eaten, but I can't find any insects. What does that?

A Probably pillbugs. They're fond of the soft, succulent stems and chew into them almost like tiny beavers. If that sounds like the problem you see, dust the ground around the plants with Sevin, or use one of the snail-slug-pillbug baits.

474

Q My begonias look like they have been boiled. The edges of their leaves are browned and the flowers are as well. They looked so good all spring, but the summer hasn't been kind to them. What more can I do to save them?

A At first we hardly used wax begonias in landscaping, then we tried to use them everywhere, full sun included. While the bronze-leafed types are somewhat resistant to sunlight, they really should not be used in full, hot afternoon sun. Above all, don't put water on them while they're in full sun. It's also important that we plant begonias early in the season, certainly by early May, so they can get well established before the really hot days arrive. Summer plantings usually scorch and wither, while plants given 6 to 8 weeks to acclimatize seem to do pretty well.

475

Q Will my begonias come back next year, and, if so, how can I help them survive the winter?

 A For some reason many folks expect wax begonias to survive our winters. Although they may come back after mild cold spells, that's usually only along the immediate Gulf Coast. Treat them as annuals, and buy new plants in the spring.

476

Can I take my begonias up and overwinter them in the house?

Absolutely, but be prepared to cut them back and reshape them as you bring them indoors. You'll need to keep them in a really bright spot over the winter, preferably in full sunlight.

Caladiums

477

When can I plant my caladiums? The nurseries start getting them in February, but I'm told that's way too early.

Caladiums are tropical plants, and they require soil temperatures approaching 70 degrees. That means you should wait until one month after the last killing freeze in your area. If you want to wait even longer than that, so much the better. You can actually plant caladium tubers into mid-summer and still get the same number of weeks of good color from them.

478

What size of caladium "bulbs" should I buy? The larger ones cost a good bit more.

For individual pots you may want to grow the largest tubers, but, for use in your flower beds, smaller sizes are great. You can afford to plant them closer together, plus they stay shorter, for a better overall look.

479

Which side of the caladium tuber goes up? A nurseryman told me they plant theirs upside-down.

Some growers do that in the assumption that they'll get more and smaller leaves, for a better-looking container caladium.

Try some each way and see if you see any difference, and, if so, if you like it. It probably isn't a critical issue.

480

Q What are the round things that are growing up in my caladiums and elephant ears? Are they some type of flower? What should I do with them?

A Those *are* their flowers. They're a jack-in-the-pulpit type of flowering plant, similar to peace lilies, dieffenbachias, philodendrons, Chinese evergreens and others. You need to pinch them off. Don't let them develop, or they will stop future production of leaves. They aren't attractive anyway.

481

Q Since I'm growing my caladiums for their leaves, do I use my lawn food on them?

A Probably not. You'll find that caladiums that get that much nitrogen often lose their bright foliar colors. You can even end up with essentially green plants. It's better to use a small amount of a complete-and-balanced analysis fertilizer.

☆482☆

 Q How do I store my caladium tubers for next year?

A The humane suggestion probably is that you don't try to save them. Most of us try it once, then vow that we'll never do it again. If you do want to try it, dig the tubers after their tops have folded up tent for that growing season, usually by mid-October. You must do it before the tubers are exposed to a hard freeze. Lay the tubers on pieces of newspaper in the garage for a few days, to let them dry. Store them in dry perlite, sawdust or other suitable material. Do not allow any two tubers to touch one another, and don't layer them in their boxes. Store them warm (60 degrees), and don't take them out for planting until one month after your last freeze.

Candletrees

483

Q When should I plant my candletrees, and will they come back year after year?

A Plant the young seedlings in late May or early June for flowering that fall. The plants are annuals, dying out with the first freeze of the winter. You can save seed if you wish, then plant it the following spring.

Cockscomb

484

Q My cockscomb plants are in flower when I buy them, but they never really take hold after that. It seems like they never look as good as the plants I see in old neighborhoods. Are those plants that have come back from seeds every year?

A If you want to try cockscomb, set out transplants that have yet to form flower buds. You'll be the astute gardener who knows that cockscombs, marigolds, zinnias, verbenas and other annuals that are already in flower when you buy them may not ever do much more flowering once they're planted. If in doubt, do a side-by-side comparison.

Coleus

485

Q I have been trying coleus now for several years. The plants look beautiful when I buy them, but they never grow very tall. They seem to be determined to bloom immediately. Is there some plant food that will keep them from flowering?

A You need to switch over to the cutting-grown types of coleus. These are selections that have been made because of their vegetative habits. They may form flower spikes late in the growing season, but all spring and summer they look fabulous. If you grow seedling coleus you'll need to pinch out the flower spikes as they first show. Pinch the growing tips out of the cutting-grown types, too, to keep the plants full and compact.

486

 Q What are the white bugs that are killing my coleus? They were fine until I brought them indoors this winter.

 A Those are mealybugs, soft-bodied scale insects. No plant is more attractive to them than coleus. Most general-purpose insecticides will control them, but be sure to hit the backs of the leaves with the spray. Let the spray run down into the leaf axils, too. The small insects seek that protection. Don't let them spread to your other houseplants. They're the most obnoxious of all our houseplant insect pests.

Copper Plants

487

 Q My copper plants are so tall. Is there any good way to keep them shorter?

 A "Pinch" out their growing tips every 4 to 6 weeks. They will produce side branches and stay much more compact.

Dahlias

488

Q My dahlias just aren't amounting to anything. They seem so lanky and weak. Why?

A They're suffering heat problems. With the exception of the dwarf seed-grown types, dahlias don't grow very well this far south. Unfortunately, there isn't anything you can do to help them, either. Switch to some other easier flower.

Dusty Miller

489

Q Is dusty miller a perennial? Mine have survived the winter, and now the summer.

A They'll live for a couple of years, but they really get ragged by that time. It's really better to use their attractive gray foliage as an annual bedding plant.

Firebush

490

Q I really have enjoyed my firebush. Are they actually shrubs? They look more like tender annual plants.

A Firebush (*Hamelia patens*) is root-hardy along the Gulf Coast. In most of Texas, however, it's far better used strictly as an annual, much as we do copper plants.

Flowering Kale, Cabbage

491

Q My flowering kale plants look terrible. They were so beautiful until the hard freeze. Aren't they supposed to take the winter?

A These newer hybrids seem to be somewhat less cold-hardy than the older, plainer types. When they freeze, they pretty much look like boiled cabbage. At that point you have no choice but to replace them. You might try growing them in containers, so you could shuttle them into the garage when it's going to be really cold. You could also try one of the floating fabric covers for a bit of added winter protection.

492

Q My flowering cabbage plants are getting too tall. They were nice large heads until a week or two ago, but now they're taller than the snapdragons behind them. What causes that?

A It sounds like they're bolting. That means they're about to flower and finish their life cycles. It's best to remove and replace them as they start this vertical growth.

Geraniums

493

Q I love geraniums, but they apparently don't like my garden. The plants turn yellow and quit growing and flowering. Is there anything I should be doing? Iron doesn't seem to green them up.

A Geraniums prefer cooler climates than we have in most parts of Texas. Ideally, they'd get full sunlight and daytime highs no warmer than 80 degrees. Grow them in pots, so they can have that full sunlight in the spring and fall. During the summer, pull them back into afternoon shade, to try to keep the plants alive. They may not bloom in the summer, but at least they won't bleach from the sunlight. Iron wouldn't help your plants. They're getting too much sun, not too little iron.

494

Q I'd like to take cuttings from my geraniums. Are there any special tricks?

A You root geranium cuttings just as you would cuttings from coleus, begonias or any other fleshy-stemmed annual. The one really important difference, however, is that you must take the cuttings by snapping their stems. Don't use a knife or shears to cut the stems, or you'll risk spreading serious stem diseases, which can ruin your new plants entirely. Lay the cuttings on newspaper for a couple of hours, to let them dry, before sticking them into the rooting medium.

495

Q I bought some ivy geraniums to use in a hanging basket. They aren't flowering very well. Are they also sensitive to the summer temperatures?

A Even more than the more common bushy type of standard geranium. Martha Washington geraniums are even more vulnerable to the heat. That doesn't mean that we shouldn't use these wonderful plants—it just means that we need to use them in the cooler months, and then be prepared to replace them later when summer arrives.

Gerberas

496

Q I buy gerbera daisies in the spring, yet they never bloom again. The plants grow well, but no flowers. Can you help me?

A Gerberas are too tempting. When they're in bloom, there are no prettier flowers. However, they don't respond well to our Texas summers, and few of us ever get a second round of blooms. The plants require copious amounts of water, and whiteflies are common visitors. Probably the best way to use gerberas is to include them in large patio containers early in the spring, then plan on replacing them once they quit flowering.

Hollyhocks

497

Q What has caused my hollyhocks to turn tan all over? It's killing the plants.

A That's spider mites. Even though they're nearly microscopic, you can see them if you thump a leaf or two over white paper. Control them with Kelthane.

Impatiens

498

Q My impatiens get too tall every summer. I use a water-soluble fertilizer on them every week or two. My neighbors' plants aren't nearly as tall. Why are mine so tall?

A Impatiens' mature heights is somewhat of a genetic factor. There are varieties that have been bred to stay very short. Ask your neighbors where they have bought their plants, or what variety they have used, then try to match it. Impatiens will also get leggy if they're grown in very heavy shade, or if they're given too much nitrogen.

☆499☆

Q My impatiens' leaves are rolled under. The plants also aren't blooming the way they should. What causes all that?

A Usually it's the heat. If you notice that the plants looked good until June, and if they look good again once it turns cooler in the fall, then the heat was the culprit. To counteract the heat we often put our impatiens in a really shady location, to protect them from the sun's intense rays. Unfortunately the plants need several hours of bright light if they're going to bloom properly. That puts them back into the heat. Probably the best compromise would be to give them morning sun, until 10 or 11 A.M., then shade the balance of the day.

☆500☆

Q My impatiens' leaves are turning tan and mottled. Is there an insect that does that damage?

A That's probably spider mites. They're the nearly microscopic pests that are usually found on the bottom surfaces of the leaves. Their damage first shows as tiny freckles, but it soon spreads to encompass the entire leaf. Control them with Kelthane.

501

 How well will New Guinea impatiens do for me?

Probably not very well. They really like maximum summer temperatures in the 70s and lower 80s. New hybrids promise better tolerance to heat, but none to date has proven itself successful in Texas' hot summers.

Lantanas

502

 My lantanas seem to have spurts of blooms, then no flowers for a while. Are there some varieties that bloom more consistently than others?

The triploid variety 'New Gold' is touted as blooming more of the time, but that may not always be true. Lantanas bloom on their new growth, so the best thing you can do to keep them flowering is to keep them growing. Apply a complete-and-balanced analysis water-soluble fertilizer to them every couple of weeks.

503

Some of my lantanas have come back after the winter. Are they truly perennials, or should I use them as annuals?

It's best that you use them as annuals, particularly in the northern half of Texas. Trailing lavender and its white variant seem to be the least winter-hardy. Other trailing types such as Gold Mound and Silver Mound are slightly more hardy, and the shrubby types are the most durable to the cold. All types seem to come back better if you cut them back to the ground the next morning after they freeze, then mulch over their crowns with 2 or 3 inches of compost. Lantanas are very late to sprout out, often waiting until 3 to 4 weeks after the last freeze. They really prefer warm soils and weather.

504

Q I have tried to keep my lantanas in my greenhouse over the winter, but the whiteflies have driven me crazy. Is there any good way of eliminating them?

A You can use Orthene spray, or you can position yellow sticky traps near the plants. Neither will be foolproof for this durable insect, but both will be helpful.

Marigolds

505

Q My marigold plants are tan and they're dying. What causes that? I'm now thinking that I'm seeing some kind of webs.

A You probably are. Spider mites are the nearly microscopic pests, and marigolds are their number-one home. Thump one of those dying leaves over white paper and you'll see the tiny mites crawling around. Control them with Kelthane spray applied to both the top and bottom leaf surfaces. For the record, once you can see webs, it's probably too late to save that particular host plant. If you plant marigolds in the spring, you can pretty well expect spider mites by early June. If you plant a fall crop in August, you probably won't have any of the pests at all. These are the Marimums™ marigolds that have been touted the past several years.

506

Q I bought some large marigolds in 4-inch pots. The plants were in full bloom when I bought them, but they stopped growing. How can I avoid that problem the next time I buy marigolds?

A By buying plants that are in bud, but not yet in full flower. For some odd reason, if you let marigolds go to bloom in their transplant pots, that pretty well shuts down further growth and flowering. Even if the plants are somewhat shorter, they'll re-establish better and bloom much more heavily.

Mexican Heather

507

Q I have had Mexican heather as a flower-bed border all season. Will it come back next year? What can I do to help it survive the cold?

A That depends on where in Texas you live. If you're in the southern third of the state it will often come back from its roots. Mulch over them after the first frost. In Central Texas it will occasionally survive, but not often enough to consider it any type of perennial. Treat it totally as an annual.

Morning Glories

508

Q My morning glory vines are beautiful, but they're not blooming. Lots of foliage. No flowers. Why?

A Morning glories need full sun and comparatively "poor" garden soils to bloom their best. If they get very much nitrogen from lawn fertilizers you can expect them to grow strongly, but at the expense of flowers. Morning glories also bloom best in late summer and fall.

Moss Rose

509

Q My moss rose and purslane flowers don't stay open past about noon. Is there anything I can do to get more hours of color, or are there better varieties?

A You'll have more hope with the latter idea. Choose from the latest varieties and you'll generally have the best chance at prolonged flowering, which is one of the main goals of the hybridizers.

510

 My moss rose plants are playing out. I planted them 8 or 10 weeks ago, and expected a longer bloom season. Is that abnormal?

No. Of all our flowering annuals, their productive time in the garden is one of the shortest, usually about 10 to 12 weeks. At that point you just need to replace them.

511

 Can I let my moss rose seedlings grow (and not have to buy new transplants this year)?

You can, but they're not going to be the same as the variety you had last year. Most modern moss roses are hybrids that won't "come true" from seed. Usually they're not as double, and the color mix may not be as interesting. Start with new transplants each spring.

Nasturtiums

512

When should I plant nasturtiums in Texas?

They can't handle the heat, partly because the plants begin to fade away, and partly because of spider mites. Avoid those problems by planting in late winter, some 4 to 6 weeks ahead of the average date of the last killing freeze.

Pansies

513

 What is the earliest I can plant my pansies in the fall? Nurseries begin getting them before it turns cool.

 You should not plant pansies until you've had some very cool evenings, usually early October and thereafter in North

Texas and mid- to late October in South Texas. If you plant them too early they'll grow too tall and lanky before they start flowering.

514

My pansy plants seem to be dying. Their stems don't seem to be able to support the tops. They are all shriveled and they are falling over. What causes that?

It could be damage from pillbugs that have eaten the stems near the ground line. In that case you'll see where they have actually chewed into the stems. Control them with Sevin dust or one of the snail-slug-pillbug baits if they haven't already killed the plants. It's also possible that a water mold fungus such as Pythium has attacked the stems. In that case the plants are probably in a poorly drained soil and in a part of your garden where air circulation is poor. Perhaps you shouldn't use pansies (or petunias, periwinkles, snapdragons or mums) there again. These plants all seem to share in the disease. Unfortunately, there is no reliable chemical control.

515

Which types of pansies are better, the very large-flowering ones, or the types that have smaller flowers, but more of them?

Most commercial landscapers plant the "multiflora" types that cover themselves in blossoms. The larger types are best in small spaces near an entry, where you can enjoy each individual flower. They're also better for use as cut flowers in shallow vases. Don't overlook the small-flowering violas and Johnny-jump-ups as well.

516

Can I start my pansies from seed myself? I want a lot of plants and would like to save some money.

Save the frustration. You certainly can't sow them into the garden directly, and you probably won't have what it takes to grow them in a greenhouse. Pansies need cool temperatures to germinate, and, by the time it's cool enough for them, it's too late in the season. The plants you buy in garden centers in the fall were generally started somewhere cooler and then shipped into Texas as small transplants. Your nurseryman buys them from a greenhouse grower who has taken them to the larger sizes. Unless you intend to get into all of this as a profession, you're usually better off just letting the growers deal with it.

517

 My pansies look terrible. It's freezing outside, and the plants look like they will be reduced to stewed foliage when they finally thaw. What could I have done to protect them?

First, don't be too concerned just yet. Pansies will always look bad when temperatures are below freezing. The good news is that they almost always come back just fine once they can thaw out. They'll do their very best if you water them just before really cold weather blows in, and if you mulch them to moderate the soil's rate of freezing and thawing. You can really protect them if you'll lay one of the lightweight fabric covers over the plants just before it turns cold. You'll need to bypass this last step if the cold will be accompanied by ice or snow that could weight the cover down.

518

Do we need to pick the seed pods off our pansies to keep them blooming?

We used to do that, but modern hybrids bloom so freely that that's pretty much wasted effort. If you want to groom plants in a very visible spot by removing their old flowers, however, do so.

Pentas

519

 My pentas are so tall. What can I do to control their height?

That's part of their nature. You can "pinch" out their growing tips periodically, but they're still going to get 18 to 24 inches tall.

Periwinkles

☆520☆

Q My periwinkles are dying. They're all wilted and they seem to be fading fast. Can they be saved?

A That's probably *Phytophora*, the soil-borne water mold fungus. Every time it rains, and every time you water, you spread it to the plants' stems. Affected plants will look like their stems have had hot knives laid against them. Your best option is to bypass periwinkles in the future. There is no affordable chemical control, and it will come back at some point in every successive year. Switch over to other heat-tolerant plants and save yourself a lot of frustration. This disease is the reason that so few people (especially commercial landscapers) plant periwinkles any more.

521

Q My periwinkle flowers aren't as large as they should be. I've been using a complete-and-balanced fertilizer, but even the plants don't seem to be thriving. What will enlarge their flowers?

A A high-nitrogen lawn-type fertilizer will perk them up and, surprisingly, result in larger blooms and more of them.

Petunias

522

Q My petunia plants look like they're gassed. They're lanky and falling over, and some seem to be dying. What can I do to get them to bloom and look good longer?

A That's a question that usually comes after petunias have been planted in late March or April. They need to be planted in the fall in South Texas, so they can bloom all winter and into the spring. In the northern two-thirds of the state you'd want to plant them before the last killing freeze date, then plan on replacing them in June. Folks from the North are accustomed to leaving their petunias in from spring into the fall, but we can't do that in Texas.

Pinks

 Will my pinks make it through the summer? They still look pretty good, even though it's hot.

Treat them as cool-season annuals and remove them by late spring. While a few of the plants might survive the summer, they won't be uniformly vigorous come fall. Things will look better if you replant with new plants every fall.

Primroses

524

Someone has told me that primroses are better than pansies, yet I don't see very many of them in landscapes. Which plant is better?

Usually pansies would win that competition. They're a lot less expensive, and they bloom for many weeks longer. Primroses are elegant flowers, but they don't show up as well as pansies and they have a tendency toward fungal leaf spot during wet weather. If you use them, start with a large patio pot and use primroses around the base of some taller centerpiece plant.

Snapdragons

525

 My snapdragons don't bloom as well as I had expected. What can I do to keep them flowering longer?

Snapdragons have blooming cycles. They'll flower beautifully for a few weeks, then they have to regrow and produce new flower buds. Keep the old flower stalks pruned off immediately after they finish blooming so the plants won't go to seed. Apply a complete-and-balanced, water-soluble fertilizer with each watering to keep them vigorous. They should bloom three or four times before late spring's warm weather finishes them off.

526

My snapdragon plants have started wilting. It looks like their stems are all dried up. What can I do? Can I plant something else there, or is the soil ruined?

There are a couple of water mold funguses that attack plants' stems near the ground line, and snapdragons are susceptible to them. There are no really good chemical sprays, especially once the diseases have done that much damage to the plants. Your best bet would be to replant, but don't use pansies, petunias, periwinkles or mums. All are susceptible to the same clan of diseases.

Verbenas

527

My verbenas are turning tan. They also don't bloom worth a hoot. I've tried them three years now, always with the same two problems. What's wrong?

The first problem is probably spider mites, and Kelthane should help. As for the flowering: Annual verbenas that we buy in full flower usually don't handle the transplanting very well. It's common for them not to flower again. In all honesty, the "perennial" verbenas make better "annuals" than the true annual types.

Zinnias

528

My zinnias have white dust all over their leaves. What will stop it? It seems to be hurting the plants.

That's powdery mildew and it may weaken zinnias some-what. More than that, however, it's also disfiguring. The plants look messy in the garden. Plant zinnias in full sunlight, in areas with good air circulation. Avoid overhead irrigation whenever possible, or at least water early in the morning so the plants can dry quickly. Fungicides can help slow the disease, and it's also less of a problem for zinnias that are set out in mid- to late summer, for fall blooming.

529

Q My zinnia transplants don't bloom very well after I plant them. They look great when I buy them, but then nothing more. What's going on?

A That's a common problem with many different annual flowers. With zinnias, as with most of the others, it's because the plants become stunted while they're still in their original pots. By the time we set them out, they've almost entirely quit growing. The best solution with most of these plants is to buy transplants that are in bud, but not yet in bloom.

9

PERENNIALS

GENERAL QUESTIONS ABOUT PERENNIALS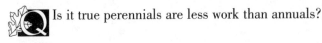

530

Q Is it true perennials are less work than annuals?

A Probably not. You still have to water, feed and trim them. You also have to dig and divide them every year (or two or three). You'll have to rework their soil as you do that dividing. So, perennials are probably only slightly less work than their annual counterparts. What perennials do offer, however, is form and character that more succulent annual plants may not have. They're interesting, and they're fun. If you're looking for months of eye-dazzling color, annuals are probably the better bet. If you want a feeling of permanence and elegance, mix in perennials.

531

Q How do I lay out my perennial garden?

A First, perennials are probably best in a dedicated bed out away from the house. Most will grow and bloom best in full or nearly full sun, and good drainage is a must. You may want to plant in raised beds, mixing in generous amounts of peat moss, compost, bark mulch, manure and other organic matter. Position a few evergreen shrubs within the bed for their off-season permanence. Plant your perennials so there will be pockets of color at any given season. Taller types should go in the back, tapering down to the trailing foreground plants. Have a planting plan grid as a permanent record of all your varieties. Many perennials become almost invisible during their dormant seasons. Be prepared, too, to shift plants around as the bed matures. You'll tire of some types and you'll want to try others. A really good perennial garden is never quite finished.

532

What time of year is best to plant perennials?

That depends on the type of perennial you're planting. As a general rule of thumb, however, plants that bloom in the spring are usually transplanted in the fall. Plants that flower in the fall are usually moved in early spring. Nurseries have excellent selections in the spring, and more and more nurseries are also well stocked in other months as well. If at all possible, buy from local sources. National mail-order houses are great supplements for the little-known and unusual varieties.

533

What kind of fertilizer is best for a planting of assorted perennials?

That's difficult, because something will always be blooming at the same time that other plants are growing vegetatively. A soil test will always be your best way of knowing exactly what you should use. For general purposes, however, a 3-1-2 ratio fertilizer, similar to what you would put on your turfgrass, will do very well. Apply 1 to 2 pounds per 100 square feet in early spring, late spring and early fall. Brush over the plants after you fertilize to get rid of any granules that may have lodged in their leaf axils. Water them thoroughly.

534

How should I water my perennials? I don't want to sprinkle them from overhead.

Drip irrigation works best, although you'll need to position the drippers near the crowns of your plants to be certain they're receiving adequate water. Gentle overhead irrigation sprays aren't bad, especially if the watering is done just before dawn, before the flowers open in the morning. Avoid impulse sprinklers, however, that could blast the blooms apart. If diseases begin to show up in the flowers and buds, discontinue overhead irrigation.

535

 Should I mulch my perennial garden, and, if so, with what?

 Absolutely. Nowhere will mulches be more beneficial. Organic mulches are ideal, since they not only perform all those normal mulch functions, but also because they break down to improve the soil later. Put 2 or 3 inches of compost or shredded pine bark mulch out at any time of the year. There are so many positives to mulching that you can make a case for it at any time of the year.

536

 What types of herbicides can I use to keep weeds out of my perennial garden?

 There are several that could be appropriate.

- Pre-emergent weedkillers prevent germination of crabgrass, grass-burs, and other annual grasses. Treatment should be made two weeks prior to the last killing freeze date and again 90 days later.

- Spot-treat with glyphosates or similar materials to eliminate bermudagrass, nutsedge, Johnsongrass and other perennial weeds, but keep them off the foliage of desirable perennials.

Always read and follow label directions carefully, and ask a Certified Nursery Professional for specific advice for your weed problems.

537

 How do I know when it's time to divide my old plantings of perennials?

There is no one rule of thumb, but if they fail to bloom properly, that's usually a good indicator. If the crowns have multiplied and are tightly congested, you probably need to divide them. If shade trees have grown larger and now cast excessive shade, it's time to move the perennials to a brighter site.

☆538☆

Specifically, which perennials will grow and bloom in fairly shady locations?

There are several good options, including violets, liriope, ajuga, hydrangeas, columbines, astilbe, summer phlox, and hostas. Combine those with shade-loving groundcovers, shrubs and annual flowers, and you can have a lovely shade garden.

539

I have many types of bulbs. They were planted on time in the fall. Even though spring is many weeks away, they're already starting to sprout. Do I need to worry about losing the plants before they can flower next spring?

No. That early growth will happen almost every year in December and January. Mulch the beds with compost or bark to conserve moisture and prevent weeds, but don't worry too much about the bulbs' foliage freezing. If we have a really cold snap the tips of the leaves might be browned. You could make a case for piling loose tree leaves over them in that kind of weather extreme, but pull the leaves back as soon as the weather moderates.

540

I have just found some bulbs cooling in my refrigerator. It's several weeks after I should have planted them. Should I just leave them there until next winter, or can I still plant them now?

Go ahead and plant them. They won't bloom quite as early as they would have, but they also won't be able to wait one entire year. Take your chances with them now.

MOST COMMON QUESTIONS
ABOUT SPECIFIC PERENNIALS ....

Amaryllis (*Hippeastrum x johnsonii*)

541

 I'd like to plant amaryllis, but I'm afraid of the ones I see at the nursery. They seem more like pot plants to grow inside the house.

Good observation. The hardy types of amaryllis have more trumpet-shaped flowers, while the tropical types that are sold around Christmas and into the New Year have wider petals that recurve back over the flowers. The most common type of hardy amaryllis is cherry red, although a pink-and-white candystripe type is sometimes seen in South Texas. You may have trouble finding the hardy types in Texas nurseries, but you can usually find a neighbor who will share with you.

Anemone (*Anemone* sp.)

542

What planting tips do you have for anemones?

Wait until late winter to plant them, generally in late January or very early February. Soak the tubers overnight before planting, then set them only 2 inches deep into well-prepared garden soil. Plant them comparatively close together (2 to 4 inches), and plan on them as annuals only, even though botanically they are perennials.

Asters, Fall (*Aster* sp.)

543

 My fall asters are tall and lanky as they bloom. Should I stake them?

 You can if you need to, but only on a one-time basis. What you really need to do is "pinch" them lightly in late May, to make them branch out and remain more compact. It's amazing that the one light pruning keeps them more compact.

Bluebells (*Eustoma grandiflorum*)

544

 I like the Texas bluebells, but my plants get too lanky. What will stop that?

 If you're talking about the plants you're seeing in most nurseries, those are hybrids that resemble our Texas bluebells, only with much larger flowers and leaves. All of that size tends to pull the stems down, although hybridizers have worked hard to bring us better types in recent years. Try some new plants of these improved forms. The true native bluebell is an upright plant with graceful foliage and, striking, smaller flowers.

Cannas (*Canna* sp.)

545

 My cannas' flowers don't open properly, plus the leaves look like someone has fired a machine gun across them. They have holes in rows across the leaves. What's happening?

That's all damage of the canna leaf roller. It encases itself within the top growth of the plants. By the time the leaves start to unfurl the flowers have often been ruined and the leaves are peppered with the damage. Use Orthene systemic insecticide to prevent and control them. Include 1 or 2 drops of a liquid detergent to help the spray adhere to the waxy leaves, and use a fine mist spray, rather than one with large droplets, for the same reason.

546

How do I prune off the old canna flower stalks? I know I shouldn't let them go to seed.

Most veteran landscapers prune the old stems back rather drastically, often way down into the crowns of the plants.

That way the plants will usually send up new side shoots and then successive flower stalks.

Q When should I dig and divide my cannas, in the fall or early spring?

A You can do it either time if you live in South Texas, but if you live in North Texas, late winter might be best. Cannas are slightly winter-tender near the Red River, and the late winter dividing time would be a safer alternative. Lift and divide them while they have no active top growth, however.

Carnations, Hardy Pinks (*Dianthus* sp.)

548

Q I like carnations, but most of the types I have tried seemed to "melt away" with the heat. Is that normal?

A Absolutely. In fact, that's why no greenhouse growers produce cut-flower carnations in Texas. It's just too warm. There are two or three types of carnations (and the related garden pinks) that will come back fairly reliably, but only when they're given perfect drainage, morning sun with a little protection from the afternoon heat, and great garden soil.

Cast Iron Plant (*Aspidistra elatior*)

549

Q My aspidistra plants are browned around the edges of their leaves. Also, they aren't growing rapidly. What should I be doing to help them along?

A The browning is probably from freeze injury or drought. They can't tolerate very much direct summer sun or they'll bleach and turn brown. Make certain that's not a concern. Trim off the dead portions and use a lawn-type fertilizer to promote new leaf growth. Aspidistras are notoriously slow-growing, so keep faith that they'll eventually look great. Keep them moist and mulch them well.

Chrysanthemums (*Chrysanthemum morifolium*)

550

Q My chrysanthemums bloom in the spring. Aren't they only fall flowers?

A Mums bloom when the nights are a certain length. Those lengths of darkness occur in the fall, but they also occur in the spring. Those spring flowers can be pretty for a few weeks, but they can get in the way of vigorous stem growth and great bud set for the fall flowering. Trim them off by early June so the plants can get on with their growth. Apply a high-nitrogen fertilizer immediately after you prune them.

551

Q My mums aren't blooming like they're supposed to. Our neighbors' plants are flowering right on schedule. What could we have done wrong?

A Check the light that might be hitting them at night. Mums measure the length of the dark period, and when lights are turned on during the night, it can keep them from flowering entirely. It may also be that your neighbors' varieties are different types of mums and that they bloom earlier in the fall. The small-flowering "cushion" mums generally bloom 4 to 6 weeks earlier than florist mums that have been planted from pots. If you pinched out the plants' growing tips late in the season, that also could slow down their bud set and subsequent bloom.

552

Q My chrysanthemums are way too tall. I need to stake them, but they already are laying down on the ground. What can I do next year to avoid this problem?

A It sounds like you have mums that were planted out of pots from the flower shop. Those are different varieties than you would buy at a nursery for landscape use. They were selected by the hybridizers for completely different reasons. No doubt they also bloom much later than garden mums. The best way to deal with the problem: Pinch their growing tips back two or three times in spring and summer. That will keep them much more compact and will encourage low branching and shorter, sturdier stems.

553

 My mums are finished blooming. Should I prune them to get rid of all the dead stems?

 Yes. If you look closely near the ground you'll see new basal shoots starting to develop. Those will be the stems for next year. Cut the old stalks back within 1 to 2 inches of those new shoots soon after they finish flowering in the fall.

554

 When should I dig and divide my chrysanthemums?

 You can either do it in late fall, after all the flowers have faded, or you can wait and do it in very late winter, before the new growth begins. The late winter time is probably better, but there is the risk that you'll wait too long and the new shoots will suddenly be 6 or 8 inches tall. By then it will be too late.

Columbines (*Aquilegia* sp.)

555

 I haven't had the best luck with my columbines. What can I do to get better flowers?

 Columbines are native to cooler areas, so our summer heat can take its toll. Many of the hybrids and species types are reluctant to grow and bloom well in our climate. One type identified as Hinckley's columbine (often sold as "Texas Gold"), is native to the mountains in West Texas. It establishes well and reseeds fairly freely in the rest of the state. Plant it in shade in well-drained, highly organic soil. Keep it moist, and cut all the old foliage off in mid-summer, after the spider mites have turned it all tan. The old foliage will die back anyway. The spider mites merely speed the process. Not only will the mother plants come back for several years, but you'll also get seedlings germinating within the bed as well.

Coreopsis, or Golden Wave (*Coreopsis grandiflora*)

556

 I like coreopsis, but the plants seem so unmanageable. What can I do to keep them more tidy?

 You've hit the nail on the head. While they're young and in full bloom, coreopsis are some of our prettiest perennials. However, by mid-season, the plants often start to lean and may look like they're tumbling over. You'll need to "dead-head" them periodically by removing all the old flower heads and fruit that forms to reduce the weight on the tops of the plants. You probably should even shear them back somewhat, to keep them more compact. Some of the newer varieties claim to be more compact, but, in some cases, they don't last as well from year to year.

Crocus (*Crocus vernus*)

557

 When should I plant crocus in my bulb garden?

 Crocus don't seem to do very well here in the sunny Southwest. If you're going to try them, plant them shallowly in late fall, just before the coldest part of winter. Yellow fall crocus (*Sternbergia lutea*) is a much better performer here.

Daffodils, Narcissus, Jonquils (*Narcissus* sp.)

558

 When can I plant my daffodils and narcissus?

 These bulbs don't require the chilling that tulips and hyacinths need in our warm soils. As a result, you can plant them as soon as you buy them in the fall. If you ever decide to dig and move established bulbs, do it in early to mid-September.

559

 My King Alfred and Mount Hood daffodils aren't blooming any more. I get lots of foliage, but no flowers at all. What happened?

That's true for their course. If you want daffodils, narcissus and jonquils that will establish and rebloom year after year, plant early flowering, small types. Large, late varieties just don't repeat as well. You might as well discard your plantings and get a fresh start.

560

How soon can I cut the old leaves off my daffodils after they flower?

Wait until the leaves have turned completely yellow. If you cut green leaves, you're cutting food-producing tissues that could make the bulbs larger and stronger the following year. Some folks will braid and tie the leaves loosely, to keep their gardens more tidy.

Daylilies (*Hemerocallis* sp.)

561

 My orange daylilies are tall and gangly. I want something more refined. What would you suggest?

If you're growing the old-fashioned tawny daylily with its spindly stems and trumpet-shaped orange flowers, you're in for some pleasant surprises. Over the past several decades, industrious hybridizers have brought us literally thousands of varieties that have:

- many more flowers,
- wider, fuller flowers,
- almost an infinite range of colors (except blue), and
- much more compact plants.

Visit Texas daylily gardens in May and June to see what is available. There may be daylily society shows in your city, and there are several fine national mail-order sources. You should have no trouble finding exciting daylilies for your garden.

562

Q How do I divide my daylilies? Will those swollen things on their roots make new plants?

A When your daylily clumps become full and crowded (usually after 3 to 5 years), you can dig the entire clump as a unit. Once it's on top of the ground, use your fingers to pry the individual plants (or "fans") apart. Sometimes you'll have to snap them into two or more pieces. As for the swollen portions of the roots, those are merely for storage of water and nutrients. They will not reproduce the plants.

563

Q What should I look for in buying my daylilies? What makes the best plants for my garden?

A Unless you're looking for novelty plants that have odd colors or flower forms, "short" and "cheerful" are the best two guide words. Types that grow to 24 inches or less at flowering usually work most easily into the landscape. You can use taller types, too, but you'll need to position them behind other, shorter perennials and shrubs. They should have multitudes of flowers, and usually the bright yellows, oranges, reds and pinks show up best.

Ferns

564

Q What types of ferns are best outdoors?

A There are dozens, but only a few are widely available. Holly ferns are good in South and Central Texas. Autumn ferns, arborvitae ferns and wood ferns are suited to most of the state. Watch local nurseries for other unusual types. Members of fern societies will have still more suggestions.

Gladiolus (*Gladiolus hortulanus*)

565

Q What should I do with my gladiolas over the winter?

A Most really good glad growers will dig and store the corms (not true bulbs) after their tops have died to the ground. You should probably dust them with a fungicide, and you'll need to protect them from freezing while they're in storage. Replant in the spring. For the record: There is a smaller perennial type of glad that is absolutely charming. A magenta form is the most common, but other colors are available.

Grape Hyacinths (*Muscari* sp.)

566

Q My grape hyacinths are running wild. They have escaped their original beds and have now spread all through my lawn. What can I use to stop them?

A First, remove any seed heads that form after they flower. Grape hyacinths spread quickly via their seeds. You can use a broadleafed weedkiller spray in the turf areas so long as the leaves are growing vigorously. You'll also want a 4-inch-deep edging at the interface between the planting area and the space where you don't want the grape hyacinths.

Grasses (Ornamental)

567

Q My pampas grass looks like it has frozen to the ground. Should I cut it back? Should I do that even when it doesn't freeze?

Do it only as needed to remove dead leaves. The fuller the clumps are, the better the fall flowering will be, so you don't want to cut green leaves back.

568

I really like purple fountain grass. Will it make it through the winter? Someone has told me it is an annual.

In most of Texas, it will be an annual, dying out with the first hard freeze. If you want to overwinter it, you'll need to dig and divide it before the first killing freeze. Plant it into 1-gallon pots and put it in a warm, sunny greenhouse until spring.

569

What can I use to get rid of bamboo? Our neighbors planted it along a bank several years ago and now it's invading our landscape.

Bamboo is one of the most difficult "weeds" to eliminate. It's a strong-growing grass with very heavy fleshy roots. You can use one of the glyphosates or similar products, but you'll need a fair amount of leaf growth. These weedkillers enter the plants only through their leaves, so the more leaves you have, the better the control. You'll certainly need to use the top rates of application listed on the label, and you'll need to protect any turf or other plants that might be hit by the spray. It would help immensely if you could dig a trench at your property line, then install some type of permanent and deep edging material. Fiberglass sheets work very well, but other things could be used, too. Your barrier needs to be at least 16 to 18 inches deep to prevent the invasion of the bamboo's roots. You'll probably have a certain amount of hand-digging as well. You're seeing living proof of why we should never use the invasive golden bamboo in our landscapes.

Hibiscus (Hardy), or Mallows (*Hibiscus moscheutos*)

570

Q I planted hibiscus plants this spring. Now I'm concerned about whether they'll make it through the winter, and how I can identify the perennial types. Can you help?

A The winter-hardy hibiscus, also called mallows, have dull leaves; tropical types have glossy, deep green foliage. Flowers of the most common hardy types will always be single, white, red, or pink. Hardy types will begin to die back in September. Usually, by the time the first freeze kills their top growth back to the ground, they have already pretty much died back on their own. Tropical types, by comparison, just keep on growing. The best help you can give the hardy types in surviving a Texas winter is to leave them alone. Leave a few inches of their stems so you can tell where the clumps are. They'll be the last of your summer perennials to sprout out and start growing again in the spring. Be patient.

571

Q How can I get more of my perennial hibiscus plants? I really like the one I got in a mixture.

A They can be divided, although you'll need to be patient. If you lift the plant in late winter, before the new growth begins, and carefully cut it into two or three pieces, you can gradually increase your numbers. You might also check seed catalogs. Most of the newer hybrids are available as individual colors. You may be able to get many more plants in a hurry that way.

Hostas, or Plantain Lilies (*Hosta* sp.)

572

Q I'm really interested in hostas, but there are so many types. Can you tell me how to pick the best ones for Texas? They're so expensive.

A Hostas do cost a good bit, so it's very important that you choose carefully. They seem to be better adapted in North and East Texas, where summer conditions are less stressful. As a general rule, smaller-leafed types are best. Beyond that, you need to experiment and ask your nurseryman questions about your exact situation. Hostas must have shade, and they do require rich, well-prepared garden soil and constant moisture (without overwatering) during the growing season.

573

Q Is there a good way to control slugs that are eating my hostas?

A Isn't it interesting how pests choose their specific host plants. For snails and slugs, hostas are home base. Use Sevin dust on the plants and on the soil around them as well. Bait-type products are also available, and you can use shallow pans of beer to attract and trap the pests.

Hyacinths (*Hyacinthus orientalis* hybrids)

574

Q My hyacinths didn't bloom very well this spring. They were beautiful last year. What did I do wrong?

A Probably nothing. Like tulips, hyacinths don't "come back" very well year after year. The first year's flowering will always be the best. It's best to replant with new bulbs, each fall.

Hypericum, or St. John's Wort (*Hypericum* sp.)

575

Q I have seen hypericum a few times, but not many people use it. Why is that? It seemed very pretty in the landscapes where I have seen it.

A Try a small planting to see how you like the results. It's a handsome little perennial sub-shrub, but it does tend to turn yellow and die away after a few years. Iron may help in alkaline soils, but you'll probably also need to replace the plants every 5 or 10 years.

Iris (*Iris* hybrids)

576

 My irises don't bloom very well anymore. Do they need a special fertilizer, or could there be something else wrong?

Usually irises that don't flower are either in too much shade, or they have become crowded and need to be divided. Rarely is a special fertilizer needed, although a general-purpose feeding in fall and again in very early spring would be good.

577

When should I transplant my irises, and how often do they need to be dug?

 Bearded irises will usually need to be dug and separated every 3 or 4 years, although frequency will vary with varieties and growing conditions. When the plants appear congested and fail to bloom properly, you probably should divide them. While irises can be moved at almost any season, early fall is the best time.

578

How deeply should I plant my new iris plants?

Plant them quite shallowly, right at the soil surface. Planting them deeper will almost assuredly result in rotted stems and poor performance.

579

 My iris plants are rotting. Their stems have a really bad aroma. What causes that, and what can I do to stop it?

 That's probably a bacterial soft rot. They're usually soil-borne, and control is difficult. Removing the affected plants is critical. Be careful, too, not to damage the crowns of the healthy plants as you cultivate around them, and don't handle healthy plants after you have worked with the sick ones. This disease usually indicates poor drainage and limited air circulation.

580

 My bed of mixed colors of iris is now all white–the old-fashioned variety of "flag." Did they mutate back to the white?

No. It's simply a stronger grower and has crowded out your other plants over a period of months or years. Dig and discard all of the white-flowering plants while they're blooming. See what you have left, then work to save them.

581

Should I trim the leaves of my iris back?

Remove only browned tissue. Some folks want to cut their plants back several times a year, but that only weakens the rhizomes. They need the green tissues to help store food in their root systems for the following year's growth and blooms.

Lilies (*Lilium* sp.)

582

 I have not had good luck with lilies. Is there a secret to getting them to establish in Texas?

Indeed. It's simply too hot for most true lilies. While they may bloom fairly well one year, they rarely establish and come back year after year, particularly in the southern 80 percent of the state. One hybrid called 'Enchantment' seems to do fairly well in most of the state. It's orange, blooming in late spring and into early summer.

Lily of the Nile (*Agapanthus africanus*)

583

Q What kind of winter care do I need to give my lily of the Nile?

A That depends on where you live. If you're north of College Station and San Antonio, you'll need to have it indoors or in a greenhouse. They are sold alongside perennials in many Texas nurseries, but, too often, folks buy them without being told that they're Zone 8 (south end, at that) plants. Mulch them 2 to 3 inches deep in compost or bark mulch if you intend to leave them outdoors.

Peonies (*Paeonia* hybrids)

584

Q I haven't seen very many peonies in Texas, since I moved here. How well will they do?

A On a scale of 1 to 10, peonies would probably rate about a 3 along the Red River and zero south of Dallas-Fort Worth-Abilene. We're just too warm in summer and winter for them to do their best. Some types will grow in far North Texas, but results can be spotty. Someone should probably do an extensive side-by-side variety trial. Give them morning sun and afternoon shade, and rake snow or ice over their crowns anytime that you have freezing precipitation during the winter. That will help chill them to initiate bud set. All things considered, for the cost of the original plants and for the few days that they're at prime, peonies are probably more trouble than they're worth.

Phlox (*Phlox paniculata*)

585

Q I've tried several types of perennial summer phlox that I had in my garden in the North. Only the hot pink types seems to establish. Is that common?

A That's the same experience most of us have had in Texas. The pink type is really good in morning sun and afternoon shade, although you may have to occasionally treat for powdery mildew. The other types just don't have the same stamina.

Ranunculus (*Ranunculus asiaticus*)

586

 How do I grow ranunculus here? When should they be planted?

Use ranunculus much as you would anemones. Plant them shallowly (2 inches deep and 4 to 6 inches apart) in late winter. They need good drainage and bright sunlight. You can also grow them in large patio pots with other annual and bulb color plants. Treat them as annuals that you replace each year.

Roses (*Rosa* sp.)

587

What kind of location is best for my roses?

Roses grow and bloom best in full sunlight. They also need excellent drainage, so avoid spots that are known to be waterlogged. Raised planting beds will help ensure good drainage. Plant them where air circulation will be good, to lessen the outbreaks of disease. From an aesthetic standpoint, modern roses are probably best left in dedicated beds, where they can be the stars and prime occupants of those beds. Many types of antique bush roses are more like conventional shrubs and may be used on their own in the landscape. Climbing roses will need the support of a heavy fence or arbor.

588

 How can I find the very best rose bushes?

Shop in full-service nurseries, or order by mail from respected national mail-order houses. Don't buy roses that have been held indoors, in warm conditions and inadequate lighting. Even if they were good when they went inside, they deteriorate within just a day or two indoors. Roses are graded as numbers 1(best), 1½ (very acceptable) and 2 (least acceptable). The better roses cost more, but they are, without question, worth the extra couple of dollars when you consider how much you'll be spending to plant and maintain them. You will find roses sold bare-rooted and packed in moss during late winter. Many nurseries pot their plants at that same time, then sell them growing and in full flower in April and May.

589

Q I see a lot of different pot sizes when I shop for roses. Are the bigger containers that much better?

A If you're talking about hybrid tea and other modern roses, you must buy them in at least 2-gallon pots. If they're in smaller containers, their roots had to be trimmed too heavily to make them fit the smaller pots. It can also mean that they were "runts" of the field, and that they will likely never regain their vigor. Antique roses, by comparison, are not budded onto old rootstocks like the modern types. They have been rooted from cuttings and are "on their own roots." You'll usually see antique roses in 1-gallon containers. Other than the fact that they'll be smaller and rather spindly looking, these 1-gallon antiques will quickly catch hold and gain their full mature size.

590

Q Where can I use miniature roses in my landscape? They're so pretty, and I don't have a lot of space around my apartment.

A Miniature roses are handled exactly like their larger counterparts, except you do everything in smaller amounts. You can plant them into the garden in the same sorts of places you would use standard roses, but they'll obviously need to be in the fronts of the beds. They're just as winter-hardy, and timing of all activities will be the same, whether it's planting, pruning, feeding or spraying.

591

 What tips can you give me for planting my new roses?

 Be sure the soil is well prepared in advance. It should have 6 to 8 inches of organic matter worked into the top foot of native soil. That will ensure the raised planting bed, and, therein, good drainage. Set the plants at the same depth at which they had been growing previously. If they're bare-rooted, prune off any broken or damaged roots. If they're in containers, be sure their roots don't wrap around and around inside the pots. Cut through them in one or two places if necessary. Ask your nurseryman for spacing require- ments for each type that you buy, then be sure you keep it.

☆592☆

 When do I prune my roses?

 Major pruning of bush roses is done in February, before the new growth begins. Climbing roses, particularly the "once-only" spring bloomers, are pruned after their major flush of spring flowers, usually in May. Climbing roses that bloom all through the summer may be shaped somewhat in late winter, although the major pruning should probably still be completed after the spring flush. More minor shaping and grooming is done all through the season.

593

How much do I cut off my roses, and how do I know where to make the cuts?

As a general rule you'll cut bush roses back by 50 percent in late winter. You'll probably prune climbers back by that same amount, generally to the 4- to 5-foot range. Always prune just above a bud that faces out from the center of the plant. That will encourage spreading and more open growth. Climbers, especially, bloom better when their branches are trained horizontally. As you're pruning, remove all weak and nonproductive twigs.

594

Q My climbing roses don't bloom well at all. In fact, I haven't seen any flowers at all for the first two years that I've had the several plants. What might be going wrong? They seem to be growing fairly well.

A Climbing roses bloom on growth they made the prior year, so first-year plants will usually not have any flowers. Most folks who ask this question also admit that they have pruned their climbing roses in late winter (by the bush-rose schedule). That removes the growth that would have been producing that season's buds.

595

Q What kind of fertilizer is best for roses? When should it be applied?

A There are many excellent specialty rose fertilizers. Most are high-phosphate types, aimed at promoting flower buds. While that's good in principle, be certain the soil actually needs all that phosphorus. Have a soil test run every couple of years to monitor progress of the stored nutrients. If you're using granular materials, fertilize monthly, starting in early spring and continuing into late summer. Liquids will be applied more often.

596

Q My rose leaves have almost perfect circles cut into their edges. What kind of insect does that? I can't find any insects on the plants, yet the damage gets progressively worse.

A That's an insect called a leaf-cutter bee. The female cuts those thumbnail-sized circles into the margins of the leaves, then carries them to an unused faucet or downspout and makes her nest. She doesn't feed on the leaf tissues, nor is she there very long at a time. For those reasons, chemical controls are completely out of the question. Any damage they do is minimal. Just learn to enjoy the unusual insect and its lifestyle. Any greater concern will merely frustrate you. The damage, by the way, will probably be less in other years.

☆597☆

Q Why do my rose flowers fail to open properly? They're brown and scorched-looking, even as flower buds.

A That's a perfect description of thrips. They're the blond whisker-like insects that inhabit buds of multi-petaled flowers such as roses. They suck at the flower petals enough that they stop their development. That scorching is the prime symptom. Look at the bases of the petals and you'll see the tiny thrips moving briskly around. Control them with a systemic insecticide such as Orthene.

598

Q My roses this summer have looked terrible. The flowers were great in the spring, but they have fewer petals and terrible form now that it's hot. Some of the pink and yellow roses aren't even the same color that they were in the spring. Why?

A While northern roses are the stars of the summer, in Texas they suffer from the heat. Some varieties are worse than others, and some years will be worse than others. Many of our common garden flowers are paler in the heat than the same flowers produced in cooler months of cooler climates, and that's true with roses, too. October roses can be the best of the year, so the battles are worth the effort. Just keep the plants themselves vigorous and you'll be rewarded with a great fall bloom.

☆599☆

Q What are those dark brown spots all over my rose leaves? The leaves turn yellow and fall off, and the plants don't seem to be very vigorous either.

A That's black spot, the number-one problem of roses worldwide. It's a fungal leaf spot that defoliates many varieties of roses, some worse than others. It spreads most quickly in high humidity and where air circulation is poor. Avoid overhead irrigation whenever possible, and spray the plants weekly with Funginex or other listed fungicide. You'll need to spray from early spring into the summer and in the fall. If the problem persists in the summer, spray then as well, but don't ever spray roses when the sun is hitting their foliage or when temperatures are above 85 degrees.

600

Q I planted a hybrid tea rose, but now I have a plant that looks like a blackberry bush. Its flowers are also very much like a blackberry. Why would a rose mutate like that?

A What you have is the rootstock of the original rose. It hasn't mutated at all, but the top must have died out. If there is any of the top growth still intact, cut out all of the shoots from the rootstock. Otherwise, just dig it out and replant with a new rose plant.

601

Q I have a rose that I'd like to give to friends. How do I root the cuttings?

A First, it may not be legal for you to do that. If it's a new variety that is still protected by plant patents, it can only be propagated by licensed growers. With that disclaimer out of the way, it also may not be a good idea for you to try cutting-grown roses. Modern roses (as opposed to antique types which are almost always grown from cuttings, on their own roots) are budded onto more vigorous rootstocks. Starting them from cuttings would risk having plants that were weak and inferior. It's always better to buy modern roses as vigorous, healthy, budded nursery stock. As for the antique types, if you're trying to root those from cuttings, choose vigorous shoots in the 4- to 6-inch range. Use loose, highly organic potting soil and dip the cuttings in rooting hormone powder. Keep them moist and in bright light, preferably sunlight, until they form roots. Pot them into 1-gallon containers, and grow them for part or all of one season before you set them into the garden. Late winter is a great time to start the cuttings if you have a greenhouse or coldframe.

602

We mulched our roses really heavily when we lived in the North. Do we do that here?

That heavy mulching in the North is to protect the bud unions from extreme cold. You'll rarely lose the top growth in Texas cold spells, so that mulching shouldn't be needed. Once in a long while rosarians will wrap the stems of their most prized plants if unusually cold weather is expected, or if it's turned quite cold after a period of warm weather, where the canes might not be properly acclimatized. Most home gardeners in Texas, however, don't do anything special to protect their roses. Mulching, of course, is a great idea during the growing season, but you won't need more than an inch or two, certainly not enough to cover the bud unions.

Salvias (*Salvia* sp.)

603

I'd like to use perennial salvias in my landscape. Which types work best, and how tall and wide will they grow?

There are many great salvias, some annuals, but most of the really good ones are perennials. *Salvia greggii* (autumn sage) is the most perennial, almost looking like a small woody shrub. In its various forms it produces red, pink, coral and white flowers. The plants grow to 18 inches tall and wide. Mealy cup sage (*S. farinacea*) may work as a perennial, but, even if you use it just as an annual, it's great. It produces 18-inch spikes of blue-violet flowers (white forms are also available). Mass it as a bedding plant and it will bloom for months. Stars of the fall show are Mexican bush sage (*S. leucantha*), with its 4-foot plants and long purple-and-white spikes. Butterflies love it. You'll also want pineapple sage (*S. elegans*). It's bright green while it grows, blooming scarlet red in the fall. Its leaves, when crushed, have the wonderful aroma of fresh pineapple. It is less tolerant of winter cold than the other types listed.

Santolina (*Santolina* sp.)

604

Q My santolinas appear to be going downhill. I have both the gray and green forms, and the gray ones seem to be hurting worse. What could the cause be?

A There are two common problems. First, if the plants try to bloom, you need to shear the flower buds off before they ever develop. They aren't all that showy, and the plants will lose their compact form if they're allowed to bloom out. Second, santolinas must have good drainage. The gray plants are the more susceptible to root problems in waterlogged soils.

Sedums (*Sedum* sp.)

605

Q I have used sedums as groundcovers in the fronts of my beds, but they keep thinning out. Is there something I should be doing differently?

A Probably not. That's the way many sedums grow over the years. Of course, you always want to give sedums full sun and excellent drainage. Beyond that, you may just need to plant fresh transplants back into the bare areas.

Shasta Daisies (*Chrysanthemum maximum*)

606

Q How often do I need to dig and divide my shasta daisies? They seem to fill in so very quickly.

A If they're growing that well, you probably need to reset them every fall. Break the clumps into strong individual plants and set them into well-prepared garden soil on 8- to 12-inch centers, depending on the variety and its mature size.

Spider Lilies (*Lycoris radiata*)

607

It seems like my spider lilies have disappeared. Why might that have happened?

Usually it's because they have frozen. Spider lilies are best adapted to Central and South Texas, although they're fairly reliable as far north as the Red River. When the soil freezes for a prolonged period, the bulbs may be lost. Otherwise, they have few demands. They need dappled sunlight and moist, highly organic soils. Given those conditions, they should bloom each fall.

Tulips (*Tulipa* sp.)

608

I'm growing tulips, but they aren't doing what I expected. Most of them bloomed the first year, and almost none of them has bloomed since. What can I do to promote more flowers? I'm not even getting very many leaves, recently.

The showy hybrid types of tulips are best used as garden annuals in Texas. They just don't "come back" and bloom again in successive years very well. You might try a limited planting of the species types of tulips. These are generally smaller-flowering, often with several flowers per stalk. They establish and colonize more readily than their hybrid counterparts. They'll generally have botanical-looking names such as *Tulipa clusiana, T. greigii, T. kaufmanniana* or *T. praestans*, among several others.

609

My tulips flowered fairly well, but their blooms were all very short, hardly out of the soil. Did I need some type of fertilizer to make them grow better?

No. Your bulbs didn't get enough "chilling." That's a process that fools the bulb into acting as if it had been exposed to a more northern winter. Tulips must have at least 45 days at 45 degrees in the vegetable bin of your refrigerator before you plant them into cool (50-degree) soils. For most of Texas that means you'd buy them in late September or October, chill them until mid- or late December, then plant them on a cool day. Doing all that, you should have great and normal tulip flowers in March.

Turk's Cap (*Malvaviscus arboreus*)

610

Q I saw turk's cap in a public garden. How well will it do for me, and how can I get it started?

A Turk's cap is a relative of hibiscus and it thrives in Texas gardens. Give it full sun and ample room. The plants will grow to 5 feet tall and wide. It attracts hummingbirds to its rolled red flowers. Although the plants die to the ground with the first freeze, they come back strongly each spring. It has few if any pests. You'll find it with native plant collections in specialty nurseries. More and more mainstream nurseries now offer it with their perennials as well.

Verbenas (*Verbena* sp.)

611

Q How would you rate perennial verbenas to their annual counterparts?

A Two green thumbs up! They bloom better over a longer period of time and in a wider range of colors. The plants are more compact, almost making a groundcover planting. They come in shades of red, pink, white and purple. Watch out for spider mites, and use Kelthane to control them. Trim the planting to keep it attractive. Otherwise, they're great plants for Texas.

Violets (*Viola odorata*)

612

Q My violets are all scorched and brown. What causes that, and how do I stop it?

A Like so many of our other plants, violets are subject to spider mite damage. Their leaves will turn tan and mottled, and you will be able to see the tiny mites if you thump the affected tissues over white paper. Control them with Kelthane miticide, but use a pump sprayer that will let you apply it to the bottoms of the violet leaves. These particular mites sometimes show up as early as March.

10

FRUITS AND NUTS

PLANTING AND EARLY CARE ....

613

 Where can I plant my fruit and pecan trees? How much space will they need, and how much sunlight?

 Fruit and pecan trees need ample space where they can grow to full height and width without encountering shade from adjacent trees. That means fruit trees will generally need 20 feet or more and pecan trees at least 40 feet. If you're planting them near shade trees, be sure you take the final mature spread of the shade trees into account, not just their current limb span. You also want fruit trees to be planted in higher locations, where late frosts are less likely to settle and ruin the flowers or young fruit. If air moves through the area, so much the better. Avoid rocky, shallow soils for all fruit and nut crops, and be sure the subsurface soil is well drained. You can always add more water, but it's much more difficult to remove excess water.

614

 When should I plant fruit and pecan trees? What about grapes?

 All of these are sold in two common ways. They are dug during the winter dormant season, then usually packed in moist sawdust or moss for planting as soon as possible, usually during January or early February. More recently, fruit and nut plants, also grapes and berries, have been widely available all through the growing season in containers. The advantage of the container-grown plants is that all of their roots will be intact, although the bare-rooted plants cost considerably less.

615

 What size of fruit and pecan trees should I buy?

Again, the answer is somewhat tied to the way you buy the tree. Bare-rooted fruit trees should be 3 to 5 feet tall. Bare-rooted pecans can be as tall as 4 to 6 feet. Buying taller trees increases the setback of transplant shock, plus it means that you'll have a more difficult time training the trees to the proper branch structure. On the other hand, you don't want to buy "runts," which may lack the necessary vigor to establish and grow actively. Container-grown trees won't suffer the transplant shock, so you can go to larger specimens. Be careful, however, that those larger trees won't have to be trimmed excessively to develop the necessary "scaffold branching."

☆616☆

 Which types of fruit crops will grow best for me in my area?

That's a very involved question. It includes many factors, most important of them all being the climate and soils. Your local county Extension office will have precise recommendations for your county. Master Certified Nursery Professionals also have up-to-date suggestions.

617

 How many years will I have to wait before my fruit trees start to bear fruit?

It varies with type of fruit and even with the varieties involved.

- Strawberries will produce the spring after they are planted. Blackberries will produce their second season.

- Grapes, figs, peaches and plums will usually begin fruiting after 3 or 4 years.

- Apples and pears will begin after 4 or 5 years.

- Pecans will produce after 6 to 10 years, depending on the variety and the plant's vigor.

You'll get limited fruit before those times, but don't let your plants over-produce too early or you'll slow their growth and development.

618

 Will I need a second tree for good pollination?

Some fruit crops are sterile to their own pollen. Others produce their pollen (male) flowers at times different from the female flowers. In both cases, you'll need a second variety that blooms at the same time. Crops that will pollinate themselves, in other words, that won't require a second variety, include blackberries, cherries, citrus, figs, grapes (except all muscadines), nectarines, peaches, persimmons and strawberries. Apricots, pears, pecans, plums and walnuts are partially self-fruitful, which means that a second variety blooming at the same time would help ensure good fruit set. You will definitely want a second variety for apples and blueberries. Remember, too, that your neighbors may have the more common fruit crops, so you may not have to plant the second variety in your own garden. Bees will carry fruit tree pollen for a considerable distance, and pecan pollen can blow for similar distances. Above all, if you're planting a second tree to improve pollination, be certain that it's a different variety. Too many folks plant two of the very same favorite fruit and accomplish nothing toward improving the pollination.

619

 What does the "chilling requirement" mean?

Some types of fruit crops have a built-in mechanism for measuring the length of the winter. They monitor the number of hours temperatures are below 45° F and above freezing. That accumulated number of hours becomes the chilling period. Along the Red River it may be 1,000 hours per winter, but in the Rio Grande Valley it may only be 200 hours, on average. Once the required number of hours for a specific variety has been met, it will begin to bloom with the next warm spell. That means if you have a 200-hour variety of peach along the Red River, it may try to bloom sometime in early January, while a 1,000-hour variety would never bloom at all in the

Valley. You have to match the chilling hour requirement with what
you get in your area. Your county Extension office can give you the
most precise help for your area.

☆620☆

Q I want to raise some fruit in my garden, but I don't want to
spend hours pruning and spraying every month. What types
are productive and comparatively easy?

A If you had room for only three fruit crops, you would have
Brazos blackberries, plums (probably Methley) and Orient
pear. All are adapted over big parts of the state, and each will produce well with minimum care and space. If you have ample room
you could mix in a pecan tree. Each of these could be given an "A"
grade. Those that would rate a "B" in most of the state include
peaches (pest problems), figs (cold-sensitive in northern half of
state), grapes (higher maintenance), apples (insect and disease
problems), and blueberries (well adapted only to East Texas's
acidic soils). Cherries, strawberries, apricots, and nectarines are
more difficult here. Citrus trees grow well, of course, in the Rio
Grande Valley.

☆621☆

Q We saved some seeds from our favorite apple and peach
fruits. How can we start them, and how long will it be until
they bear fruit?

A Run, as fast as your legs can carry you, away from those
seeds. The fruit from which they were saved came from
hybrid trees. Those seeds won't "come true," that is, you won't get
the same kind of fruit. You need to buy grafted trees of the variety
you want. For those folks who say they "...just want to try the
seeds," you're wasting your time and space. By the time you spend
all those dollars and hours on fertilizers, sprays and pruning, the
few extra dollars you might pay for a really good type of tree are a
great investment.

622

 What kind of soil preparation do I need for my fruit trees?

These are trees. As they grow and develop they're going to outgrow any soil improvements you make, so you don't need to do a lot of heroic soil preparation. Put the same soil back in the holes around their roots. Pack it lightly and water them thoroughly, and all should be well.

623

 How deep do I plant my fruit trees?

As with any other tree or shrub, you want to plant them at the same depth at which they were growing in the nursery. You'll see the bud union near the ground somewhere. Be sure that's above ground by several inches. Use the old soil line on the trunk as your depth guide.

624

How much do I prune my new fruit trees back after they have been planted?

The general rule of thumb is to cut bare-rooted plants back by 50 percent and container-grown plants as needed to shape. That means you'll be paying for a 5-foot apple tree, but you'll be cutting it back to 30 inches. Part of the reason for that is to compensate for roots lost in the digging, but you also need to establish that new tree's branch structure early. As it grew in the nursery, it was probably crowded against other trees. As a result, it grew tall and slender. Pruning at planting lets you develop the scaffold branches the tree will need to hold its full load of fruit.

GENERAL CARE OF ESTABLISHED FRUIT CROPS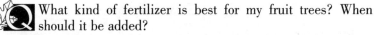

625

 What kind of fertilizer is best for my fruit trees? When should it be added?

As always, that depends on your having a soil test run periodically. Don't be surprised, though, if the tests indicate you need to add primarily nitrogen. While we think of phosphorus as being important for flowering and fruiting, it has become excessive almost to toxic levels in some Texas clay soils. Follow the guide of your soil test. As for timing, very early spring works well, as the trees start to grow. You probably will not need other feedings during the course of the growing season. In many cases, figs and pears being classic examples, you actually don't want too much new growth in any one year. Overfeeding can actually be very damaging.

626

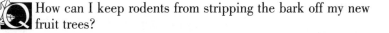 How can I keep rodents from stripping the bark off my new fruit trees?

Putting a piece of aluminum foil (shiny side out) around the trunk will usually discourage rodents such as field mice and rabbits from stripping the bark. The foil will also reflect the sunlight off the trunk, so sunscald won't be a problem.

627

 I think my fruit trees have mutated. My pear tree has thorns and little round fruit, and my plum fruit isn't the right color.

That can be one of two things, but it's not usually mutation. In the case of your pear, the top of the original tree has died out. What you have now is the growth of callery pear, the rootstock onto which pears are grafted. It's a lovely shade tree, although its fruit is not edible and the plant has thorns. You need to plant a new tree of the variety you wanted.

As for the plum, you probably got a tree that was mislabeled at the nursery.

MOST COMMON QUESTIONS
ABOUT SPECIFIC FRUIT CROPS

Almonds

628

 Can I grow almonds in my part of Texas?

Almonds don't grow well anywhere in Texas. They have very low chilling requirements, and they generally come into bloom weeks before it's safe, only to be caught by a late freeze.

Apples

629

 What varieties of apples are best?

Apples are best suited to North and North Central Texas. In that area you'll do best with Gala, Golden Delicious, Jonathan, Holland, and several of the Red Delicious types. In South Texas you can plant Anna and Dorsett Golden. Remember that red apples won't develop their really deep red colors as they ripen in Texas's summer conditions.

630

 How should I prune my apple trees?

When you plant a young apple tree it will probably have few, if any, side branches. Cut its top back by half at planting to encourage side branching. The bottom branch should be 26 to 30 inches from the ground, and you will want two or three other scaffold branches evenly spaced around the trunk. After the scaffold branches have been established you'll do little regular pruning each winter. If strongly vertical "watersprouts" develop, however, you'll want to remove them during the dormant season.

631

My apple tree has suddenly died. What would cause it to go from a healthy, pretty tree one week to completely dead the next?

 That's usually cotton root rot. This soil-borne fungus seems to love apples. It's a potential problem anywhere that soils are alkaline. Some growers have actually used massive amounts of agricultural sulfur as they planted their apples to try to prevent the development of the disease. It may help, but it isn't a guarantee.

632

My apple trees have spots all over their leaves. What kind of fungus does that?

Cedar apple rust. The same organism that causes eastern redcedar trees to develop those gelatinous rusty masses on wet days in the spring also invades apples. You can try fungicides, but the disease will still be there. Actually, apples shouldn't be planted near native stands of the redcedars.

633

 I'm losing one limb of my apple tree. It has turned almost black, and it's done it almost overnight. What disease does that?

 Fire blight can. It's a bacterial disease that is specific to the rose family of plants. Spray your tree while it's in full bloom with agricultural streptomycin. Prune out the dead wood, cutting back to healthy tissue. Disinfect your pruning saw with a 10-percent chlorine bleach solution between each cut.

Apricots

634

 Why is it that my apricot tree doesn't ever have fruit? It forms buds, but I don't get the fruit.

 Apricots are difficult in almost all of Texas. The problem is that they meet their chilling requirement fairly early in the winter, then come into bloom almost immediately thereafter. Too often there are weeks of potential bad weather ahead, and they usually get caught in bud, bloom or even in fruit. There is no solution to the problem, although planting apricots where you have the warmest night temperatures (higher on a hill, rather than in a valley, for example), and where they get good air circulation when frost might occur, both help. Expect one crop every four years, and feel lucky when you get it.

635

Q What is causing the sap to form at the base of my apricot tree?

A That's damage from peach tree borers. Spray the last week of August with a chlorpyrifos borer preventive to stop further invasion.

Blackberries

636

 What varieties of blackberries are best for Texas?

Long-time Extension recommendations include Brazos, Rosborough and Womack in North and North Central Texas; and Brison, Brazos, and Rosborough in South Texas.

637

 How do I start new blackberry plants?

 You use root tissues, either actual rootsprout plants or root cuttings. Nurseries sell them in January, or you can buy potted plants in the spring. One established plant from a friend's garden can actually yield dozens of new plants and never bother the mother plant. Blackberries will produce their second year after planting.

638

 How do I prune my blackberries?

 You trim the plants drastically the day after you harvest the last fruit. Cut any canes that had fruit clear to the ground, because they will never bear fruit again. Take the growing tips out of the new, vigorous canes at 40 to 45 inches, to encourage side branching and to keep the plants more compact. Otherwise, no additional pruning should be needed.

639

 Can I take dewberry plants and plant them into my garden?

 Dewberries are far less productive than their more upright counterparts, square-foot-by-square-foot. If you decide you do want dewberries, you might want to plant the improved variety called Austin instead of transplanting plants from the wild.

Blueberries

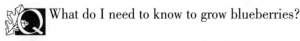

What do I need to know to grow blueberries?

Lots. First, they need a more acidic soil mix than almost any plant we try to grow in our landscapes or gardens. Unless you live in East Texas and have naturally acidic soils, plant them into a mix of peat moss and bark mulch. Soil preparation, if you live in an alkaline area, can cost many times as much as the plants themselves. Blueberries need morning sun and afternoon shade, and you'll need to keep them moist at all times. They make large shrubs, so don't crowd them together. Unless your soil conditions are absolutely perfect, you probably should initially try a limited planting. Woodard and Tifblue are the best types.

Cherries

I want to grow cherries, but my nurseryman has discouraged me. Is he correct in doing so?

Yes. They have a very high chilling requirement which will be met only in the Texas Panhandle. They're certainly not happy with the rest of Texas's mild winters and hot summers. The sour cherry Montmorency is your best chance.

Citrus/Satsumas

I bought a satsuma citrus tree for my patio. It has grown very well. Can I plant it outside?

Most citrus varieties, satsuma included, can't take hard freezes for any prolonged period of time. If it drops into the 20s in your area, and if it stays there for more than an hour or two at a time, better leave it in a large patio pot and shuttle it into protection when it's really cold.

643

Q I have whiteflies all over my satsuma. I almost hate to bring it indoors. They seem to get worse while it's inside over the winter.

A Whiteflies are difficult to control. You're right, they are usually less of a problem when natural predators can work on them outside. Try Orthene spray (not if the plant has fruit on it), or use yellow sticky traps within your plant's canopy to capture them.

Figs

644

Q My figs are terrible. They taste really bad. What causes that?

A Usually it's the dried fruit beetle. This tiny insect invades the fruit through its open end, or "eye." The insects carry an organism that causes the fruit to deteriorate, or "sour." There is no chemical control for the pest, but you can plant varieties like Texas Everbearing or Celeste. Each has closed eyes, so the insects cannot invade.

645

Q How do I fertilize my figs?

A Little, if any. Figs grow vigorously, even without supplemental feedings. Avoid high-nitrogen fertilizers that would stimulate succulent new growth.

646

Q How should I prune my figs?

A Do very little pruning. If a shoot is too tall and needs to be cut back, do so. If it would make the plant look better if you were to cut that limb clear back to the ground, do so. Prune, if needed, in March, to remove winter-killed branches.

647

 Why do my figs never ripen? They stay small, too.

 Give them time and they will eventually ripen. Texas Everbearing will often produce a second crop in a given season. Those fruit will come late and they'll be considerably smaller than the first, or "breba," crop. Unless you can control the weather, there is nothing you can do to speed things along.

648

 How can I start new fig plants? I have one that was in my old home garden, but I don't know its variety.

Figs are started from cuttings. Hardwood cuttings are taken in late winter, or semi-hardwood cuttings can be taken in early summer. In either case, your cuttings should be 4 to 6 inches long. All figs are started this way, and you'll get exactly the same variety as the original.

Grapes

649

 When should I plant grapes?

Most grapes are sold bare-rooted, which means winter planting is a must. You may also find 1-gallon plants in nurseries, which can be planted at any season.

650

What kind of planting site is best for grapes?

They need good air circulation to lessen the chance of disease. They also grow and produce best in deep, sandy loam soils. Avoid planting them in shallow, rocky, alkaline soils.

☆651☆

 What varieties of grapes are best for Texas?

Unfortunately, it's much more specific than that. You should probably check with your local county Extension office for the most precise information and the latest variety suggestions. Old stand-bys for big areas of the state, however, have always been Seibel 9110 and Champanel. With the resurgence of interest in wine grapes, however, many other varieties are proving suitable. You do need to be careful to select types that are adapted to the area, however. Many of the finer table grapes from California and elsewhere have major disease problems in the eastern two-thirds of Texas.

652

What kind of support do I need for my grapes?

You can grow grapes on almost any kind of substantial fence or trellis (6-inch posts are excellent); however, simple wires are probably easiest. You will do major pruning to grapes each winter, and it's easiest to remove the canes if you have a single wire or rail. Be sure it is well anchored and rust- or decay-resistant.

653

 How much room will my grapes need on the trellises?

Space grapes 8 feet apart when you grow them on trellises. If you're planting a grape to cover a patio or arbor, space it 10 or 12 feet (or more) from any other vine.

654

 Where do I put the wires on my trellis, and how do I train the vines to them?

 Traditionally, grapes have been grown by the cordon system, with two wires running between posts, one at 4 feet and the other at 6 feet. Plant your vines against the stakes, and spend the first two years developing the scaffold branching. Tie the vines to the stakes. When each vine reaches 4 feet in height, pinch out its growing tip to encourage side branching. Remove all the side branches that develop, with the exception of the two you select to be the main scaffold branches along the 4-foot-high wire. Using plastic plant ties, secure those lateral shoots to the wire and allow them to grow horizontally. After the first growing season, prune each of the lateral branches back to 4 feet in length from the main trunk. The second year, allow the buds along each of those 4-foot lateral branches to develop upward shoots that will grow toward the 6-foot-high wire. When they reach the higher wire, attach them to it with the plastic plant ties. Remove all fruit that forms that second year. That will establish the basic configuration of your cordon grape planting.

655

 What season should I prune my grapes?

 In mid-winter, certainly before any new buds start to swell.

☆656☆

 How do I prune my grapes once they're established?

 In a word: heavily. You'll probably remove 80 to 85 percent of the cane growth off each vine each winter. From all of the upright cordons you'll want to select 15 to 20 that are 4 to 6

inches apart on the lateral branches. Prune all of these cordon stems back to two buds each. The next year's fruiting cordons will originate from each of these buds. Their vigor will determine how much you prune the plant the following winter. Vigorous vines can be left somewhat longer, while those that grow less vigorously should be pruned more heavily, leaving fewer buds. In general, however, you'll always end up with the main stem and its two 4-foot lateral branches, and 15 to 20 cordon spurs and their two buds per spur. Repeat this process each winter as long as you have the grapes. If all of this is too confusing, your county Extension office has materials that illustrate it; and other garden references have devoted pages to outlining all the particulars.

657

 Do I need to thin my grapes like I do peaches and plums?

 Yes. Don't allow your plants to overproduce or you'll lessen the quality of the clusters and weaken the plants themselves.

658

 Are there any specifics I need to know about watering grapes?

 That's a really critical issue. Because they grow vigorously, they also use water really quickly. Drip irrigation lines (with several emitters around each trunk) work especially well. Mature plants may use 20 to 30 gallons of water per week, during peak growing season.

659

 What kind of fertilizer should I use on grapes, and when should it be applied?

Grapes need one annual feeding of a 3-1-2 ratio fertilizer in very early spring, ¼ cup per plant.

660

Q My grape plants look like they have measles (brown spots all over them), and the fruit is turning black and many of the grapes are drying up. What can I do to save my fruit and the plants?

A That's the most common disease, called black rot. You can spray with a listed fungicide early in the spring. Keep water off the foliage to lessen its spread.

661

Q The leaves on my grape plant are dying back from their tips. It looks like I might lose entire plants. I assume it's a disease. What can I do to stop it?

A That may be Pierce's disease. It's a serious problem for many high-quality types of grape plants in the humid eastern portions of Texas. It's spread by insects, but insecticides really don't help much in stopping its spread. Choose adapted varieties, instead. This disease is becoming more common as more grapes are grown in Texas. Your county Extension office will have the latest information.

662

Q My grape plants are mustard-yellow. I know my soil isn't the greatest, but what can I do to get them to green back up?

A If your soil is rocky and alkaline, it's probably iron deficiency. Symptoms on grapes and other plants include yellowed leaves with dark green veins, most prominent on the newest growth first. Apply a sulfur soil acidifier along with iron.

Kiwifruit

663

 I planted hardy kiwifruit several years ago, but they haven't had any fruit to date. What might I try?

There was a big push on these plants at that time. What they told us was that they would be hardy to our Texas winters. What they didn't tell us was that these plants originated in New Zealand, where temperatures seldom exceed 80 degrees in the summer. They can't cope with our heat. Your experience is the same as almost everyone else's, if that's any consolation.

Peaches

664

What types of peaches are best for my part of Texas?

Again, we're going to refer you to your local county Extension office for a reliable suggestion for your specific conditions. You need to match the chilling hours your area receives with the needs of any variety you choose. Plant a couple of varieties for the very best pollination. If you plant several different types, choose so that you'll have different varieties ripening all through the summer, not just over one or two weeks in June. Some of the best types for North Texas include Ranger, Sentinel, Denman, Harvester and Redskin. Some of those you might want to include in South Texas, where chilling hours are far fewer, include Early Amber, Rio Grande and Sam Houston.

665

How large should my peach tree be when I plant it?

Not very. Tall trees don't bear any sooner; in fact, they can actually die from the shock of being transplanted at such a mature size. Usually a 4- or 5-foot tree will be perfect, especially since you'll have to cut it back by 50 percent after you plant it. While that's a guideline left over from the day when all fruit trees were sold bare-rooted, you still need to cut a container-grown tree back by half, just to get it to establish its main scaffold branches 24 to 28 inches from the ground.

666

 Would you describe how I get my peach to establish those scaffold branches?

After you prune the tree back by half it will send out many side branches. Remove all but three or four. They should originate between 24 and 28 inches from the ground, and they should be evenly spaced around the trunk. Those will be the main branches for the entire life of the tree. Remove all other side shoots that try to develop.

667

 What pruning do I need to do to my peach tree in subsequent years?

Peaches should be pruned rather heavily in January of each year, by as much as 40 to 50 percent. The next year's fruit will be borne on the small red shoots produced the prior season. You want to remove any vertical shoots, always pruning just above buds or branches that face out from the center of the tree. Your ideal would be to maintain a bowl-shaped tree that is 8 to 10 feet tall and 15 to 18 feet wide. It's critical that you begin your pruning program the day the tree is planted, and that you continue it annually thereafter.

668

 I know that I prune my peaches heavily to lessen the fruit load. Aren't we supposed to thin the fruit that do form, too?

Yes. Ideally, you'd have 5 or 6 inches between peaches on each branch. That may mean that you remove half or more of the fruit that set, but you're doing it with the intent of improving the quality of the fruit that remain. Thin the fruit as they reach marblesize. By then the danger of late frosts should be past. Wind, strong rain and hail also will thin the fruit for you.

669

 What kind of fertilizer is best for peaches?

A 3-1-2 ratio lawn-type fertilizer also works well on peaches. Have a soil test run periodically to be certain the high-nitrogen fertilizer is in order.

☆670☆

My peaches have worms in their fruit. What can I do to prevent that next year?

That's the plum curculio. Apply a listed insecticide according to the spray schedule you can pick up at your county Extension office. The schedule will call for spraying when the buds are fully formed and showing color, but before they start to open, again when 75 percent of the petals have fallen (this spray should be in late evening, to lessen chance of damage to bees), and on 10-day intervals until harvest.

671

My peaches are dropping off the tree, even though they've only been on the tree for a few weeks. What should I have done?

Often that's because late frosts have killed the seeds within the fruit, but it also can be from wind, hail or other natural phenomenon.

672

My peaches' leaves are badly deformed, enough so that I can't really tell that they're peaches. It's happened other springs, and it never really seems to hurt the tree. Is it something I should worry about?

That's peach leaf curl, a disease that overwinters on the dormant buds. It won't harm the fruit quality, nor does it seem to shorten the trees' life expectancies. However, spraying with Bordeaux mixture or other copper fungicide soon after all the leaves drop in the fall should lessen its impact.

673

 The fruit on my peach are turning soft and brown. What causes that?

 Probably the disease called brown rot. Include a labeled fungicide with each of your spring insecticide sprays, and be careful to collect and destroy all mummified fruit on the tree and on the ground after harvest.

674

My peaches have large brown spots. It looks like there is a tiny hole in the center of each of the large spots. What causes that, and what can I use to stop it?

Stink bugs will do that. They carry micro-organisms that cause decay and ruin the fruit. The insects themselves are quite large and very mobile, so there is little hope of controlling them with a specific spray. Their damage shows up just before harvest, anyway, and most conventional insecticides would probably have too long a waiting period to keep the fruit usable. The insecticide sprays that you'll be applying for other purposes during the growing season will usually keep their populations in check.

☆675☆

I have globs of hard sap at the bottom of my peach tree. Now the tree seems to be dying. Is there an association?

Absolutely, and those aren't good symptoms for your tree. Peach tree borers probably account for the death of 90 percent of all our Texas peach trees. They're larval worms that tunnel through the trunks near the ground line. The sap flow that results plugs the tunnels and seals the borer larvae from any insecticides you might try to get to them. In short, it's much easier to **prevent** borers than it is to **cure** them. Apply a chlorpyrifos borer preventive spray between August 25 and September 5 to keep additional borers from invading the trunk. Hopefully, the tree isn't damaged so badly that it can't recover.

676

 I have globs of sap all along the trunk and limbs of my peach tree. What causes that?

Usually that's from bacterial stem canker, an especially troublesome disease. The copper spray you make for peach leaf curl in November will usually help. This is more of a problem with plums, but it can also damage peaches.

677

 In looking at the trunk of my peach tree I see a nasty crust adhering to it. The tree seems to be weaker. What causes it?

It's probably a scale infestation. These insects are mobile for part of their lives, then they affix themselves to the trunks and limbs. Their effect on a tree is much as a tick outbreak is to animals. Control the scales with a horticultural oil spray during the dormant season. You can often use the same materials at different spraying strengths during the growing season. Orthene works well, too, but do not use it when you have fruit on the tree.

Nectarines

678

What about nectarines? I really enjoy them, but I don't hear much about them here.

Nectarines are treated exactly as you would peaches. Their problem is that they lack the protective fuzz peaches carry. As a result, they're much more likely to develop disease and insect problems. They're more commonly grown in the more arid areas, where these pests are less likely to invade.

Pears

679

Q I enjoy pears. Are they fairly successful here in Texas?

A Yes, if you choose the right varieties. We have a real problem with fire blight. It's a bacterial disease that can kill large limbs, even entire trees of susceptible types. For that reason you should never plant Bartlett pears in Texas (except in far West Texas). The best type of pear for most of the state is Orient. It's resistant to the disease, yet it still has good fruit quality. The old Texas variety Kieffer is really resistant, but its fruit is quite hard. Pears have the added advantage of being attractive trees, so they can be tucked into a corner in the landscape where they will visually carry their own weight.

680

Q What kind of fertilizer should I use on pears?

A You can use a lawn-type 3-1-2 ratio fertilizer early in the spring, but do so sparingly. You really don't want very much vigorous growth on pears, since that soft, succulent tissue is more vulnerable to fire blight. Your pear will probably get adequate fertilizer simply from what filters in from adjacent turf.

681

Q How much should I prune my pears? When will they need to be pruned?

A Prune pears in late winter, before new buds start to swell. Remove any damaged or dead branches, and try to maintain strong branch angles where limbs intersect the trunk. What that means with pears is that you may remove one of two branches that join in a very narrow crotch. Such branch angles accumulate bark and other debris and are more likely to break apart in windstorms. Otherwise, unlike peaches and plums, no regular pruning is required for pears.

682

Q There are two or three dead limbs in my pear tree. A couple of weeks ago they were green and alive, but now their leaves are black. They're just hanging on the limbs. What causes that?

A That's probably fire blight, a common visitor to Texas pear plantings. You must have a variety that is susceptible to fire blight. Should fire blight kill an entire limb during the growing season you should remove the dead portion, cutting back into living tissues by several inches. Disinfect your pruning tools between each limb that you cut to prevent spread of the bacterium. Use a diluted solution of chlorine bleach (10 percent bleach, 90 percent water). Rinse and oil the tools after the final cut to prevent them from rusting.

683

Q My pear sometimes blooms in the fall. Does that mean it's sick?

A Pears, like several other spring-flowering trees, shrubs and vines, bloom when they come out of a prolonged dormant period. In the spring these plants are breaking cold-weather dormancy. In the fall they're responding to the end of the hot, dry Texas summer. The fall bloom should in no way diminish their performance the following spring.

684

Q My pear has grown very well since I planted it 3 years ago, but it doesn't bloom, hence no fruit. What is going wrong?

 A Old-time gardeners quickly found that pears flower best on horizontal limbs. It probably has something to do with hormone content of the tissues. They found that they could encourage

earlier flowering and fruiting by pulling the young trunks and branches out of their vertical habit. If you give a pear several years to grow
naturally, it will accomplish the same thing itself by the weight of the
large limbs pulling branches down out of their vertical positions.

685

 My pears develop large, dark brown splotches on their surfaces just as they start to ripen. What causes that, and is
there a good control?

That's stink bug damage. The insects carry a fruit-rotting
bacterium on their bodies. You won't be able to spray specifically for the stink bugs, since they come and go in a short period of
time, but regular spraying for other pear insect problems will probably keep their damage in check.

686

My pears are so hard. I have a hard time telling when to harvest them. What tips can you give?

That's a characteristic of many of our old-fashioned pears,
most notably Kieffer. Those grit cells seem to go hand-in-
hand with each variety's resistance to fire blight. The types with more
grit cells seem to be more resistant. Pears ripen for several days or
weeks after harvest. You can harvest the fruits, then wrap them in
newspapers and let them continue ripening. Once they're somewhat
softer to the touch, they'll be easier to eat.

687

My pear tree has thorns, and the fruit aren't any bigger than
marbles. I thought I was getting a good variety. What is the
problem?

The problem is that your good pear variety has died back to
the rootstock. What you're seeing is probably callery pear.
It's a more rounded, open tree. The branches have thorns, and the

fruit will be the size you describe. Look closely at the trunk. If you can't see the bud union where it was grafted onto the rootstock, it has died back below that point. You'll either need to learn to enjoy the callery pear or replace it with a variety of your choosing.

688

 I see Asian pears in the grocery store, and I'd like to grow my own if I can. I have seen them in the nurseries, but I don't hear much about them. Can you give me some advice?

 Asian pears seem to be quite susceptible to fire blight. If you want to try one in your landscape, do so. However, limit larger major plantings until more research can be done toward finding a resistant variety.

Pecans
Note: Many questions of a landscaping nature and relating to pecans are covered in chapter 3, Trees.

689

 How far apart should I plant pecans in my home orchard?

 Pecans should be at least 35 feet apart in all directions, preferably 40 to 50 feet. When their limbs begin to touch, pecans will start to lose their lower branches.

690

 What type of soil is best for raising pecans?

 Deep soils are best, preferably 5 to 6 feet at a minimum. However, with proper management, satisfactory yields can be attained from shallower soils. Avoid shallow, alkaline and rocky soils. Be certain, too, that the water table doesn't stay at or close to the soil surface for prolonged periods of time. Lake banks, for example, can have excessively wet soils for pecans and the trees won't do their best.

691

 How should I buy my pecans for an orchard? Should they be bare-rooted or in containers?

 Containers are always a great choice, but only if they're affordable and of the variety you would want to be planting anyway. Most large orchards use bare-rooted 4- to 6-foot trees and plant them in the winter.

.

☆692☆

 What are the best pecan varieties for Texas home "orchards?"

Assuming you need only a few trees you'll probably want to plant one each of several varieties. The best types for the drier western half of Texas: Cheyenne, Choctaw, Sioux, Western, and Wichita. The best types in the more humid eastern half of the state where diseases are more prevalent: Cheyenne, Choctaw, Desirable, Kiowa, and Caddo.

693

 I bought some pecans that were really high quality. Can I plant some of the nuts where I'd like to grow several trees?

Yes, but you won't get the same varieties back. You'd be far better advised to buy budded trees of a named variety. Plant the seeds and you would essentially be growing native pecans—good trees, but unpredictable for growth form, pest resistance, fruit yield, and quality.

694

I have a native pecan that is probably 20 years old. Is there any way to graft a better variety onto it? How is that done?

It certainly can be done, although it may involve some very serious and (initially) disfiguring pruning. Your county Extension office will have a fact sheet on "topworking" established pecans. They can probably recommend two or three local people who can do the work for you for a reasonable price.

695

If I want to grow several pecans near our house, what kind of fertilizer can I add to them and still keep the lawn underneath happy?

You're in luck. Both pecans and turfgrass benefit from high-nitrogen fertilizers. If you keep the grass "happy," the pecans will probably be satisfied, too.

696

Why do my pecans not fill out? When the tree was younger they were excellent, but now they only fill out about halfway out the kernels.

That's a characteristic of several older varieties, most notably Mahan and its daughter Mohawk. Once the trees get large and have heavy yields of pecans, they simply can't pull enough moisture and nutrients into the roots to supply the needs of the elongated kernels. There isn't much you can do for them, and, as a result, they simply haven't been recommended much in recent years.

697

My pecans try to sprout while they're still on the tree. What can I do to stop it? Does it completely ruin them?

That's a physiological process common to a few varieties, most notably Burkett. It's worse in wet falls, and, yes, it does ruin those particular pecans. Unfortunately, there is nothing you can do for it.

698

 My pecans' limbs seem to die back, then they try to regrow, then the whole process happens again. What stops this odd growth pattern?

That's pecan rosette, and it's caused by a lack of available zinc. It occurs west of Interstate 35, where soils are more alkaline. Oddly, this highway divides the state rather accurately from Oklahoma to Mexico. Pecan rosette will occur almost exclusively west of the line. You can add the zinc to the soil, but most of it will be lost to the soil's alkalinity. It's much better, instead, to spray the tree with a mixture of a zinc product. Include the zinc with each insecticide or fungicide spray you make, during the growing season.

Plums

699

 What types of plums are best for Texas?

Plums are among our best fruit trees. They're small, reasonably attractive, and highly productive. Best varieties include Bruce (large, red), Methley (medium, deep purple), Morris (large, red), and Ozark Premier (large, yellow and red and very sweet). Methley is an excellent pollinator, of both itself and the other varieties as well. Cross-pollination is needed for Bruce, Morris, and Ozark Premier.

700

 What type of plum is it that has red leaves and edible red fruit? I thought that all the purple-leafed plums were fruitless.

That's probably the variety called Allred (for obvious reasons). Its leaves will take on a greenish-red tint once it gets hot, and the fruit is of very acceptable quality. It's an interesting dual-purpose tree for ornament and fruit production.

701

What size of plum trees should I buy, and should I get bare-rooted or containerized trees?

Plums are among the smaller fruit trees when we buy them. You can find 3- to 5-foot trees that will take off and grow quite well for you. While you can usually find them in garden centers in containers, you can also do very well with bare-rooted trees in the winter. Decide on the variety you want. If you can find it in a container, buy it. Otherwise, go with a bare-rooted tree.

702

What kind of fertilizer is best for plums? When should it be applied?

Follow the guide of your soil test. For many plums in many Texas soils, however, a 3-1-2 ratio fertilizer will work quite well. Apply it in early spring, just before the tree starts to grow—1 pound per inch of trunk diameter.

703

How do I prune my plum tree to keep it vigorous and so I'll get the most possible fruit?

Prune plums just as you would peaches, that is, to a bowl shape. Remove all the strongly vertical growth, always trimming above buds that face away from the centers of the trees. That will keep the tree shorter and help it spread more, so the fruit will ripen to its full color. It will also let you reach the fruit from the ground as you harvest. You will be removing as much as half of the twig growth each January or early February.

704

Q My plum is dropping most of its fruit. They're not any bigger than marbles. What can I do to stop it?

A Several things can cause fruit drop. Wind will blow them out of the trees, and hail can knock them loose. If you've had a late frost, that can kill the embryos, resulting in aborted fruit a few days later. Insect damage can cause them to fall as well. A certain amount of drop isn't all that bad, since the fruit needs to be thinned anyway. Hopefully, it won't be excessive. By the time you see it there isn't much you can do to stop it.

705

Q My plums have worms in them. Can they be stopped?

A Those are plum curculio worms, the most common problem for both peach and plum fruits. You need to spray several times during the spring to prevent their entry. Apply Malathion or other listed insecticide while the tree is in full bud (before the flowers begin to open), when 75 percent of the petals are on the ground (this spray should be made in late evening so you won't harm the bees), and on 10- to 14-day intervals until harvest. Include a fungicide with each spray to protect the fruit from disease.

706

Q My plum tree looks like someone shot it with a shotgun. All of the leaves are full of holes. Please help.

A That's bacterial leaf spot. Spraying in the fall with a copper-based material will help, or you can use a labeled fungicide in the spring as the leaves are emerging. This disease usually runs its course by the middle of May, so you should only need one or two sprayings.

707

Q My plum tree's trunk is covered with beads of dried sap, clear up into the limbs. What causes that, and what can be done to help the tree regain its vigor?

A That's the same bacterial stem canker that bothers peaches. Plums are often devastated by the disease. Use a copper-based fungicide in November, after the tree has lost all its leaves. It's much easier to prevent this particular disease than it is to cure it.

708

Q My plum tree has large globs of sap near the soil. It bloomed very heavily and had a good fruit crop this year, but now it looks like it's dying. What should I do?

A That's peach tree borer damage. As you can tell, these two related trees share many of the same problems. You need to spray every plum tree every year, from the time they are planted, to protect them against this insect. Use a chlorpyrifos borer preventive between August 25 and September 5. Apply it to the trunk, just to the point of run off.

709

Q Birds are devouring my plums, just as they ripen. Can I use any kind of spray to repel them?

A There are tree nettings you can drape over peach and plum trees to keep the birds from having access to the fruit. Take them off as you harvest the fruit and store them for another year. Otherwise, you're going to have to resort to noise makers or things that have movement to scare the birds away. Those are frustrating ways to accomplish the task. You should never pick the fruit before it's ripe, however. Unlike tomatoes, which can ripen indoors, peaches and plums will not ripen more once they have been harvested.

Pomegranates

710

 My pomegranates flower, but I never get any good fruit. Are there some varieties that don't produce fruit?

Indeed. As hard as it is to believe, not everyone loves the seedy pomegranate fruit. What we do seem to agree on, however, is that this deciduous shrub is very attractive while it's in flower. If you want fruit, probably the best type to plant is one named Wonderful.

711

 My pomegranate looks like it's dying. We had an unusually cold spell this winter. Are they not winter-hardy?

Pomegranate plants can suffer damage with single-digit temperatures, particularly if they follow a warm spell. That means occasionally in the northern half of the state you may see freeze injury. In that case the plants will die back to the ground, or selective limbs will be dead when the plant tries to leaf out in the spring. Trim out the dead wood first in early spring, then reshape the rest of the plant as needed.

Strawberries

712

 I'd like to grow strawberries, but friends have told me they're difficult to grow in Texas. Is that true? How can I grow them?

Strawberries don't like our high summer temperatures. That's why folks in the southern third of the state will plant them in the fall and harvest the fruit the following spring. The plants are usually discarded at that point. Winters in the northern two-thirds of the state are too cold to allow the plants to establish and bear that quickly, so you plant them in February, pick off the flowers that first spring, and harvest your fruit the second April, 14 months after planting. Those plantings may succeed for several years. Carefully prepare the soil for your strawberries. Eliminate all existing weeds prior to planting. Add several inches of organic matter, and work the planting beds up 3 to 5 inches above the surrounding grade. Soil-borne diseases are a problem for strawberries, and good drainage is your best way of slowing their progress. It can also help if you erect some type of shade over the plants for the hot summer afternoons. They still will need very bright light, but you'll want to give them any extra help you can when it's extremely hot.

713

Q What varieties of strawberries are best for Texas, and where can I buy them? How good are the everbearing types?

A You want most of your planting to be of the spring-bearing types. You'll get all of the fruit at one time, granted, but those spring-fruiting types will greatly out-produce the everbearing varieties. Your county Extension agent will have a list of the recommended varieties for your part of Texas, but it's likely to include Chandler, Douglas, Sequoia, and Tioga for South Texas; and, Cardinal, Pocahontas, and Sunrise for North Texas. Check with farm supply stores and nurseries at the appropriate planting time. Some will even sell potted transplants in the spring. Out-of-state specialty mail-order nurseries offer disease-free plants, a nice bonus, but be sure of your sources before you buy through the mail.

714

Q Do I need to cover up my strawberries in the winter?

A No, in Texas it's not necessary. For the record, however, that's how the plant got its name (because of the straw that is placed over them in colder areas).

11

VEGETABLES

PLANTING AND EARLY CARE

715

Q What is a practical size for a home garden? This will be our first experience with it.

A Start with 100 to 200 square feet. You'll be able to maintain it easily, and you can always expand it another season if you enjoy the experience.

716

Q What are the easiest crops for a home vegetable garden?

A First, start with types your family enjoys. It doesn't matter if they're easy. If the family hates them, you're wasting your time, space, and effort. Having said that, here are some that produce well with few major problems: cabbage, broccoli, radishes, leaf lettuce, potatoes, squash, beans, cucumbers, tomatoes, peppers, okra, and black-eyed peas. Don't limit yourself just to these, however.

717

Q I don't have a lot of sunlight in my yard. How much will I need to grow good vegetables?

A Most flowering and fruiting vegetables will need at least 6 to 8 hours of direct mid-day sunlight to yield well. Horticulturally, we'd call that "full or part sun." Leaf and root crops can get by with less direct sunlight, but, again, the less light they get, the poorer the yields.

718

How do I prepare the soil for my vegetable garden?

Raised beds are requirements. That means you'll want to elevate the vegetables' soil by 5 to 6 inches above the surrounding grade. That will ensure perfect drainage, even in the wettest of seasons. It also will allow you to incorporate 4 to 6 inches of organic matter (peat moss, cotton burrs, bark mulch, compost, rotted manure, etc.) into the native soil. If you're thinking ahead and preparing your garden soil in the fall, use a glyphosate spray to eliminate all existing vegetation, before you start tilling. These materials will not contaminate the soil; in fact, they must enter the plants through active, vigorous growth.

719

How do I know when I should be planting various types of vegetables? Don't their planting dates vary a good bit?

Yes, they do, and people make their biggest vegetable-growing mistakes by planting at the wrong times. You want to meet your crops' temperature requirements above all else. For example, English peas and onions need to be planted 6 to 8 weeks before the last killing freeze, while black-eyed peas and okra should never be planted prior to one month after the last freeze. Let's group the plants as best we can.

- Those that are planted 4 to 8 weeks before the average date of the last killing freeze include asparagus, English peas, onions and potatoes.

- Those that should be planted 2 to 4 weeks prior to the last killing freeze date include lettuce, spinach, beets, turnips, broccoli, cabbage, cauliflower, Brussels sprouts, carrots, kale and radishes.

- Those that are planted on or after the last freeze date include tomatoes, beans, peppers, eggplant, corn, melons and cucumbers.

- One month after the last freeze plant okra, southern peas and sweet potatoes.

720

Q How do I time things for my fall plantings?

A Know the number of days each of your crops will take until you can make your first harvest. Usually that time will be described in the seed catalog or on transplants' labels. Allow that much time plus 4 to 6 weeks for peak harvest in fall's cooling weather conditions. Because the average date of the first freeze varies so much north-to-south in Texas, it would be impractical to try to list every crop's planting date. Tomatoes will be the first, however. Set transplants out around June 20 for the Panhandle, by July 1 along the Red River, by July 10 in Central Texas, and by late July in South Texas. Almost all fall vegetable plantings will be finished by September 1, except in deep South Texas.

721

Q Are there any vegetables that grow well indoors in pots during the winter?

A Stick with leafy vegetables such as herbs and leaf lettuce, and grow them on your brightest windowsill. If you have a greenhouse (or similar structure that is heated in winter), you can also try tomatoes, peppers and cucumbers, among others.

722

Q How important is it that I rotate my crops in my vegetable garden? I don't have much room, and I don't have much sunlight. I really can't move the plantings very far.

Crop rotation, as farmers will tell us, keeps problems from accumulating. If you grow the same plant in the same soil year after year, insect and disease problems that are specific to it can eventually build up to serious proportions. Until that begins to happen, however, you can stay with your existing planting plans.

723

I have been told that my vegetable garden has a problem with nematodes. The plants have been stunted the past two or three years, and now they're hardly growing at all. What can I do now?

Nematodes infest many of our common vegetables. When your crops show stunted growth (and, more specifically, if you ever see knots on the roots of okra, tomatoes, peppers, potatoes, or others), you need to have a soil test run through the Nematode Diagnostic Laboratory at Texas A&M University. There is a charge for the test. Your county Extension office will have all the details. If the test comes back positive, plant Elbon rye in October. Allow it to grow all winter, then plow it under in late January or early February. While it won't eliminate the nematodes, it certainly will reduce their population by entrapping them in its root system. You do not have to worry about removing the root systems as you rototill. The nematodes will be dead by that time. You should also choose varieties that are resistant to nematode damage. Cool-season vegetables, for example, are less likely to have problems. Some tomatoes will carry the initial "N" after their variety name, indicating that they are resistant to the microscopic pests.

724

 Are hybrid seeds worth the added cost?

Absolutely. Resist the temptation to buy "bargain" seeds off discounted racks in discount stores. Choose the very best varieties of vegetables. By the time you have gone to the trouble and expense of getting everything else ready, that extra cent you pay for a hybrid seed will be a tiny additional investment. Hybrids are more aggressive and far more productive. They often have better insect and disease resistance, and they frequently offer superior color or flavor, or both.

725

 Can I save seeds from my vegetables for next year?

 If they were hybrid plants, no, you cannot. They won't "come true" from the seeds they produce. That means you'll get some other variety, probably inferior, than the one you had grown. Buy fresh seed. Inbred varieties, by comparison, can be saved. Porter tomatoes are the best example. You can cut the fruit open, spread the seed out to dry for several days, then store it cool until the following year's planting time rolls around.

726

 When are vegetable transplants better than planting seeds?

Plants that have smaller seeds will often be better as transplants. If the seed is very expensive, you'll want to use transplants, and, if you're trying to get a jump on the season, transplants will be of great help. Plants we most commonly plant from transplants include onions, cabbage, broccoli, cauliflower, Brussels sprouts, tomatoes, peppers, eggplants and sweet potatoes.

727

Should I put some kind of fertilizer alongside my seeds when I plant them?

Probably not. All plant foods, whether they're organic or inorganic, contain mineral salts. Those salts can be concentrated enough to cause root damage to tender new plants. Wait until

the seedlings have been up and growing for two weeks, then apply a
diluted solution of a water-soluble plant food. If you're trying to do
things organically, you may be able simply to mix generous amounts
of well-composted manures into your garden soil as you prepare for
planting. Over a period of several growing seasons the manures may
add sufficient nutrients. In the meantime, you may need to add a little of the water-soluble inorganic material.

728

 How far apart should the seeds be planted? Will I need to
thin them?

That depends on each crop's mature size. Tomatoes will be
perhaps 36 to 48 inches apart in their rows, while lettuce,
by comparison, can intermix with itself. Vegetable plants can compete with one another just as much as weeds, so keep them
well spaced.

729

How far apart should the rows in my vegetable garden be?

Again, it will depend on the crops you're growing. Tomato
rows should be 4 feet apart, while lettuce, spinach and
radishes can be grown as vegetable "groundcovers."

730

What is a "hill" that I see mentioned on seed packs?

In cooler, wetter parts of America gardeners used to plant
their vegetables in raised areas, or "hills." It was their way
of ensuring great drainage. Today, however, with our amended soils
and careful and attentive watering, you'll be able to plant directly
into the garden rows.

CARE OF A VEGETABLE GARDEN ....

731

Q What kind of fertilizer is best for my vegetables?

A Have your soil tested every couple of years to monitor the levels of the various nutrients. Don't be surprised, however, if the tests show that you need to add high-nitrogen fertilizers for the foreseeable future. That frequently happens in landscapes and gardens, and it's difficult to convince yourself to add nitrogen to that vigorous tomato plant, when all you really want are the fruits that plant will produce. What the soil test may show you is that you already have ample (or even excessive) amounts of phosphorus and potassium in the soil. Trust the test.

732

Q How often do I need to fertilize the garden?

A If you're using a quality granular material, probably just once a month through harvest. If you opt for a water-soluble fertilizer, you'll probably need to apply it once a week. Organic fertilizers break down much more slowly, so just two or three applications per season will be needed, but be prepared to supplement them with inorganic nutrients if your plants appear stunted or "hungry."

733

Q How can I best water my vegetables? How often?

 A Drip irrigation is the best way to water vegetable gardens because it allows you to apply the water directly around the plants' root zones. It also keeps the water off the leaves and produce, and it eliminates evaporation and runoff. Space the emitters so each small plant such as beans or lettuce will have one or two emitters, while larger plants such as tomatoes will have three or four. You can also use sprinkler hoses turned upside-down on the soil, or you can slowly fill the furrows with water. Overhead irrigation is the worst choice, since wet foliage and produce is far more likely to develop diseases and sunscald.

734

 Is it necessary that I mulch my garden?

 While it may not be completely necessary, mulching is certainly a great idea. Nowhere in your landscape or garden will mulches have more benefits than they do in the vegetable patch. Mulches:

- keep the produce off the soil surface, protecting it from insect and disease invasion;

- reduce splashing, so your produce is cleaner when you bring it indoors;

- cut down on weeds;

- moderate soil temperatures; and

- conserve moisture and lessen runoff.

735

 What weedkillers can I use in my garden?

 You always want to read and follow label directions before you use any product in your garden. Once you do that you'll find that there are really very few weedkillers that are registered for use around existing vegetables. That doesn't necessarily mean that they would do any harm to you or your family. It merely means that the manufacturers have not gone to the expense of proving that their products can be used around edible crops. You must always follow the labels' directions. You can use a glyphosate herbicide during the "off-season"

to eliminate existing grassy weeds such as bermuda and Johnsongrass. Otherwise, mulching and cultivating should serve you well.

736

Q How can I get ants out of the garden?

A Again, you'll have to check the labels and their restrictions. Some of the inorganic insecticides have label clearance for use around existing vegetables—so long as you respect the required waiting period before consuming the produce. If it's fire ants that are bothering you, you can also make a band treatment around the perimeter of the garden with one of the registered baits.

737

Q Is there anything that will discourage rabbits in the garden?

A Fencing will be your best bet. Use chicken wire to keep them out. Make sure there are no gaps, and, if the garden is large, be sure the rabbits are out of the garden when the fence goes up. One friend discovered that he had actually fenced the rabbit inside his large garden plot! You might also try low-voltage electric shock fencing, or try to capture the rabbit with a humane trap.

738

Q How will I know when produce is ready to harvest? I want to get as much as I can, of course, but I don't want them to go past their prime.

A As a general rule, you want to harvest produce when it's about two-thirds its full mature size. Letting carrots grow longer, or cucumbers longer and fatter, will merely diminish their quality. Large beans develop strings and are chewy to eat, and overly mature radishes can be woody and hot. In two words, "harvest early."

739

What time of day is best for harvesting produce?

Early in the morning is best, while the plants are still turgid (full of water). Avoid mid-afternoon harvests during the heat of early summer. That produce won't have the same quality as the morning pickings.

740

How can I protect my plants from frost? I'm interested in getting a jump in the spring, but I also will need to cover them the night of the first freeze in the fall.

There are special lightweight spun fabrics that can be laid over the tops of tender plants. You can also use old sheets or burlap bags. When temperatures are above 32 degrees, cover the plants to keep frost from forming directly on their leaves. If it's going to drop below 32, however, enclose the plants in plastic and put some type of heat source in with them. Perhaps you have a heating cable, or maybe you use a drop light from the shop. This little bit of heroic covering can actually extend your garden's productive season by many weeks. It's definitely worth the effort.

741

What types of plants grow best in a container vegetable garden?

Types that stay small and produce heavily. Avoid crops like okra, corn, watermelons and potatoes that either need more space than any conventional container would allow, or that produce so little per container that they wouldn't be practical. Best bets: lettuce, cabbage, spinach, radishes, tomatoes, peppers and cucumbers. Use a really good potting soil, and water and fertilize the plants more often than you would if they were in the ground. Container gardening lets you get a head start in the spring, and it allows you to shuttle tender plants into the garage on the first cold nights of late fall.

MOST COMMON QUESTIONS
ABOUT SPECIFIC VEGETABLES ....

Asparagus

742

 Q What kind of special soil preparation will I need to make for an asparagus bed?

 A You'll have to work the soil much better than you would for other vegetables, because asparagus stays in the same soil for many years. Rototill to incorporate 6 to 8 inches of organic matter such as peat moss, compost, bark mulch and rotted manure into the soil. If you're amending a clay soil, include 1 inch of yellow washed brick sand, as you rototill.

743

 Q When and how do I plant asparagus?

 A Buy dormant two-year-old roots in January. Choose one of the improved varieties such as UC-157 or Jersey Giant. Set them into 10-inch-deep trenches, spacing the roots 15 inches apart in the trenches. The trenches, if you have more than one row, should be dug 5 to 6 feet apart. Asparagus plants grow quite large as they mature. Cover the roots with 2 to 3 inches of the soil mix, then soak them heavily. As the crowns start to grow, gradually add more soil until the trenches are filled.

744

 Q How soon can I start harvesting spears from my asparagus?

 A You really should leave the plants alone for their first two growing seasons. Those spears develop into stems, and the stems bear the leaves that make the foods, which are then carried down into the fleshy storage roots. If you cut off too much top growth one year, you'll pay the price the following year.

745

 When is asparagus harvested?

When the stems shoot out of the ground in late winter and early spring, you can cut them with an asparagus knife. Be careful not to damage adjacent stems, and harvest only for 6 or 7 weeks. Quit by April, so the plants can grow and produce bigger and better roots systems to propel the next year's shoots.

746

 My asparagus spears are small, not as large in diameter as I had hoped. What causes that?

That is usually due to our warm climate. Asparagus develops its best spear size where winters are cold and summers are mild. There isn't much you can do about it in Texas, other than to give the plants the best possible care in all other respects.

747

When do I fertilize asparagus, and with what?

Apply a high-nitrogen fertilizer in late winter, just before the stems start to grow, and again immediately after you finish harvesting the spears in April.

748

 How can I get bermuda out of my asparagus bed?

That's really difficult, because there are no labeled products that will eliminate bermuda without damaging the asparagus. Best bet would be to wipe a glyphosate weedkiller directly onto the bermuda, then cover the ground with a roll-type mulch to keep it from sprouting again. Give the asparagus ample room to send out its new shoots, however.

749

Q Someone told me about using rock salt around my asparagus plants to kill any weeds. Does that work?

A Whether it might kill the weeds is a moot point. The real issue is that you don't want to be introducing all that sodium around your plants and into the soil. It can contaminate the garden for years to come, and affected plants will scorch and burn.

750

Q Do I need to cut off the old brown asparagus stems during winter?

A Asparagus needs to go dormant in the winter, if you are going to expect any size to the following spring's spears. In South Texas you often have to cut green stems back in early December, just to force the dormant period. In North Texas, however, your plants will turn brown with the first hard freeze. At that point you can cut them back near the ground, or just leave them in place until late winter.

751

Q Can I move a clump of asparagus when we move to our new house? It had just gotten old enough to start producing.

A It's best just to leave asparagus behind when you move. By the time you disturbed the old clump and moved it to its new home, it would set it back enough that a new planting would probably out-produce it.

Beans

752

Q How early can I plant my beans? Also, will they do well in the fall garden?

Plant beans one to two weeks after the last freeze in the spring. They won't germinate in cold soils, so early planting gains you nothing. Beans do quite well in the fall garden, but plant them early enough that they will have time to mature before frost. The timing will vary with varieties.

753

What types of beans are easiest and most productive for my garden?

Bush green beans and wax beans are the quickest and easiest, which is why they're among our most popular Texas garden vegetables. Pole green beans are also good choices—although they're somewhat slower and more labor-intensive. By comparison, lima beans are far more difficult to grow.

754

How do I know when to harvest my beans? They get much bigger if I leave them, but the quality goes down. Is there a good guideline?

Yes. You want to harvest beans just as you see the swelling of the seeds start to develop. If a particular pod is really lumpy with seeds, you can bet it's going to be tough and stringy at the table.

755

 My beans have been producing for about one month, but they don't appear to be setting any more beans. Is that normal?

That is very normal. You usually will get 4 or 5 really good pickings off any planting of beans. If you fail to harvest them punctually and let them get overmature on the plants, you'll reduce the yield from that point. It's extremely important that you have someone pick the beans for you if you're going to be away for a few days as they reach harvest size.

756

 My bean plants have turned tan and the plants appear to be dying. What causes that?

That's damage by your old friends, spider mites. They attack many vegetables, but beans are among their very favorites. You can use the miticide Kelthane to eliminate them, but harvest all the beans that are of the proper size before you spray. Be sure you spray the backs of the leaves as well, since that's where spider mites are most active. If the plants are as tan as you indicate, it may not be possible to save them.

757

I noticed knots on the roots of my bean plants when I took them out of the garden. Are those anything I should worry about? The plants grew and produced well.

There are two candidates, one good and one bad. Beans are legumes, and, as such, they have nitrogen-fixing bacteria that form nodules on the plants' root systems. They convert gaseous nitrogen from the soil-borne air into a form which plants utilize through their roots. Those nodules you have seen may be nothing more than that. However, beans are also susceptible to nematodes, the microscopic soil-borne worms that attack many plants' roots. Galls will form on the roots, and thereafter the plants will usually be stunted. Having the soil tested for the presence of root-knot nematodes is the only way you can be certain of the problem. Your county Extension office has all the details.

Broccoli

758

 When should I plant broccoli?

The spring planting is made 4 to 6 weeks before the average date of the last killing freeze. This early planting is critical to the quality of the heads that will develop. Producing broccoli does not tolerate high temperatures well at all. Fall plantings should be made 3 months prior to the average date of the first killing freeze.

759

 Can I sow broccoli directly into the garden?

 Yes, but it's better to start the transplants in pots, then introduce them to the more hostile outdoor conditions.

760

 How will I know when to harvest my broccoli? I want the heads to get big, but I don't want to wait too long.

We eat the flower buds of broccoli, with a heavy emphasis on "buds." If you wait until the heads start to show actual yellow flowers, you've blown it. Cut the heads just below the lowest florets and encourage the plants to send out secondary side shoots. The shoots will give you subsequent harvests of smaller heads in a couple of weeks.

761

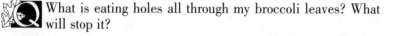 What is eating holes all through my broccoli leaves? What will stop it?

That's cabbage looper damage. This small caterpillar ruins almost any broccoli planting that isn't protected by *Bacillus thuringiensis* spray or dust. "Bt" spray or dust can be used as late as the day of harvest.

762

 When I harvest my broccoli heads I notice many small green plant lice on them. What can I do that won't ruin the quality of the heads?

Those are aphids, also known as plant lice, as you indicated. You probably should be using an insecticide spray a week or 10 days prior to harvest, to keep them from becoming such a problem at the last minute. Carefully rinsing the heads prior to cooking will get rid of them.

Brussels Sprouts

763

Q When should I plant Brussels sprouts? How successful are they here?

A Brussels sprouts aren't easy in Texas, but they can certainly be grown here. Plant them in late winter, 4 to 6 weeks prior to the last killing freeze date. Your fall planting may be more rewarding. Set the transplants out 3 months prior to the average first-frost date.

764

Q My Brussels sprouts plants grow well, but they aren't developing "sprouts." What can I do to speed that along?

A When the plants are 20 to 24 inches tall, pinch out their growing tips. That will force them to send out their side shoots (the sprouts you will later harvest).

765

Q My Brussels sprouts' leaves are chewed full of holes, like Swiss cheese. What insect does that?

A Cabbage loopers. Control them with *Bacillus thuringiensis*. Ask your nurseryman for "Bt." It can be used as late as the day of harvest.

Cabbage

766

Q I'd like to plant cabbage. Should I use transplants, or can I start seeds?

Cabbage is sensitive to hot, dry conditions of late spring, so it's best to use the head start that potted transplants give you. Set them out 4 to 6 weeks prior to the average date of the last killing freeze. Your fall crop should be planted 3 months prior to the first freeze of the fall. If early light frosts happen before you harvest the heads, however, they will survive and continue to develop. Harvest before a hard freeze, however.

767

My cabbage heads are splitting open. It looks like they're being ruined. What causes that, and what can I do now?

You need to harvest the heads as soon as possible. Sudden changes to hot, dry weather can cause that, especially if it's been cool and moist. Next time try planting earlier, so you can harvest before the weather takes its toll.

768

My cabbage heads are full of worms. What are they? Sevin didn't work very well at all.

Those are cabbage loopers, and Sevin isn't particularly effective on them. Use *Bacillus thuringiensis* ("Bt") as a spray or dust. It can be used the same day as you harvest, although you'll probably need it long before that time. It will take several hours to kill the caterpillars, but they will stop feeding almost immediately after you treat the plants.

Carrots

769

My carrots are always stubby and mangled looking. What can I do to get better quality?

 Long, tapered carrots need sandy, loose soil to grow to full length and good, straight shape. If you have garden soil that is less than ideal, you'd be far better off to plant some of the stubby-rooted types. Even with that, you'll want to plant them in raised beds filled with really good garden loam.

770

Q My carrots are tough and woody, not at all tasty. What did I do wrong?

A They probably didn't grow fast enough, or else you're leaving them in the garden too long. Carrots should be harvested when they're half to two-thirds of their expected mature length. Also, when carrots are challenged by heavy soils, poor drainage or drought, high temperatures or other environmental factors, their response is to turn corky, as you described. Be sure you're planting early enough, too. Carrots need to be seeded 2 to 3 weeks prior to the average date of the last killing freeze for your area. That way they'll be harvested and gone before it turns really hot.

Cauliflower

771

Q When should I plant cauliflower? Will it do well here?

A Cauliflower takes a longer time to mature than its other relatives, cabbage and broccoli. As such, it can be difficult in springs when it turns hot and dry unusually early. Plant it 4 to 6 weeks before the average date of the last killing freeze. Keep it growing actively. Fall plantings are often the most productive. Plant it 3 to 4 months before the average date of the first killing freeze.

772

Q Do I have to tie the leaves up around my cauliflowers' heads like my folks used to do?

A We have done that for decades in an effort to keep the heads pure white. When they're exposed to sunlight they may develop chlorophyll and take on a green shade. That's not the least bit harmful, however, so you can certainly bypass tying the leaves if you wish. If you do decide to blanch the heads, use large, soft rubber bands to pull the top leaves up and over the heads as they mature.

773

 Q My cauliflower leaves are full of holes. I see a small green worm feeding voraciously on them. What will stop the worms?

A Use *Bacillus thuringiensis* ("Bt") to stop these cabbage loopers. Left unchecked they can certainly ruin an entire planting in just a few days.

Corn

774

 Q When can I plant corn?

A Plant it on the average date of the last killing freeze in the spring to one week later. Corn doesn't do as well in fall's cooler weather, so it's not a prime candidate for the fall garden.

775

Q What special feedings will my corn need?

A Corn is a grass, and, as such, benefits from a high-nitrogen fertilizer applied when the plants are 6 to 10 inches tall. You can use a complete-and-balanced analysis fertilizer one month later.

776

 Q My corn ears aren't filled out very well. What could I have done differently?

A Corn is wind-pollinated, so it relies on having many plants producing pollen at the same time. If you ever plant corn in one long, straight row, you're going to see this sort of uneven filling of the ears. You always need to plant corn in square blocks, to ensure good pollination.

777

As I harvest my ears of corn I'm finding a small worm eating away at the ends of the ears. What is it, and how do I eliminate it?

That's the corn ear worm, and it ruins great-looking ears faster than anything else. You can use 1 drop of mineral oil on the flower silks as they form. That will keep the larvae from getting into the ears in the first place. Insecticides such as "Bt" may help.

778

How can I know when it's time to harvest my ears of corn? When do they go past their prime?

Pull the ears while they're at the "milk" stage, that is, when the kernels squirt sappy milk when you press against them with your nail. Once they get to the stage that they have dents at the outer ends of the kernels, they will have lost some of their sweetness.

Cucumbers

779

My cucumbers bloom, but they don't set fruit very well. What can I do to get more cucumbers to form?

They may not be getting pollinated. Cucumbers bear both male and female flowers. You can tell the difference by the small primordial fruit at the bases of the female flowers. Male flowers have straight stems. If you have a shortage of bees working your garden, you can increase the fruit set by snipping off one or two male flowers and using them to pollinate the female flowers manually.

780

 My cucumbers are hot and bitter, not at all the flavor we like. What causes that?

Anything that puts the plants in stress as their fruit ripens can give them the unusual flavors. Keep them moist and well fertilized to keep them actively growing.

781

 How do I know when to harvest a cucumber? When is it ripe?

Don't let cucumbers develop to their full size. Big, tough cucumbers aren't very appetizing. Harvest them when they're approximately half their normal mature size, even smaller if you're going to use them for pickles. Don't leave overly mature cucumbers on your plants or you'll stop further production.

782

 My cucumbers' leaves are starting to develop small tan spots all over them. Is that caused by an insect? What should I do?

That's the beginning of spider mite damage. Thump one of the leaves over white paper. You should be able to see the nearly microscopic mites moving on the paper. Control them with Kelthane miticide spray.

Garlic

783

 When and how do I plant garlic in Texas?

 Unlike onions, garlic is planted in the fall. Set each clove fat-end-down, 2 inches deep and 3 or 4 inches apart in their rows. Allow it to grow through the winter and early spring, then harvest it in late spring, when the tops begin to fall over. Store it in a cool, dry spot in your garage.

Herbs

784

 What kind of a planting area do I need for herbs?

Any spot can do quite well. Include herbs everywhere. They're great in a vegetable garden, of course, but they also look wonderful with flowers. You can use several types as low border plants, and they're perfectly suited to patio pots and hanging baskets. Most important: Have fun with your herbs. Use them in some unpredicted way.

785

How do I pick the best herbs for my garden? Which types do well?

Entire books are written on herbs, and most will tell you to grow the types your family enjoys the most. Some of the easiest and most rewarding include all the different and lovely types of basil, chives (great as a low border plant in the landscape), dill (with its graceful textures), scented geraniums with their wonderful foliage, all the types of mints (be careful of their invasive nature), parsley (makes a lovely annual edging plant), rosemary (as a semi-hardy small shrub), all the beautiful sages and the various thymes. All of these are readily available at their seasons (usually in spring).

786

 Do most herbs need sun, or can they take shade?

Most herbs will grow best in nearly full sun, although they seem, as a group, to be tolerant of half shade. Experiment and you'll find types that will grow almost anywhere. Sage and basil are good in baking heat, and mint can tolerate almost complete shade, as three extreme examples.

787

 When is the best time to harvest my herbs?

 Morning is usually best, just after any dew has dried. Do not harvest them while they're hot and wilted.

788

 Which types of herbs should I freeze, and which are dried?

 You'll want to freeze basil, dill, chives, parsley and tarragon. Tie their stems in bundles and carefully rinse them. Remove any damaged parts, then dip them into boiling water for 1 minute. Rinse them after you remove them from the water, then place them into the freezer as soon as possible. For the types you intend to dry, you'll want to hang bundles of the herbs upside-down in a clean location. Let them dry for a couple of weeks, at which time you can break them into smaller parts and store them dry and dark until you're ready to use them. Seeds are dried on wire frames. Herbs that are frequently dried include basil, chives, dill, oregano, parsley, rosemary, and sage.

Lettuce

789

 When should I plant leaf lettuce?

 Sow the seeds 2 to 4 weeks prior to the average date of the last killing freeze for a spring garden, and 8 to 10 weeks prior to the first killing freeze date for a fall garden.

790

 Can I grow head lettuce successfully here?

Not easily. You're much better off planting leaf types. Use several varieties of green- and red-leafed lettuce for an extended season and for the prettiest salads.

791

 My lettuce isn't sweet, but very bitter. What causes that?

Hot, dry weather will cause lettuce to be bitter. If you plant the seeds too late in the spring the plants will mature too late. If you cut several harvests of lettuce, then leave the plants in the garden too long, they'll get tough and strong-flavored. Fall lettuce often has a sweeter flavor, since the leaves are growing during more favorable temperatures.

792

What tips do you have for harvesting leaf lettuce? Do I cut it all at once, or let it keep growing?

If you're making your first harvest you can pluck the leaves individually. Don't pick the oldest leaves, and leave the growing tips to produce more leaves. As the plants mature and you've made one or two harvests already, you can begin to take more of each plant, including their growing tips. Once the plants start to bolt to flower, you need to complete all harvesting immediately.

Melons

793

 How well will I do growing watermelons in a home garden? When should they be planted?

Watermelons take huge amounts of garden space, often as much as 100 square feet per plant. Grow them only if you can give them that room to grow. Plant them a week or two after the last killing freeze date for your area. Watermelons are not as productive in fall gardens. They really prefer the hot days of early summer.

794

How can I know when to pick my watermelons?

 Watch for several indicators of ripeness. When the white spot under the melon starts to turn yellow, the melon is probably ripe. You'll also see two tendrils on the stem on either side of the melon. When they begin to turn dry and brown, the melon is probably ripe. Folks who have commercially harvested melons also know the dull "thud" sound the ripe melons make when thumped. If they hear a higher "ping" sound, they leave the melons for a few more days.

795

My melon leaves have a white powder on them. Will it hurt the plants?

That's powdery mildew. It can weaken the plants, so, if the problem seems severe, you can use a labeled fungicide. Keep irrigation water off the leaves, and don't handle the plants while the leaves are wet.

Okra

796

 I have ants all over my okra. What can I use to kill them, assuming they are doing some type of damage?

Ants aren't really that harmful to the okra itself. However, if they're fire ants, they can be damaging to you as you harvest. You can use any registered insecticide to control them.

797

 My okra roots are all full of knots. What caused them?

 Those are root knot nematodes. They're microscopic worms that sting the plants' roots and interrupt normal growth processes. Plant Elbon cereal rye in your garden in October to entrap and kill the nematodes. Move your okra patch to another part of your garden, or perhaps move your plantings to an entirely new garden. There is no chemical control for nematodes.

Onions

798

 When should I plant my onions?

 Bulbing onions should be planted from bundled transplants 6 to 8 weeks prior to the last killing freeze in your area. Later plantings will lead to inferior onions. Should severe cold ruin your planting you'll need to start again, although that won't be a common problem.

799

 How deep do I set the onion transplants?

 Plant them very shallowly. In fact, it's not uncommon for many of them to topple over and have to be reset, if they were initially planted properly.

800

 My onions are flowering. Doesn't that ruin the bulbs? Why do they do that?

Yes. Harvest and immediately use those onions. They won't store well at all. If anything interrupts an onion's growth patterns, it is likely to bolt prematurely to flower. Sudden turns to hot, dry weather can trigger it. When you plant the transplants in late winter you even need to sort out and discard the larger ones, since they're more likely to flower prematurely.

801

 I think I planted my onions too close together. Now they seem to be crowding one another. Can I harvest part of them as green onions?

 Yes. Thinning them is the perfect solution. The final spacing for your bulbing onions should be 2 to 3 inches between plants.

802

 My onions have grown well. How can I tell when it's time to harvest them?

Harvest bulbing onions once two-thirds of their tops have fallen to the ground. Dig the bulbs and lay them out on top of the ground to dry for a couple of days. Lay their foliage over their tops to prevent sunscald. Don't water them for a few days prior to harvest, and move them into the garage if there is a threat of rain. (Moisture promotes decay during storage.) Store them cool and absolutely dry.

Peas, English

803

When do I plant my English peas?

Early. Sow the seed 8 to 10 weeks prior to the last killing freeze date for the spring. Peas take longer than most other cool-season vegetables to mature, plus they need to produce their pods before it gets really hot.

804

 Will I need some type of trellis for English peas?

Many types of peas will need some type of support, either from wire fencing or from lattice. Newer bush types of snap peas require far less support.

805

My English peas have a dusty covering on their leaves. Is that mildew? What can I use to control it?

That's powdery mildew, and it's common with English peas. Plant them where they get good air circulation and they may not have the problem in future years. There are several good fungicides that can be used to control powdery mildew in vegetable gardens.

Peas, Southern

806

My southern peas are producing nothing but stems and leaves, that is, no fruit at all. What causes that?

Southern peas are quite sensitive to nitrogen levels in the soil. When soils are too fertile the plants will grow luxuriantly, but they won't flower and fruit. Think back to your feeding program. If nitrogen was included, don't do it again anytime soon. Be certain, too, that your plants are in full sunlight. Southern peas won't produce well in shady conditions.

Peppers

807

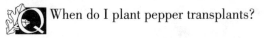 When do I plant pepper transplants?

Set them out 1 to 4 weeks after the last killing freeze date of the spring, and 12 to 14 weeks prior to the expected first freeze in the fall. You can extend peppers' productive season by growing them in large 5- or 7-gallon containers in your fall garden, then moving them into the garage the nights of the first frosts.

808

 My peppers quit setting fruit this summer. Why?

Peppers and their cousins tomatoes both do that. It's a reaction to the high temperatures we have here in the summer, and it's more a problem with bell peppers than it is with the smaller types. Keep the plants healthy and vigorous and they should come back into flower and fruit with fall's cooler weather.

809

My bell peppers, also some sweet banana peppers, have scorched-looking blotches on the sides of the fruit. What causes that?

That's sunscald. Those parts of those fruits were exposed to hot sun as they started to ripen. You may need to harvest a day or two earlier.

810

 How do I know when it's time to harvest peppers?

They have a wide margin for error. You can harvest bell peppers, for example, while they're somewhat immature and green, or you can wait until they turn their mature red, yellow or other color. Jalapeños, for example, will be a deep green while they're young, then yellow and red as they ripen. Flavor will vary through the maturation of any pepper, so harvest at your favorite stage.

Potatoes

811

 When do I plant potatoes?

 One month prior to the average date of your last killing freeze in the spring.

812

 Can I use potatoes from the grocery store as my starts?

Buy only certified "seed" potatoes from nurseries and farm stores. These are intended for garden planting and have not been treated with chemicals to retard sprouting. Cut the seed potatoes into several sections, each with at least one "eye." That will become the growing stem of the new plant.

813

 What kind of soil is best for potatoes?

As for any other root crop, it needs to be deep and very loose and well-drained. Mix in generous amounts of organic matter to loosen tight clays. Some folks even grow potatoes in rotted compost, which they pile up around the developing plants.

814

 How can I tell when it's time to dig my potatoes?

Watch their top growth. When the plants are in full flower you can harvest a few new potatoes. Once the tops die to the ground you can dig the mature baking-size tubers. Eat them as you wish, and store the rest cool and dry. Save the small potatoes as seed potatoes for your fall garden. Nurseries almost never handle seed potatoes for the late summer planting.

Pumpkins

815

Q When should I plant pumpkins in order to have them by Halloween?

A Some of the timing depends on the variety you grow. Larger types obviously take longer, but they're not as well adapted to growing conditions in most of Texas. It's best to plant medium-sized varieties, and to sow them around the end of June.

Radishes

816

Q My radishes are so hot and peppery that we can hardly eat them. What causes that?

A Stress during their time in your garden. Most often, it's caused by planting too late. When the weather turns hot, so do the radishes. Sometimes folks leave them in the garden too long and they get overly mature. If you let them get too dry, that can also result in hot radishes. The secrets in growing good radishes are to plant them at the right time (cool weather) and to grow them quickly so you can harvest them within just 4 to 5 weeks, depending on the variety you're growing.

Squash

817

Q When should I plant squash? What is the difference between "summer" and "winter" squash? Are those the seasons in which I should grow them?

It's a matter of terminology. "Winter" squash mature over a much longer period of time, and they have harder outer skins. In the North they mature in early fall and are often stored well into the winter. Here in Texas, however, they can mature in early to mid-summer from spring plantings, or you can sow them in mid- to late summer to mature in the fall. Summer squash, by comparison, start producing mature fruit within 50 to 60 days, so they can be sown in both early spring, as the danger of frost has passed, and again in late summer, for fall harvest.

☆818☆

My squash plants bloom, but I don't get any fruit. What is wrong?

Two possibilities. Either your plants are still producing only male flowers, or you don't have adequate bee activity. Squash and their relatives produce both male and female flowers on the very same plants. The female flowers actually will show the very immature fruit as a part of the stems at the bases of the petals. Male flowers have straight stems. You'll also see pollen in the male flowers. For the first couple of weeks that a squash plant blooms, it produces almost exclusively male flowers. If that's all your plants are producing, just wait and you will be rewarded. On the other hand, if you have female flowers and you're still not getting fruit, you probably don't have enough bees in your neighborhood. Pick a few male flowers and use them to transfer pollen onto the female flowers by peeling their petals away and simply rubbing the pollen across the female flowers' sticky surfaces.

819

My squash fruit never matures. It just dries up and shrivels. Why?

If it's dry as it shrivels, then it probably hasn't been pollinated. Squash fruit will often proceed for a day or two before it aborts from lack of pollination. Try cross-pollinating the flowers yourself, as described in question 818.

820

Q My squash fruit starts to rot almost as soon as it forms. What causes that?

A There are fungal fruit rots that hit squash fruit. The disease sometimes originates with the old petals. If the petals are wet, and if they stick to the surface of the fruit, they can lead to almost overnight decay. You need to be careful in handling the deteriorated fruit so that you don't spread the disease to other near-by fruit. Wash your hands frequently, and use a listed fungicide to stop the disease. It might also help if you put a layer of mulch under the plants, to keep water from splashing from the soil onto the plant during rainfall.

821

Q How do I know when to harvest my squash?

A Summer squash should be harvested when they're half to two-thirds their potential mature size. Old, overgrown squash is not desirable at the dining room table, so discard any that have grown too old. If you're out of town for a few days in the summer, arrange for someone to harvest your squash for you, so those mature fruit won't slow further production. Winter squash are harvested when their skins harden and the vines begin to die. Often there will be a distinct light-colored spot where they have rested on the soil. Leave an inch of stem attached to prolong their storage life.

822

Q What will control squash bugs? They're all over my plants, and the plants seem to be dying.

A All the true "bugs" (shield-shaped backs) are notoriously resistant to insecticides. Sevin dust will help with the young squash bugs, and you can hand-pick the mature ones. Perhaps the best way, however, is to prop a board under each plant. At mid-day, when the temperatures are high, the squash bugs will congregate in the shade of the boards. You can merely knock the props out and eliminate the squash bugs with one heavy press of the foot.

823

 I have a lot of dusty mold on the leaves of my squash plants. What products will control it (assuming it's harmful)?

Squash plants will be bothered by both powdery mildew and downy mildew. Neither will kill the plants, but both do harm. Listed fungicides will help.

824

My squash fruit is mottled green and yellow. Is that a disease, and can I eat the fruit?

That's probably a mosaic virus. Although it disfigures the fruit, it does not affect its edibility at all. It is spread by insects such as squash bugs and aphids; also by handling affected plants, then healthy ones. Practice good sanitation, but don't worry about the virus.

825

My squash plants' leaves are tan and dead. It started with the bottom leaves, but now I'm afraid I'm going to lose the entire planting.

That sounds like spider mite damage. They will cause tiny tan specks all over the leaves, usually showing up in late May and June. Spider mites are the most damaging vegetable garden pests that we have. As the problem gets worse the leaves eventually turn brown and crisp. Control them as soon as you see the first mottling by spraying with Kelthane miticide.

826

 There is a big worm in each of my squash stems. What will control them?

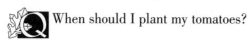 Those are squash vine borers. There is no chemical control you can spray onto the plants for this pest, but, if you get at them before they kill the plants, you can often slit the stems with a single-edged razor blade, then pry them out with a fine wire. If they have enough native vigor, the vines will usually heal across the wound.

Tomatoes

827

 When should I plant my tomatoes?

This is where most folks fall down on the job. Spring tomatoes should be planted around the date of the last killing frost. Earlier plantings often freeze, and later plantings run into the summer heat. Fall plantings need to be timed back from the first expected frost. Allow 4½ months from planting until the average first frost date. That means mid-June in the Panhandle, late June in North Texas, early July in Central Texas, and late July in South Texas. The fall crop will be the better crop, so don't miss the opportunity. Those fruit will ripen without all the traditional problems of the spring tomato planting.

☆828☆

What varieties of tomatoes are best suited to Texas gardens?

There are many varieties of tomatoes that are well suited to Texas, but a general rule applies to them all. Large-fruiting tomatoes like Big Boy and Beefsteak, among many others, will not set fruit when it gets really hot. Avoid these unless you're prepared for very poor yields. The small and medium-sized types are best in Texas. Your county Extension office will have a listing of the best current varieties. Select types that are resistant to common disease problems as well as nematodes.

829

 Nursery tomato transplants that are available are often too tall and lanky. Can they still be used? Also, is it better to buy tough transplants that have been grown in cooler weather outdoors, or the soft, green ones I find in greenhouses?

 You can use those tall transplants, but lay them angled on their sides in trenches in the garden. They will form roots all along their stems. Always buy the toughened transplants. They'll reestablish much more quickly than the succulent plants, which may suffer wind burn or sunscald.

830

Can I plant tomatoes in containers and hope to expect any good production? Are some varieties better than others? What size of container should I use, and what type of potting soil?

Tomatoes are very well adapted to container gardens. Use at least a 5-gallon, preferably a 7- or 10-gallon container and a loose, highly organic potting soil (no native soil, please). Stick with "determinate" varieties. They grow to a manageable height, then quit getting any taller. You'll still want a cage for support, however.

831

I understand that I can root tomato plants from cuttings. How do I do it?

Sometimes you have a really good spring tomato plant and you either can't find the same variety for your June or July planting for fall harvest, or you don't know exactly what type you have. Those are times when you might want to root new plants from stem tip cuttings. Take 4- or 5-inch cuttings from the ends of the growing shoots. Root them in a loose, highly organic potting soil, one cutting per 4-inch flower pot. Keep them in bright shade until they root, then get them acclimatized to the sun and heat before you set them into the garden. You'll be amazed at how quickly they'll develop new roots. They should be ready for setting into the garden within 15 to 20 days. You may be surprised at how durable they are to sun and heat right from the start, much more so than young succulent seedlings.

832

How can I protect my young fall tomato transplants from the damage of mid-summer sun until they're established?

If you buy transplants that have been grown and held in the sun, you should have no trouble. However, you can always erect some type of shade over them. You can use an A-frame made of wood shingles, or a couple of pieces of cardboard taped together. Let them get morning and late afternoon sun, giving them one hour per day of additional sunlight until, after a week, you remove the covers entirely.

833

Do I need to stake my tomatoes? Do the cages work well?

The best way to grow tomatoes in Texas is to put them in homemade cages constructed from concrete reinforcing wire. Cut it in 50-inch lengths, so you'll end up with 16-inch-diameter cylinders. The prefabricated cages you see in garden departments are for northern climates where tomatoes don't get very tall. In Texas we need the added height the concrete wire will give us. Put one or two stakes alongside each cage to prevent the plants from blowing over in the wind.

834

 What kind of fertilizer is best for a tomato planting?

Let a soil test guide you. Don't be surprised, however, if it comes back saying that you need only nitrogen; that is, increasingly, the report—particularly with clay soils, which accumulate phosphorus and potassium.

835

 Do I need to remove the "suckers" from my tomato plants?

Old thinking was that those side shoots should be pinched out, but we have come to realize that they, too, will produce fruit. They also will shade the ripening fruit, lessening the chance of sunscald and cracking. Push the side branches back into the cages and let them grow.

836

I'm seeing red plant lice on the new growth of my tomatoes. What damage do they do, and how do I control them?

Aphids, or plant lice, transmit diseases. They also cause distorted growth. Most general-purpose insecticides, both organic and inorganic, will eliminate them.

837

How can I prevent the birds from pecking holes in my ripening tomatoes?

For one thing, you can harvest the fruit just as it starts to turn red. The birds aren't quite as attracted to green fruit, so this can prevent their damage. The fruit will ripen with no loss of flavor or nutrition. You can also drape bird netting (available at garden centers and hardware stores) over the tops of the plants to prevent the

birds from getting to the fruit. Some folks even use red glass
Christmas tree balls as substitute fruit. The birds peck them and are
annoyed by the results. If you start early enough in the season, you
may be able to change their feeding habits before the actual fruit
starts to ripen.

☆838☆

 Why don't my tomatoes set fruit? They flower, but it looks
like something is cutting the flowers off before they are
pollinated.

In many cases that's tied to the variety and temperatures.
Large-fruiting types such as Big Boy and Beefsteak, among
many others, won't set fruit when temperatures are in the low 60s at
night, or when they're in the 90s in the daytime. In the Midwest,
those temperatures fit almost all summer, but here in Texas we have
only a narrow window of time in late spring when temperatures are
right for fruit to set. Medium-sized types, by comparison, will set at
both cooler and hotter temperatures.

☆839☆

I'm growing the recommended varieties of tomatoes, but
even they aren't setting fruit. What gives?

Assuming they're in full sunlight and are producing flowers,
then they probably aren't getting pollinated. Tomato flowers
are self-pollinating, and it's the action of the wind that vibrates the
pollen loose within the flowers. If you're growing your tomatoes in a
sheltered area, and if they're not exposed to much wind motion, you
may have to thump the flower clusters with your finger every couple
of days to ensure good pollination. Try it. It really can help.

840

 What causes the sunken brown spots on the bottoms of my
tomatoes?

 That's a physiological disorder called blossom-end rot. It has
been attributed to a lack of calcium in the soil, but you'll see

it in soils that are quite high in calcium. The fact is, you seldom see blossom-end rot until it gets really hot and dry in the summer. The soils have the same amount of calcium in late spring as they do in the summer, yet the problem doesn't show up until then, so there are obviously other things going on. Generally it happens when we let our tomatoes get too dry between waterings. Just as leaves turn brown and crisp at their ends when they have gotten too dry, fruit will do the same thing. Try mulching the plants and watering them more religiously and see if the problem doesn't resolve itself.

841

 My tomato plants have plenty of fruit, but many of them are rotting. When I pull them off the vine, they're nothing but stinking fluid. What causes that?

There is an especially nasty bacterial soft rot that hits tomatoes, leaving them hanging like water balloons on the plants. Usually you can see the discoloration a few days before the fruit turns putrid. Try to remove the fruit at that point. Wear a disposable plastic glove, and take care not to touch other fruit or foliage. A registered fungicide may help.

842

My tomato plants wilt, but then they rebound before the next morning. Are they in trouble?

Probably not. This is a fairly common occurrence in late spring, when we've had several days of cloudy, cool weather. Suddenly, the clouds clear away and it's 90 degrees and the plants are unprepared for the change. They temporarily wilt until they can catch their overnight breath. Usually, this is a good thing that ends up toughening the plants.

843

My tomato plants are wilted and appear to be dying. They've been this way for several days. That's even though the soil is wet from recent rains. What can their trouble be?

Tomato roots are very sensitive to overwatering. Look closely at the stems just above the ground line. If you see swollen root-like growths (called adventitious roots) arising from the stems, that's good evidence that the plants have lost much of their root systems. You may or may not be able to save them. Next year, do whatever you can to improve the drainage, including raising the bed and installing tile drains.

☆844☆

My tomato plants are turning yellow from the ground up. There are large, bright yellow blotches on the leaves, then they turn brown and dry. What advice can you give me?

Yellow blotches on the leaves are the operative clue here. Early blight is a fungal disease that attacks the plants, usually in mid- to late May, depending on your location in Texas. It quickly knocks the foliage off the bottoms of the plants as the leaves go from yellow to brown. Your nurseryman will have registered fungicides to stop it. Keep water off the foliage as well.

845

My tomato plants' leaves are cupped and rolled. Is that a disease? There are no other symptoms, and they seem to keep producing fruit.

When the temperatures climb above 90 degrees in late May and June tomato plants respond by rolling their leaves. It makes the plants look odd, but it does nothing to the fruit that is on the plants. It will usually start with the bottom leaves.

846

My tomato plants' leaves are pointed and very odd looking. In fact, you would hardly recognize them as being tomato foliage. What causes that?

 Usually they have been hit by a drift of a broadleafed weed-killer. No plant that you grow will be any more sensitive to this entire category of garden product. Be especially careful when you treat for dandelions, poison ivy, clover and other non-grassy weeds if tomatoes are growing anywhere nearby. There is nothing you can do other than wait and see if the plants outgrow it.

☆847☆

Q My tomato plants' leaves are turning tan and mottled, then dry and brown. It started at the bottoms of the plants, but now the entire plant is affected in most cases. I think they're going to die. What can I do?

A Spider mites are at work. They start at the bottoms of the plants, then spread upward. Affected plants will have tiny tan mottling before the leaves turn brown and crisp. In severe cases you'll even see fine webbing between the leaves and the stems. Control spider mites with Kelthane miticide. Read the label directions carefully for the best results. Be sure you spray the backs of the leaves, since that's where the mites congregate.

848

Q My tomatoes have cracks or rings around their tops. It turns the fruit corky and ugly. What can I do to stop it?

A That's hot weather damage. Harvesting the fruit a day or two earlier, then letting it ripen indoors, will usually help. Fall tomatoes will almost never have that problem.

849

Q My tomatoes have cracks that run vertically on the fruit. The cracks penetrate clear into the flesh of the fruit and essentially ruin it. How can I stop the problem?

A That's caused by sudden exposure to hot, dry weather and probably also hot sunshine. Just as a windshield cracks when the temperature changes quickly, so will tomato skin. Again, harvesting a day or two early will help. Leave the side shoots (suckers) in place to shade the ripening fruit.

850

 My tomatoes have worms in the tops of their fruit. What can I use to prevent them?

 Fruit worms in tomatoes can be stopped with Sevin applied as early as you see the problem. Curiously, this is the same insect that bothers corn ears.

851

Our tomato leaves are being stripped, but we can't find any signs of an insect. What type of pest does that?

Tomato hornworm is almost always the culprit. You're going to be embarrassed when you finally do find the caterpillar. It's probably as big as your finger, but it's bright green, just like the tomato stems and leaves, so it's almost impossible to see. For the record, its large horn is actually harmless. Hand-pick the worms when you do find them. Sevin dust or "Bt" can help, if the worms are still active.

852

When the first freeze comes in the fall, can I harvest the green tomatoes that are on my plants? Will they ripen indoors?

Many of the immature tomatoes will go ahead and ripen. Cut through a couple of representative fruit with a very sharp knife. If the seeds move out of the way of the knife, then that fruit would have ripened indoors quite well. If you cut through the seeds with your knife, those fruit will make great relish. Use them right away. They will ripen no further.

12

HOUSEPLANTS, GREENHOUSES AND PLANT PROPAGATION

GENERAL QUESTIONS ABOUT HOUSEPLANTS

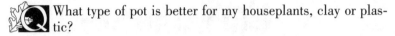

853

 What type of pot is better for my houseplants, clay or plastic?

Both are entirely satisfactory. You will need to make minor adjustments in watering, however. Plastic pots retain water longer, since none escapes through the pots' side walls. Plastic pots are much easier to clean and reuse, but clay pots are more natural looking, plus they're heavier and less likely to tip over. Plastic pots are far less likely to break. The choice is yours.

854

How essential is a drainage hole for a pot?

It's required. Most folks think that it's because you would overwater a plant if you didn't have the drain hole, and that is, of course, possible. However, a good gardener can avoid that pitfall. What you cannot avoid is the accumulation of mineral salts in the potting soil. Each time you water a plant, and every time that you feed it, you'll be introducing more salts to the soil mix. It's exactly the same problem as the Great Salt Lake, and, unless you can leach out the soil periodically, the plant will eventually die.

855

 Can I drill a drain hole in a flower pot?

Absolutely. Use a special carbide drill bit from the hardware store. Support the inside of the bottom of the pot against a scrap piece of wood, and drill the hole at a very slow speed. Keep your drill bit well lubricated as you drill, and take your time. If the bit isn't very large, drill more than one hole.

856

 What can I do if I have a valuable container that I'd like to use for a flower pot, but I absolutely cannot drill a hole in it?

 "Double pot" the plant. Grow it in a conventional pot with a drain hole. Nestle that pot down inside the larger decorative container. Use bark mulch, potting soil or some other cushioning material between the two pot walls. Every time you want to water the plant, lift it out and carry it to a sink. Water it thoroughly, then let the excess water drain away before you return it to the outer container.

857

 Do gravel or broken flower pots in the bottom of a flower pot improve the drainage?

 No more than gravel in a stopped-up bathtub would improve its drainage. No commercial growers use that technique anymore. What it might do is keep roots from exiting the drain holes and growing into soil beneath the pot. You can accomplish the same thing, however, merely by moving outdoor containers once in a while. With your houseplants, gravel in the bottoms of the pots does nothing more than take up valuable space that soil should be filling.

858

How do I know when it's time to repot my houseplants?

There are several clues.

- If you're having to water the plant far more often than you once did, it's probably rootbound.

- If the plant is more than three or four times as tall or wide as its pot, it probably needs a larger home.

- If, on taking it out of its pot, you can see that the roots are wound around and around inside the pot wall, it's time to repot.

859

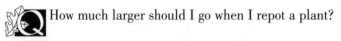

How much larger should I go when I repot a plant?

 Most times you'll want to go to the next larger pot size. They move in 1-inch increments for small pots and 2-inch steps for larger sizes. Over-potting a plant into a pot that is considerably larger than necessary can be very harmful. The plant won't be able to take up all the water that the soil will hold. It's far better to make gradual moves.

860

 How can I get a plant out of its old flower pot?

You need to work when its soil is moist, not wet, and certainly not dry. If it's a small pot that you can hold in one hand, tap it upside-down on a table or countertop. It should pop loose easily. If it's a large pot you'll probably have to work outdoors, where you can lay it on its side and gently roll it until the plant comes loose easily from the pot. If the pot has a tapered top and the soil ball won't come loose in one piece, it's usually better to crack and discard the pot rather than risk ruining the plant.

861

Our clay pots have green moss growing all over them. It's slimy and ugly. What can we do to get rid of it?

Maybe not much. You can soak the pots in a 10-percent solution of chlorine bleach for a few hours, then carefully rinse them. That will kill the algae, but some of the residue may remain. Scrubbing them with a wire brush will likely help. In the long run, however, they're still going to be discolored. They'll work great outdoors, but they may not be quite as attractive as you'd want inside your house. That algae, by the way, usually starts in the potting soil and spreads to the pot walls. If you cut back ever so slightly on the water you give the plants, you may be able to discourage its growth in the future.

862

Q I understand we can paint clay pots. How do we do it?

A You can match interior colors in a home or office by using flat latex wall paint in the appropriate shades. Work only with new dry pots, preferably white. Seal the insides of the pots with roofing sealant or pruning paint. Let them dry for a day or two. You can use masking tape to mark off the areas to be painted. Brush the paint in place and let it dry for several days before you fill the pots with potting soil. It should hold for many years.

863

Q What makes up a really good potting soil? How can I select one at the garden center, and how could I mix my own?

A Great potting soils are lightweight. When you pick up a bag at the nursery you should have the conscious thought that it's lighter than you expected. Your homemade blend should include about 50 percent brown Canadian peat moss (no heavyweight domestic American black peat, please), 20 percent fine bark mulch, 20 percent either perlite or vermiculite, and 10 percent sand. Use no native Texas soils. They're simply too variable. Mix the soil thoroughly.

864

Q Will I need to amend that soil (see question 863) any for specific types of plants?

A Absolutely. For example, with cactus and succulent plants you'll want to cut back to 40 percent peat moss and use that other 10 percent to include blasting sand from an aquarium supplier. It's coarser still than washed brick sand, almost like fine gravel. It provides still better aeration. In other cases, such as

orchids, some bromeliads, and a few ferns, you'll use entirely different growing media.

865

Are plastic hanging baskets better than wire ones?

A lot depends on the type of plant that you're trying to grow.
If it's a variety that roots freely through the sides of a wire
basket like a Boston fern does, you probably ought to use that type of
basket. On the other hand, if it needs more moisture than you might
be able to provide in a wire basket, go with plastic. Bougainvilleas
are a good example. They dry out quickly and are easier to maintain
in plastic containers. If you're dealing with larger plants you'll probably go to wire, particularly if you want something very attractive.
There are welded wire baskets up to 4 and 5 feet in diameter.

866

How do I line the wire baskets so they'll hold soil?

Use either moist sphagnum moss packed an inch or two
thick around the outer edges and up over the top of the wire
basket, or one of the pressed fiber liners made to fit the wire baskets.
The moss will allow you to plant through the sidewalls; the fiber liner
will not.

867

Are there any tricks to make hanging baskets easier to maintain?

Use a pulley so you can lower the basket to groom the
plants and change the plantings. Hang it from a stout swiv-
el which will let it rotate with the breezes, for more even lighting to
all sides of the plants. Use drip irrigation to water the baskets. All
are good, long-proven "tricks."

868

I'd like to add lights for my houseplants. What types are best?

First, just to be completely honest, it's very difficult to add enough lights to grow medium- and bright-light plants in otherwise dark spots indoors. The lighting they receive in their native tropical homes is hundreds of times greater than a bright artificial light—enough so that you're not even going to be in the ballpark. Instead, use lighting to highlight your plants and accent them, not to grow them. There are a few exceptions, of course. African violets and other low-light plants can be grown under fluorescent tubes, so long as the tubes are installed within a few inches of the plants' leaves. There are special color-corrected plant lights that work quite well, or you can use "daylight" types. Leave the lights on daily for at least 16 hours.

869

Does the solar screening film that is on windows hurt houseplants?

It cuts the amount of light that comes into the house, so it certainly will affect the plants that you're trying to grow. Where you might have been able to grow bright-light types, you'll probably have to switch over to kinds that can take darker conditions.

870

How often should I mist my plants?

That's probably wasted effort. With today's homes having forced air heating and cooling, most of the moisture you might add to the plants' immediate environment will quickly be dispersed throughout the house. Better ways to prevent problems of low humidity are to group the plants together so they can add to one another's moist air, and don't put them anywhere near heating and cooling registers, the fireplace, hot windows, or drafty doorways.

871

 How good are the moisture meters for determining when it's time to water my houseplants? How else can I tell?

 Commercial interiorscape maintenance people use sophisticated meters that let them read soil quickly, but many of the home models are pretty much useless. You have 10 of the best moisture meters at the tips of your fingers and thumbs. Learn to stick your finger into the top inch of soil. When it's dry to the touch, that's the time to water the plant. Also, the potting soil will probably turn a lighter color, plus the soil may separate ever so slightly from the pot wall. Growers can tell merely by lifting a small or medium-sized pot. Dry soil is light, and thus they can monitor the differences.

872

 Does wick watering work?

You can Over the years there have been many special flower pot products that used different types of wicks to carry water up from a reservoir and into the potting soil. Most times these seem like overkill. Watering houseplants isn't all that special a science, and you really don't need all these sophisticated tools to accomplish it. In some specific cases, again using African violets as an example, wicks can help.

873

Should I water my houseplants from below?

You can do that occasionally, but it's not the best regular practice. When water is taken up from below it fills all of the pore spaces. Oxygen, much needed by the plants' roots, is driven from the soil. Mineral salts are pushed higher in the soil, rather than being leached out as they would be from top watering. However, if you have a really porous potting soil such as you might have in a wire hanging basket, this may be the very best way of saturating the soil mix.

874

 Should we leave our houseplants standing in water in the bathtub while we're on vacation?

Absolutely not. You'll ruin their root systems with that prolonged soaking, plus most bathrooms are too dark for plants to survive for more than a couple of days before they start dropping leaves. If you're going to be away a couple of extra days, and want to be sure your plants don't get dry, you can soak them in the tub beforehand; but let them drain and return them to their normal locations before you leave.

875

How heavily should we water our houseplants?

Nobody wants to have water running out the bottoms of flower pots and across the floor, but you do need to water your plants heavily enough that water drains out at least every four or 5 times that you water. That will eliminate the buildup of mineral salts. Be sure, however, to discard the water that drains out. Don't leave it in the plastic saucer under the plant, or those mineral salts will be picked right back up again.

876

 Is water from a water softener bad for my houseplants?

Yes. It has sodium added, a definite problem for any plants, houseplants included. Standard city tap water would be better. Rainwater is best.

877

 What is the best type of plant food for my houseplants?

 There are many fine water-soluble products on the market. Most folks get best results from complete-and-balanced analyses such as 20-20-20. Several companies include important trace elements with these fertilizers. You can also buy encapsulated, timed-release plant foods that will supply needed nutrients for several months per feeding. A few of your houseplants may benefit from specialty fertilizers. You may want a higher phosphorus content, for example, for flowering types.

878

 How often should I be feeding my houseplants?

Sparingly, unless conditions are satisfactory for normal and vigorous growth. Usually it's too dark for that kind of growth indoors, so folks are better advised to buy plants that are already grown, then maintain them *status quo*. If you fertilize houseplants in normal indoor conditions every five or six times that you water them, that should be adequate. Even with that infrequent feeding schedule you'll want to use a very diluted solution.

879

My houseplants drop their leaves soon after I get them home. What causes that?

A change of lighting, generally to lower light intensities. The plants were adjusted to certain levels of lighting in their nurseries and greenhouses. When you brought them home and put them in your own environment, they didn't get those same levels of lighting. If the leaf drop happened somewhere around the two to four week mark, it was almost assuredly the change of lighting. Letting a plant get too dry between waterings can also lead to leaf drop, and so can certain insect outbreaks.

880

Q My houseplants have cupped leaves. The newer leaves just don't look like the leaves that were on the plants when I bought them. What causes that?

A That's usually low light intensities. The same thing happens to our outdoor landscape plants, too. When they're grown in dark corners they are more open, with larger and differently shaped leaves than when they have full sunlight. Try moving the plants gradually to brighter conditions and see if the subsequent growth isn't more normal.

881

Q My houseplants often have weak stems, with their leaves too far apart on the stems. They just look ugly and lanky. Is that caused by the wrong kind of plant food, or too much water, or what?

A Both of those could contribute. Using too much nitrogen could cause stretched growth, as could excessive water. By far the most common cause, however, is lack of light. Plants' cells elongate when they're exposed to darkness. That's why plants will stretch out of shadows toward a light source. When they're in generally dark conditions, all of the cells will elongate that way, resulting in weak, spindly growth.

882

Q How long does it take a plant to sunburn if it's been in the house for a few months, then is moved out onto the patio to be repotted?

A Bright sunlight can ruin a plant's leaves within 10 or 20 minutes in the heat of the summer. You really need to do all your outdoor spraying, repotting, and other maintenance work in the shade, away from sunlight.

883

 Do we have to worry about bringing pests indoors when we move patio plants in for the winter?

Yes. It's always a good idea to set the plants aside for a week or two and watch for any serious pest problems. Be especially careful to control whiteflies, mealybugs and other scales, and also spider mites, before you bring the plants inside.

884

We have some serious pest problems on our houseplants. What is the best way to spray for them?

It's probably better if you take the plants onto a shaded patio or into the garage so you won't have to use the pesticides inside your house. Just don't put them into direct sunlight. You can use a small hand sprayer to apply the sprays directly to the problem. In some cases, as with mealy bugs and other scales, for example, you can also use a cotton swab dipped in insecticide to remove them manually.

☆885☆

The edges and tips of the leaves of our houseplants are brown and crisp. What causes that problem?

Generally it's from letting the plants get too dry between waterings or from putting them in a hot, dry environment. In some cases you can trim the tips of the leaves back to a rather natural look, or you may want to remove them entirely.

☆886☆

My houseplants have some type of little gnats that fly up in my face whenever I touch the plants. What are they? Are they harmful? What will control them?

 Those are fungus gnats. They live in the algal growth on the surface of the potting soil, and also on the sides of the pots in the green slime. They indicate that you're keeping the plants somewhat too moist. Either cut back on the amount of water you give them, or wait an extra day to water them. Replace the top 1/4-inch of soil with fresh potting soil. Use a tender houseplant insecticide spray over the plants and then down onto the soil surface to eliminate them. They're more annoying than they are harmful.

☆887☆

 What are the very best houseplants that will give me the least amount of trouble indoors?

 There are many great choices, but some of the very best include dracaenas, pleomeles, aglaonemas, spathiphyllums, sansevierias, pothos, vining philodendrons, pony tails and syngoniums.

888

 What are the best large houseplants?

Large plants, by their nature, often develop into trees in their native homes. What that tells you is that they also are likely to prefer full sun. If you have a really bright spot, consider any of the many ficuses and rubber plants, scheffleras, *Dracaena marginata*, and the various palms, among others. Other dracaenas are also good, and many can tolerate less light. Consider Janet Craig, Warnecki and corn plant dracaenas.

889

What are the best flowering houseplants?

Here we have to make the distinction between plants that we buy in flower and enjoy as long as the flowers last and those that will flower repeatedly indoors. The best of the latter category include African violets, episcias, spathiphyllums, begonias, orchids, bromeliads, and cacti and other succulents.

MOST COMMON QUESTIONS
ABOUT SPECIFIC HOUSEPLANTS ·······································

African Violets

890

Q My African violets aren't blooming as well as they used to. What can I do to help them flower better?

A Usually that's either tied to light, or the plants are congested. African violets need to grow on a bright east windowsill, or you need to have them very close to fluorescent light fixtures that are left on daily for 16 hours. If the plants are clumped and very full in their pots, that overcrowding can also keep them from producing good flowers. Use a high-phosphate water-soluble plant food.

Aglaonemas

891

Q My aglaonemas have white insects on the backs of their leaves. The plants appear to be dying. What will kill the insects?

A Those are mealybugs, and you can use a general-purpose houseplant insecticide, or you can clean most of them off with a cotton swab dipped either in the insecticide or in rubbing alcohol. They are quite prolific, and they can spread to many other types of plants. You really do need to eliminate them quickly.

892

Q I have aglaonemas in my greenhouse, but they look bad every winter. They are wilted looking, and many of their leaves turn yellow. What's happening?

That's almost assuredly chilling damage. Where some tropical plants hang on to the freezing point, aglaonemas go downhill anytime temperatures are below 60 degrees for a prolonged period. Move them to the warmest part of your greenhouse, or bring them indoors with you during the winter.

Aloe vera

893

How can I get my *Aloe vera* to bloom? I have seen photos of it in flower, and it's really pretty.

Look at those photos again and you'll notice that those are big, single plants that are flowering. If you let your plant send out all the side shoots it will try to, the mother plant will probably never flower. Pinch off those side shoots and you'll also end up with a very spectacular foliage plant with large, very succulent leaves. As it matures, it will also bloom.

Amaryllis

894

I have a potted amaryllis, which was given to me for Christmas. It's through blooming now. What can I do with it to get it to bloom again? Can I plant it outdoors?

That's a tropical type of bulb that is winter-hardy only in South Texas. You'll have the best luck if you leave it in its pot and grow it all spring and summer. Around the first of September you can set the pot on its side, so the soil will dry out. This plant goes dormant and dies back to its bulb in its native home to get through dry periods. If you let it get dry for 4 to 6 weeks, then repot it into fresh potting soil, it should bloom for you again in late fall or early winter. It won't work every time, but generally the plant will re-flower. Give it bright light and moist soil.

Aralias

895

 My Ming aralia is dropping most of its leaves. It was so pretty when I bought it, but it doesn't look like it's going to last more than a few weeks in my home. Can you help?

It's not happy with the lighting. Get it near a really bright window. It will continue dropping leaves for a week or two after you move it, but it should recover and put out new foliage.

Avocados

896

 How can I start an avocado from a seed?

Save the large seed and either plant it into a pot with good potting soil, or stick three toothpicks into it so that you can suspend it part-way down into a glass filled with water. Remember, always, that the flat end goes down. It will gradually sprout roots and stem tissues and start growing. You can leave it in the water for a while, but eventually it will need to be potted up as a conventional plant and grown in potting soil.

897

I have an avocado that I have grown from a seed. How can I keep it from getting too tall and lanky?

You need to trim it way back, to keep it compact. Ideally, you would do that from the time it is very small. Pinch the growing tip out, in the hopes that you'll get two branches in its place. That sometimes happens, but not often. Above all, don't get too attached to your avocado. They're large trees where they grow well, and, as a result, they're not too well suited to indoor conditions.

898

Q Can I plant my avocado outdoors?

A You can, but it will freeze at 32 degrees. Unless you're south of Brownsville, it's not going to grow outdoors in Texas.

Begonias

899

Q I'd like to grow begonias indoors. Are the wax begonias my best choice? How about the types with the colorful leaves?

A There are hundreds of good begonias to grow inside your house. Many of them have spectacular foliage, and most will also bloom at some time during the year. Rex begonias are more challenging, but ever so rewarding. There are many beautiful rhizomatous types with fancy leaves and low, clumping habits. A lot of the cane types, such as the many angel wing begonias and their relatives, will be beautiful, especially in brighter light. Wax begonias like we grow outdoors, while lovely, aren't really as special indoors as the other houseplant types.

Bromeliads

900

Q I enjoy bromeliads of various types. What special kind of potting soil and care do they need?

A There are many kinds of bromeliads, some terrestrial and many epiphytic. The latter group is more popular as flowering houseplants. Since they grow natively suspended in air from tree trunks, they have very modified root systems. You'll also notice that their leaves are arranged as cups, or vases, that hold water for long periods of time. You should use a loose, highly organic potting soil. Keep it moist, but remember that their root systems will not be as well developed as those of other terrestrial plants. You will also need to water the plants within those vases. Periodically, include a very diluted liquid houseplant fertilizer, both in the soil and in the vases. Don't over-feed bromeliads, though, or keep them in low-light conditions, or they won't develop their richly variegated colors.

901

Q My bromeliad has finished blooming and now it looks like the plant may be dying. What can I do to get it to grow and bloom again?

A Probably nothing for the mother plant. That's the way many bromeliads operate. The better news, however, is that there will be many new plants that will form around the original plant. These "pups" can be cut loose and potted separately.

Bulbs, for Forcing

902

Q I'd like to grow paperwhite narcissus and hyacinths indoors, for flowering in winter. Should I grow them in water or soil? Do I need to feed them? Can I set them into the garden after they bloom?

A You can do it either way. There are special hyacinth vases for those bulbs, or you could use shallow bulb pots that are half as tall as they are wide. Paperwhites are grown in shallow decorative dishes filled with gravel, or you could grow them in pots filled with soil. In both cases, the bulbs will grow and flower much more quickly than you might imagine, often within just a few weeks. Both types are wonderfully fragrant. They will need no special fertilizer. They probably won't grow very well in your garden—after they have been manipulated this way indoors.

Christmas Cacti

903

Q How can I get my Christmas cactus to bloom again next year? It was so pretty when I bought it this season.

A Christmas cacti are from rainy tropical forests, where they grow suspended high in treetops. They need really loose potting soils and cool conditions to come back into flower in early winter. The biggest factor, however, is lighting. They need almost full sunlight all fall, but they also must have 14 hours of total darkness at night, just like poinsettias, if you expect them to produce their flower buds.

904

Q My Christmas cactus plant's stems are shriveled, and the plant is toppling over. What causes that?

A It's usually because of spider mites attacking the stems at the ground line, or it can be caused by really sunny locations where the plant's tissues actually scorch. Use Kelthane spray for the mites, and, if lighting is excessive, move it to a bright, but shaded, location.

905

Q Small parts of my Christmas cactus plant's leaves are falling off. Can I use them to start new plants?

A Those are actually stem tissues, not leaves, and, yes, you can certainly start new plants from them. Use them as cuttings, and stick them into pots filled with a very loose soil mix. Keep them slightly moist as they form roots and start growing. You'll be amazed at how well they will root and grow.

Crotons

906

Q I have a croton, but it isn't as colorful as it was when I bought it. All of its newest leaves are bright green. Is there some nutrient I need to be adding?

A That's caused by darker indoor conditions. If you move it to a spot where it gets more light, the new growth should regain the colorful variegation. You also may have to prune it back somewhat to eliminate some of the green foliage and to keep the plant from getting too lanky.

907

Q My croton seems to be dying. The leaves, especially at the bottom of the plant, are turning crisp. I can't see any insects, and I'm sure I'm watering it properly. What could go wrong?

A That's probably spider mites. Crotons are very susceptible, although the mites can be stopped if you identify the problem early enough. Where plants' leaves will turn tan and mottled when spider mites hit, that's hard to identify with a brightly variegated plant like a croton. Spray the top and bottom leaf surfaces with Kelthane to control these nearly microscopic pests. You can see them before you spray if you'll thump one of the leaves over a sheet of white paper. As large as crotons' leaves are, you could eliminate most of the spider mites with warm, soapy water. Use two sponges, one on top of the leaves, the other beneath, and wipe them clean.

Dieffenbachias

908

Q My dieffenbachia is so tall it's touching the ceiling. How can I cut it back, and can I use the stem to make more plants?

A If they're fairly healthy and vigorous at the time, dieffenbachias can be cut back rather drastically. Spring or early summer are great times to do it, since lighting is better then to foster vigorous regrowth. You could probably cut the plant back almost to the soil line. Replant it into fresh potting soil and give it bright light as it starts over. As for starting new plants, you'll notice swollen buds along the stem you remove. Each of those has the potential to make a new stem. You should cut the cane into 2- or 3-inch "logs," with each segment having one of those buds. Lay the stem segments on their sides in 4-inch pots, half-submerged in loose potting soil, with the buds all facing upward. The old stem segments will develop roots, and the buds will begin to grow into new stems. Once the plants are 4 or 5 inches tall you can repot them into larger containers, perhaps grouping some of them together. You're likely to have enough to open your own nursery!

909

Q My dieffenbachia's stem is weak, and the plant is leaning. Its leaves aren't as colorful as they used to be, and they're even somewhat cupped and rolled. What can I do differently to help it?

A It's not getting enough light. You may want to trim it back somewhat and move it to a brighter location. It may have enough vigor to recover and grow back.

Dracaenas

910

Q I have a corn plant dracaena that is too tall. How do I cut it back so I can keep it in my house? Can I use the top to start new plants?

A Most corn plants were started from dormant canes that were potted, then encouraged to send out shoots with leaves. Usually you can cut the plant back fairly close to the old cane stump and it will regrow, often with two branches where you had one before. Frankly, it's difficult to describe exactly how that cut should be made without seeing the specific plant in question. As for starting new plants, your best bet would be to air layer the top before you cut it. If you happened to have a greenhouse with a mist propagation bed, you could probably root the severed top; otherwise, it will be quite difficult.

911

Q What can I do with a corn plant that has browned leaf tips and edges?

A First, determine what caused the problem. It almost has to be one or more of the following: too dry at some point, excessive mineral or fertilizer salts in the soil, or too hot (under a heat register or in a bright west window, for examples). Correct the original problem, then trim the leaves with a pair of really sharp scissors. You can actually restore the pointed tips to the leaves and you'll conceal the fact that the plant was in distress.

912

Q I have a red-leafed *Dracaena marginata*. I've had other dracaenas, and they have been excellent houseplants, but this one seems quite angry to be in our home. It looks wilted, and it's lost most of its leaves. What should I do?

A That one dracaena needs more light than any of the other common varieties. Fact is, it really needs to be grown in a bright west window or under a bright skylight. Move it and watch it regain its vigor.

913

Q I couldn't figure out where the sweet smell was coming from, and now I have found a flower spike on my dracaena. Is that unusual?

A For many of the different types, no, it's fairly common. Corn plants will do it once or twice a year once they're mature, and *Dracaena fragrans* actually gets its species name from its fragrant flowers. In tightly closed buildings the flowers can almost be too sweet. If they begin to bother you, just cut them off.

Easter Lilies

914

Q Can I plant my Easter lily outdoors now that it has finished blooming?

A Yes, and it will probably flower for a year or two. They don't seem to be able to establish and thrive in our hot Texas conditions. Nonetheless, nobody wants to throw them away, so give it a whirl. Grow it where it will get morning sun and afternoon shade. Outdoors, it will probably bloom several weeks after Easter.

Ferns

915

Q I'm really having trouble with my houseplant fern. It's losing its leaves. It started in the center of the plant, but now all of the fronds are elongated and ugly. What can I do?

A That's a fern that isn't getting enough light. Move it immediately into a south or east window. Don't put it in direct sunlight, but get it as close to that as you otherwise can. We think of ferns as shade-loving plants outdoors, but they need really bright light inside our homes. Withhold fertilizer, and water carefully until you're sure the plant is in good recovery.

916

Q How do I start new ferns? Are spores the prime way, or can I use those runners they produce?

A The best way is to divide the mother plant. Use a large butcher's knife to cut through moist soil. Cut the mother plant into four or more parts, then pot them individually. You'll need to trim their fronds back to make them look more normal once you have divided them. Within a few months you'll have four or more plants that will look like they've been growing for a much longer time. Spores are best left to the serious greenhouse grower. The long stolons the plants produce will eventually make new plants, but you would need to put a pot alongside and peg the stolons to the soil until they rooted and developed a new plant.

Ficuses, including Weeping Figs and Rubber Plants

917

 My rubber plant's leaves are rolled and abnormal looking. What can I do to get it back into better growth form? It also has dropped many of its leaves.

Move it to a brighter location. Those are, guaranteed, the symptoms of a rubber plant that is in too dark a location. If it didn't freeze outdoors, rubber plants would actually make great large shade trees. That's how much light they can tolerate.

918

My rubber plant is way too tall for our room. Can I cut it back severely?

Yes, although rubber plants are huge trees in their native homes in the tropics. Eventually you'll either have to find it a larger room or start over. Move it into the garage as you cut it back, or put plastic drop cloths beneath the stems. They will drip a sticky white latex all over your floor after you make your cuts.

919

 How are new rubber plants started? Can I take cuttings from my plant?

 It's better to start them by air layering, where you clasp a handful of moist sphagnum moss around a "wounded"

portion of the stem, then wrap plastic film around it all to keep the moisture around the developing roots.

☆920☆

Q I have a weeping fig that is dropping most of its leaves. I'm really wondering if I'll be able to save it.

A Weeping figs are related closely to rubber plants, and many of their problems are shared. They're odd plants, in that they produce leaves that are adapted to the amount of light they're receiving. The actual physiological makeup of those leaves will be different if they're in bright sunlight than if they're in a medium-light situation. As soon as you move a weeping fig from one light level to another, you can expect it to start dropping leaves. Even if you merely turn it in its current location near a bright window, you can expect it to shed some of the leaves. The best advice is to give weeping figs extremely bright light indoors, then leave them alone. If you rotate them at all, do it only a quarter of a turn each week. Be careful in pulling the drapes or closing the blinds that you don't seriously alter the amount of light the plant receives. They're great plants, but they're really touchy about lighting.

921

Q My weeping fig is dripping sticky material all over our carpet. I've looked closely and there don't seem to be any insects. What might the problem be?

A Usually, it's scale insects or aphids. You should have been able to see either of those, however. The aphids are pin-head-sized, pear-shaped insects that congregate on the tender new growth. Scales are more common, and the one that is most prevalent on weeping figs is a hard-shelled insect that resembles, in both size and color, half of a BB. Use a cotton swab dipped in rubbing alcohol to eliminate the adult scales, and use a general houseplant insecticide spray to control the rest of the immature scales, as well as the aphids that might be present.

922

Q I have noticed a small brown corky spot on the bottoms of all my weeping fig's leaves, right at the base of the leaf blades. It's about the size of a pinhead, and I can't peel it off with my fingernail. Is that caused by an insect, or what?

A That's a spot at which the leaf flexes. That corky dot is common to most weeping figs, and it doesn't appear to be affiliated with any particular problem. Don't worry about it.

Fuschias

923

 Q Can I grow fuschias in Texas, either as a flowering houseplant or out on the patio?

A They can't handle temperatures above 80 to 84 degrees. If you had a cool, bright, winter greenhouse, fuschias would probably have a good chance, but don't count on them after April. Unfortunately, it's hard to find fuschia transplants in the fall or winter, and by spring their time is limited.

Jade Plants

924

 Q My jade plant is dropping most of its leaves. They are shriveling up and falling all over the countertop. What causes that? It almost looks like I haven't been watering it enough.

A It isn't getting enough light. The problem will begin a couple of weeks after you move it to a darker location, and it will proceed until the plant dies. Moving it to a really bright location is the only cure.

Kalanchoes

925

Q I was given a kalanchoe as a gift. It has bloomed for many weeks, but now it seems to be finished. Can I get it to regrow and flower again?

A Yes, but it would help if you had a greenhouse. Cut it back by 50 percent or more and repot it. Grow it in very bright light for several months, until the plant is 8 to 10 inches tall. At that point you can give it artificially long nights by pulling shade fabric over it for 14 consecutive hours every day. You can also put a cardboard box over the plant–anything to keep the light away from its growing tips. During the day, however, it will still need that really bright light. It should start flowering a couple of months after you start this process.

Norfolk Island Pine

926

Q I have a Norfolk Island pine. It's beautiful, but it has grown too tall for our living room. It also is dropping many of its lowest branches. What do we do now? Can we plant it outdoors?

A In their native homes, Norfolk Island pines grow to be very large trees, often taller than 50 feet. Most living room ceilings are far lower than that, so our houseplant Norfolk Island pines are really living on borrowed time. Once they get too tall, unfortunately, there isn't much you can do. If you trim them back you'll ruin their shape. The lower leaf drop is caused by lack of available light. It sounds like you need to find a greenhouse or bank lobby that needs a tall plant. The only place Norfolk Island pines grow outdoors in Texas is in the very tip of the Rio Grande Valley.

Orchids

927

Q What types of orchids are easiest for growing indoors?

A There are many genera and species of orchids. In fact, it's one of the largest plant families in all the world. From all those different types, the very best for growing in a houseplant collection would be, perhaps, *Phalaenopsis*, *Paphiopedilum*, *Dendrobium*, and *Cattleya* varieties. All of these will grow well in bright east or south windows. Their specific planting mixes vary somewhat, but most will do well in a bark mix available where you buy the plants. Pick up the appropriate fertilizers at the same time. They will grow quite deliberately, so be patient. Most will bloom at specific seasons, and most will remain in flower for many weeks, even a couple of months.

Palms

928

 Q My palm's leaves are turning brown at their tips. Is it a serious problem?

A That means, in most cases, that you've let it get too dry at least once. Water more regularly and, perhaps, more at a time. Trim off the browned ends, and remove any leaves that are totally yellowed.

929

Q My palm's leaves were turning tan in fine specks, but now they're brown and dead. What's going on?

A That's the old nemesis, spider mites. Control them as quickly as you see their telltale tan mottling. Use the miticide Kelthane, and be sure to spray both top and bottom leaf surfaces. All palms are highly susceptible.

Philodendrons

930

 I have a *Philodendron selloum* that has gotten so large that I can't get it through the door. Can I plant it outdoors?

 Only in deep South Texas. Elsewhere it will freeze when temperatures drop into the high 20s. Either find a way to keep it alive during the winter, or make plans to switch over to the much more compact variety called Xanadu. It's much more household-friendly.

931

How important are those trailing roots on my *Philodendron selloum*? Can I cut them off?

They are quite incidental. Prune them to keep the plant tidy. You won't hurt it at all.

932

My splitleaf philodendron's leaves aren't splitting any more. What causes it to revert?

The vining type of splitleaf philodendron will have the cut leaves so long as their stems are growing upward. As soon as they reach the top of their pole and start hanging downward, the new leaves will be full and rounded. Supply a taller pole, or trim them back to the top of the old pole. Be sure, too, that the plant receives adequate light.

Pineapples

933

 I'd like to grow a pineapple plant. I understand I may even be able to bring it into flower and fruit. How do I do all that?

 Select a fresh pineapple with a vigorous-looking top at the grocery. Cut the top off and set it aside, then use the fruit as you normally would. Let the top dry for a couple of days, then pot it into an 8-inch clay flower pot, using the portion of the top of the fruit which you have left attached as its anchor, almost like roots. Use a loose, highly organic potting soil. Place the new plant in bright light, and keep it moist. It will start to form roots and then new leaves. Within a few months the leaves will take on an entirely different look as they elongate and develop spines. After 12 to 18 months the plant will be 24 to 36 inches tall and wide, and you'll be able to try your hand at bringing it into flower. Place an apple core in the center of the plant, and cover it to make it airtight with dry cleaner's plastic. The apple core will give off ethylene gas as it decays, and that gas will trigger the flowering process in the pineapple. Leave it covered, in bright light, but out of direct sunlight, for 4 to 6 weeks. You may want to open it up halfway through the process and place a fresh apple core in the center of the plant, then reseal it. You should see the flower starting to form after a month or two, and the fruit will then follow. The fruit will be much smaller than pineapples from the grocery store, but it will be edible—if you wish to try it.

Poinsettias

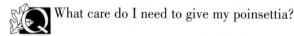

 What care do I need to give my poinsettia?

 First, carefully transport it home. Paper plant sleeves help protect the bracts from being broken, and can also shelter it momentarily from freezing temperatures. Just a minute's exposure to below-freezing weather can kill the plant. Keep your poinsettia cool, bright and moist. Those were the conditions under which it was grown in a greenhouse, and that's what it will need in your home over the holidays. If you let a poinsettia dry out to the point of wilting (even once), you can kiss half or more of its lower leaves good-bye. You won't need any special fertilizer as long as it's blooming. There will be ample nutrients in the potting soil. Keep it near a bright window, and keep it away from hot drafts.

☆935☆

How can I get my poinsettia to re-flower next year?

Be certain that you actually want to. Poinsettias get really large if they're given one entire year of good growing conditions. The plant you got at Christmas was nothing more than an unrooted cutting in August. That's how fast they grow. However, if you still want to try it, repot your plant once its bracts are no longer attractive. Prune it back by half or more, and plant it into loose, highly organic potting soil. As the plant grows, pinch the growing tips out every three or four weeks to keep it compact. Don't overfeed it, but do give it really bright light all spring and summer. You may have to repot it another time or two, since it will be getting larger and larger. To bring it into flower you should give it 14 hours of total and uninterrupted darkness each night beginning October 1. During the daytime you'll want to have the plant in full sunlight. Some folks misunderstand these directions, thinking that the plants need total darkness 24 hours a day. Re-read if you're confused. What you're trying to accomplish is fooling the plant into thinking it's later in the winter than it actually is by giving it those artificially long "nights."

Pothos

936

 I have a giant-leafed pothos whose leaves aren't as big as they used to be. All the new leaves are much smaller. What has happened?

 That's almost the same answer as for the splitleaf philodendron whose leaves aren't splitting. When a pothos is allowed to grow up a support such as a tropical tree trunk, or a pole as a houseplant, its leaves get larger and larger. However, once they reach the top of the pole and start hanging downward, they revert to their smaller form. All the fertilizer in the world won't make them grow any larger. All you can do is trim the stems back to the top of the old pole and enjoy the older leaves, or you can put a taller pole alongside it. Somehow you need to keep the plant ascending.

Prayer Plants

937

My prayer plant's leaves are browned around their edges. What did I do wrong?

Prayer plants need higher humidities than most homes have, plus you must never let them dry to the point of wilting.

Moisture stress is the reason for the browned edges, and most gardeners who have grown this plant have seen those symptoms more than once.

Scheffleras

938

Q My schefflera has lost many of its leaves. Those that remain are cupped and rolled. The plant just doesn't look healthy. What could be the problem?

A Lack of light. Scheffleras are large trees in their native homes. When we grow them indoors they require extremely bright conditions or they will die back. The cupped leaves are the best proof. Move it to a really bright south or west window and it should recover. You can take it outdoors in the shade for the summer, but it will drop the new leaves it puts on within a couple of months of your bringing it back indoors.

939

Q My schefflera's leaves are tan and drying. What causes this?

A Usually, spider mites. Thump a leaf over a sheet of white paper. You'll very likely see the almost-microscopic mites start to move around on the paper. Control them with Kelthane. Spray the plant in the garage.

Ti Plants

940

Q I brought a ti plant log home from Hawaii. Now how do I grow it?

A Pot it up as if it had roots, leaving about half of the cane out of the soil. It will develop a lovely red top. It will do best near a bright east window. Keep it moist, and keep it away from drying furnace drafts.

QUESTIONS RELATING TO GREENHOUSES

941

Q What side of my house would be best for my greenhouse? How much will shade trees impact it?

A It's probably best, as hot as our late springs, summers and early falls can be, to provide natural shading from noon on. For that reason, a spot that is either east of your house or east of a large shade tree would be ideal. If you're growing cacti, flowering houseplants or many different types of seedlings and cuttings, you may need even brighter light; if you're growing primarily foliage plants, you could even stand a little more shade.

942

Q What kind of covering is best for my greenhouse?

A To a degree, that's an economic question. Glass is the most attractive, and it's certainly more permanent than most other choices. However, you need a really good support for a glass greenhouse, and that's what runs the cost up. There are glass substitutes that cost less and are reasonably attractive, but you'll probably need to replace them every few years. Clear polyethylene plastic is the least expensive, and it's quite functional. Its only problem is that it isn't exactly handsome. If you're using your greenhouse strictly for function, it should be your choice.

943

Q How large should my greenhouse be?

A As large as your budget and space allow. There has never been a home hobby greenhouse that was large enough. By the time all the neighbor's big hanging baskets move in for the winter, the greenhouse is full to the rafters. Smaller houses heat up much more quickly, a problem in cold weather when you dare not leave vents or doors open. A 10-by-20-foot (or larger) greenhouse is probably ideal.

944

 What kind of heat source should I have for my greenhouse?

If you use gas, it must have a vent to prevent buildup of toxic fumes. Electric heat works well for small greenhouses, but you'll have to have an emergency backup heat source should the power go out. A portable kerosene heater would work well, but use it only as long as necessary to prevent accumulation of toxic fumes and smoke residue. Have a temperature alarm to alert you to developing problems. If your greenhouse is fairly large, you'll want some type of fan to circulate the warm air.

945

 Should I try to insulate my greenhouse to conserve energy?

You can use a double covering of plastic to create dead air space, which can save 25 percent or more of your heating costs. If it's more convenient to place bubble packing plastic against a flat greenhouse surface, that, too, can cut into the heating bills.

946

What temperature range should I try to maintain for my greenhouse?

It depends on the plants you're trying to grow. To keep really tropical plants such as hibiscus, bougainvilleas, aglaonemas and others, you'll need 65 to 70 degrees minimum. Many other plants will prosper even at 50 to 55 degrees, and, if you're just trying to keep plants from freezing, 40 to 45 degrees may be adequate for short periods of time. Try to keep the daytime summer temperatures no warmer than the low 90s.

947

 What kind of shading can I use for my greenhouse?

Cover your greenhouse with one of the special shade fabrics. They come in varying degrees of shade, but 50 to 62 percent is ideal. Have it made 15 percent larger than your greenhouse to allow for shrinkage, and have grommets installed so you can easily attach it to the structure—you may want to remove it during the winter.

948

What is the best way of cooling my greenhouse?

Evaporative cooling works fairly well, especially in Central, North and West Texas, where humidities are lowest. Put the cooler on the south end, so the prevailing winds in the summer can blow through it and into your greenhouse. You may prefer simply to take the covering off part of your greenhouse when it's really hot, so the air can blow through it. Have gravel under the benches, and keep the gravel moist to help cool the greenhouse.

949

 What is the best material for making my greenhouse benches?

Use pressure-treated pine, redwood, or other decay-resistant lumber. Space the boards 1/2-inch apart to allow for good drainage. You might also want to use one of the expanded metal bench systems available from commercial greenhouse sources.

950

 What is the best and easiest way to fertilize plants in my greenhouse?

Use a siphoning proportioner installed between the faucet and your garden hose, or install a fertilizer injector in-line. Read the installation instructions carefully and check with your city to make sure you're meeting all of their safety codes to prevent backflow of the fertilizer solution into your water source. You may also want to use timed-release encapsulated fertilizers.

QUESTIONS RELATING TO PLANT PROPAGATION

Seeds

951

 What types of plants can best be started from seeds?

Any standard (non-hybrid) type of plant can be started from seeds, if it produces viable seeds, of course. Annual flowers and vegetables are at the top of the list, and many trees are started this way. Many perennials are also started from seed, but not the hybrid types, which must be asexually (without pollination and resultant seeds) propagated to ensure the same genetic traits.

952

 What kind of planting medium should I use?

You'll want a highly organic, finely shredded potting soil mix. Some growers use finely milled sphagnum moss, while others merely find a good lightweight potting soil and use it. Sometimes they will dilute it ever so slightly with perlite or vermiculite to ensure good drainage.

953

 What type of container should I use for starting seeds?

 You can use any type of shallow pot, cut-off milk carton, plastic butter tub or other low container. If you're sowing lots of seeds, you may prefer to use shallow florists' flats. If your container doesn't have holes, either punch or drill holes for drainage.

954

 Should I broadcast the seeds over the surface, or sow them in rows?

Again, it depends on how much of the crop you're going to be growing. Row plantings certainly are safest, since diseases will be slow to jump from one row to the next. You can also dig and transplant one small part of a row, where it would be more damaging to disturb an entire grouping of seedlings growing *en masse*.

955

How much light will my new seedlings need as they germinate and grow?

If you're talking about late winter and early spring sowings, the more the better. Full sunlight would be ideal. Later in the season, when it turns really hot, you might want to give them light shading from mid-day sunlight. If you're growing the seedlings under fluorescent fixtures you'll want to keep the light tubes as close to the plants as possible, certainly not more than 4 or 5 inches above them.

956

 My seedlings are tall and lanky. Some even appear to be falling over. What went wrong?

 They aren't getting enough light. Either you need to put them in brighter surroundings, or sow them farther apart, so the seedlings won't be competing so much with one another for the available light.

957

 How soon should I transplant my little seedlings into pots?

 Dig and transplant them as soon as you can easily handle them by their first few leaves. Do not touch their stems. If you damage a leaf, the leaf dies. If you damage the stem, the plant dies.

958

 What kind of potting soil should I use for transplanting the seedlings?

You probably should use something very similar to the planting medium you used to germinate them. That will make the transplanting and repotting as easy on them as possible.

959

How do I get the seedlings ready to go out into the real world?

You need to toughen them up. Growers refer to it as "hardening" their plants. You need to expose them gradually, over a period of a few days or a week, to increasingly difficult conditions. They'll get more sunlight, a little wind, and perhaps cooler weather than they have had in the greenhouse. In the case of summer sowings that you intend to plant into the garden during hot weather, harden them to the sun or they'll cook within minutes of being planted outside.

960

 I bought bigger seed packets than I really needed. How can I save seeds from one year to the next?

Keep the seeds cool and dry. Seal them in plastic bags or small glass or plastic jars. Most types will do best in the refrigerator at 45 degrees. You can test their viability when it comes time to sow by putting 10 seeds in a moist paper towel. Watch them daily for a couple of weeks. If half or more germinate, you probably won't need to buy more seeds.

Cuttings

961

 What plants are most commonly started from cuttings?

 Most shrubs, vines and groundcovers, some trees, many houseplants, and a few annuals and perennials.

962

 What part of the plant do I want to use for cuttings?

 That depends on the types of cuttings you'll be taking. Some plants are started from leaf cuttings and a few others by root cuttings, but most are rooted from stem cuttings.

963

 What time of year is best for taking cuttings?

 Those cuttings that are made in late winter, just before the burst of spring growth, are called "hardwood" cuttings. "Softwood" cuttings are taken during really active growth spurts, and "semi-hardwood" cuttings, the most common type, are generally taken in late spring or early summer, as the current season's growth is becoming somewhat mature.

964

What kind of rooting medium do I need to start cuttings?

It will vary a little, depending on the types of plants you are trying to start. It needs to drain well, yet it will need enough organic matter to hold moisture around the developing roots. If you do not have access to a greenhouse rooting bench, you should probably use a mix of half peat moss with half perlite. In a greenhouse mist bed, you can use totally perlite.

965

Can I ever use water to root my cuttings?

It's usually not best. Roots that develop while a cutting is submerged in water are not physiologically the same as roots produced in potting soil. When you take those cuttings out of the water and plant them in the soil, they'll be set back much more than similar cuttings that have been rooted in potting soil.

966

How do I take leaf cuttings?

Plants such as African violets, Rex and other fancy-leafed begonias, and some peperomias are started from leaf cuttings, where one single leaf has the genetic ability to reproduce roots and more leaves. Select mature, healthy leaves and cut them cleanly with a sharp knife. Insert several such leaves into a pot filled with loose, highly organic potting soil, and keep them moist until they form roots and develop new clusters of leaves.

967

What plants are grown from root cuttings, and how do I take them?

Blackberries and other bramble berries can be started from root cuttings, where a portion of a major root is cut into sections and replanted. It will regenerate stem and leaf tissues, so one root can actually yield many new plants.

968

 How long should stem cuttings be?

 Cutting lengths will vary from 3 to 6 inches, depending on the species involved. Choose only healthy wood, and take care to keep the basal portions of each cutting identified. If you accidentally try to root cuttings upside-down, they will fail to grow properly.

969

 Should I use rooting hormone powder for stem cuttings?

 It's not essential, but it can speed the rooting process and help the cuttings produce more roots. It's not advisable with soft succulent cuttings such as impatiens, begonias or coleus, but it's almost a must for woody things such as hollies, junipers and crape myrtles.

970

 I've heard that you should cut the sides of the stem cuttings to expose more tissue for rooting. How do I do that?

 That's a process called "wounding." Use a very sharp knife to cut a slice up one side of the base of the cutting. The wound should probably only be ½- to 1 inch long. Turn the cutting over and repeat the process on the other side. Be certain that you only remove the outer bark of the cutting with each wound, barely exposing the cambium layer beneath. That will give you much more exposed surface area on which new roots can form than if you simply inserted a freshly cut cutting into the rooting bed.

971

Q How can I tell when my cuttings are rooted and ready to be potted?

A Pull on them very gently. If they offer slight resistance, they are beginning to form roots and will soon be ready to be dug and potted. If they are firmly rooted you'll be able to tell with that gentle tug. Timing for rooting will vary with species, time of year and the conditions under which you're rooting them. Some types may form roots within a few days, while others will take many weeks, even months.

972

Q What do I do with my cuttings after they're rooted?

A Pot them into individual pots filled with a high-quality potting soil. They may wilt somewhat for a few days after transplanting, so be prepared to protect them from hot, sunny conditions until they have adjusted. With some plants you may want to stick several cuttings in each pot. Low, dense shrubs can be handled that way, but groundcovers especially will benefit from having fuller transplants when they go into the garden.

Layering

973

Q What exactly is "layering," and when can I use it?

A "Layering" is the process of causing roots to form on a portion of an existing plant while it is still attached to the mother plant. It sometimes occurs naturally, and it has been a horticultural technique for centuries.

974

 How do I make a tip layer? What plants grow best this way?

 If a portion of a plant either trails along the ground, or can be pulled down into contact with the ground, it may form roots where it makes that contact. Strawberries and airplane plants do it naturally, but many other plants can be encouraged to form tip layers simply by pulling their branches to the soil. Wound the bottom of the branch lightly with a sharp knife, (as you would for a stem cutting), dust it with rooting hormone powder, then secure it with a small piece of a coat hanger or similar wire bent into a wicket shape. You can also cover the area with topsoil, both to give the new roots soil in which to form and also to weight the stem down. Once the new roots have formed, you can cut the stem and replant the newly rooted plant.

☆975☆

How do I make an air layer?

Air layering is done on stems that are above the soil line. You would select a branch that is healthy and vigorous. Work 6 to 8 inches back from the growing tip of the branch. Strip the leaves off a 4- to 5-inch segment of the stem, and cut a shallow flap through the bark of the stem. Use a toothpick or small twig to hold the flap away from the rest of the stem, then dust the freshly cut surface with rooting hormone powder. Use sphagnum moss as your rooting medium. Soak it for an hour or two before you start layering, then wring it almost dry before you place a handful of the moss around the wounded stem tissue. Use fine string to hold it in place around the stem, then wrap polyethylene plastic film around the moss to hold in the moisture. Seal all the seams with electrician's tape to make them airtight. Roots will form in the moss, at which point you can sever the stem and pot the new plant. You may want to cut the mother plant back to reshape it.

976

 What plants are most often started by air layering?

 Plants that are commonly air layered include crotons, ficuses and rubber plants, scheffleras, dieffenbachias and many other woody foliage plants. It also can be used very successfully on many woody outdoor shrubs.

Budding and Grafting

977

 How do I graft plants? How successful am I likely to be?

 Budding and grafting involve taking dormant buds or small stems from a plant of known merit and causing them to grow together with rootstocks of another variety. Fruit trees, pecans, grapes, ornamental pears and plums, roses and other plants that do not root easily from cuttings (or that need the vigor of some other type of rootstock) are started this way. The main problem for amateur plant propagators is that your first 100 buds and grafts will probably not be as successful as the next ones you do. Speed is a critical issue here, so don't leave the tissues exposed very long. What may take you 15 minutes the first time you try may honestly only take 15 seconds once you're skilled. If you want to invest the time and practice it takes to get good at budding and grafting, and if you study the comprehensive books and Extension Service fact sheets showing you how to do it, this can be fun and rewarding. Otherwise, it's probably best left to the folks who will devote the time to get good at it.

13

GENERAL QUESTIONS

GARDEN MISCELLANY
••

978

Q I'd like to help my child with a science fair project. What suggestions do you have?

A That's a very common question every spring, often days before the project is due. Plan ahead, and do something innovative. "The Effects of Light on Seed Germination," and "How Plants Respond to Music" are overdone and worn out. Pick something with a useful message to gardeners, something that is truly informative and applicable.

979

Q What can I do to eliminate cicadas? They're keeping me awake all night with their buzzing.

A Unfortunately, cicadas are quite difficult, probably impossible, to eliminate. They don't feed on the plants in which they live and buzz, and they're spread over such a wide area that spraying isn't very successful. They generally run their course within a few weeks, so buy some ear plugs and ignore them. Curiously, they seem to be especially common in cottonwoods and willows. If you have either of these trees, and if they're the host plants, you might consider choosing another species when time comes to replace them.

980

Q What are the very large insects that look like bumble bees and hover near the ground? They look ferocious. Do I need to worry about them?

A Those are cicada killers. They're beneficial predatory insects that intercept the cicadas in mid-flight, paralyze them and carry them back to their in-ground homes. They are harmless unless you try to corner them. Just ignore them.

981

Q I was working around some shrubs the other day and got stung by what I thought was probably a harmless caterpillar. How common are these pests?

A There are several different types of stinging caterpillars in Texas. Most common of them all is the puss caterpillar, called "asps" by many Texans. They're cream-colored small larvae that have ridged backs. It's along those ridges that the stinging hairs are found. You can control them with most general-purpose insecticides, including "Bt." The best advice for kids and adults alike: Assume any caterpillar is capable of stinging. Most won't, but if you don't handle any of them, you won't have to worry.

982

Q We have had an outbreak of paper wasps and mud dobbers making their nests all over our house this summer. Is there an easy way to stop them?

A These pests seem to migrate to rural and sub-rural landscapes when adjacent areas are dry. The easiest way of controlling them is merely to break their nests apart as soon as you see them being formed. Most types will not be aggressive unless cornered. Yellow jackets, by comparison, will attack with no provocation. You can use one of the long-throw, quick-knock-down sprays to kill them at the nest site, but be careful not to let the spray drift onto adjacent trees and shrubs. Most have propellants that will burn foliage.

983

Q We have large holes in our landscape, each surrounded by very coarse soil that has been kicked out. Someone told us we have crawdads. How do we control them?

A Crayfish are indicative of really wet soil. While there is no product you can use to eliminate them, drying the soil out with tile drains or by cutting in some way to let the water run off will usually get rid of them.

984

Q Will ants hurt our plants? We have ants crawling in and out of a large tree in our landscape.

A Most ants are harmless to plant life. In most cases they're merely living in the trees' voids. If you have an outbreak of aphids you may notice ants working alongside them on some of your flowers and vegetables. Again, there isn't much reason for concern. If carpenter ants seem to be damaging plant tissues or wood products in the landscape, insecticides will help control them.

☆985☆

Q Specifically relative to fire ants, is there any one really good way to eliminate them?

A We don't currently have the technology to *eliminate* fire ants. We can suppress the individual mounds, but they will move back in from adjacent untreated lands. Use mound treatments of conventional registered insecticides, as well as area-wide baits. The baits are slower acting, so you'll probably want to use the mound treatments where the ants threaten children or pets near your home. There are many unusual products for fire ant control on the market today. Some work reasonably well and many do not. Ask plenty of questions before you buy, then read and follow label directions very carefully.

986

Q Will storing firewood near our house increase the chance of termites invading the structure?

A It should not. It is a good idea, however, to keep the firewood away from wooden surfaces of the house, just to keep moisture and dirt away from the paint or stain. You do need to be careful about storing firewood where borers can invade it. Those same insects that love tunneling through the stored firewood can later invade trees in your landscape. Be extremely cautious about oak firewood. Beetles that carry oak wilt will proliferate in firewood. Cover the pile with clear polyethylene plastic. Overlap the seams by several inches.

Black plastic film develops holes, and the insects can sense the light, then use the holes for their escape and spread. With clear plastic, they are far less likely to escape.

987

Q How can we reduce the chance of snakes in our landscape?

A If you live in an area where snakes are still present, near open native land, for example, you probably are going to have an occasional snake on your property. Learn which types are poisonous beforehand, then leave the others alone to do their beneficial work. Beware of any piles of lumber, sheet metal or other cozy spots where snakes might spend their hours. Move those materials with a hoe prior to putting your hands near them. While groundcovers might encourage snakes somewhat, you're just about as likely to have them under shrubs and in turf areas as you are in the ivy or mondograss. Cats are great repellents, too. If you enjoy cats, you'll be happy for their good services in keeping snakes away.

988

Q Mosquitoes are eating us alive. What will control them safely? We'd like to be able to clear the area before we have friends over for an outside party.

A If you remember your biology classes, mosquitoes must have standing water for the early part of their life cycle. Start by eliminating any pools, puddles or containers of water around your landscape and, where possible, in adjacent public land. You can also use conventional insecticides to eliminate the adults, but you'll need to spray back under shrubs and in quiet corners and groundcover beds. Mosquitoes stay where the air is still, most of the time. You can use the vaporizing foggers to control them in a confined area. That's probably what you would want to do several hours before you had guests. They leave very little odor compared to conventional insecticide sprays. The repellent sprays work very well, and newer formulations don't leave oily residue on your clothes and skin.

989

Q I have seen a plant that was called something like "mosquito plant." It was supposed to repel mosquitoes if you just grew it in your garden. Is that true?

A The plant is a genetically altered form of a scented geranium. Folks who have tried it in their own home gardens have reported that they like the plant and its good looks, but they still have plenty of mosquitoes.

990

Q Every time I go out in the yard I come back with chiggers. What spray will help them, and how long will they be around?

A Chiggers are a problem for 8 to 12 weeks in late spring and into mid-summer in most parts of Texas. They require daily high temperatures in the high 80s and 90s, and they go dormant once it turns really hot and dry for a few weeks. In between, though, they can ravage your ankles. They're far more common in bermuda than they are in St. Augustine, and they're more of a problem in turf areas that are not mowed as often. You can control them with insecticides. Spray your socks, pants cuffs, feet, and ankles with an insect repellent intended for this purpose and you should have few problems. Beware, if you're pulling or cutting high weeds, to spray the rest of your body as well.

☆991☆

Q Birds are roosting in our trees. Is there any way to discourage them? We don't want to hurt them.

A Cover the trees with plastic mesh tree netting. It is sold in nurseries and hardware stores, often to keep birds away from ripening fruit such as peaches. It can be draped over the trees like a giant hair net. Use long poles to put it in place. You can also create motion in the trees by hanging aluminum pie plates, inflatable owls and fake snakes. Warning: The fake snakes may alarm visitors!

992

 Squirrels are stripping the bark off our trees' limbs. How can we encourage them to move on? How serious is that damage?

 There are several animal repellents on the market. Some may work, and others probably won't. If you find a time when there are no squirrels in the trees, and if no other trees' limbs or power lines touch the trees' branches, you can put sheet metal collars around the trunks of the trees to keep the squirrels from getting up into them. Humane traps also can be used. The squirrels may ruin a few limbs as they sharpen their teeth, but they usually won't do serious long-term damage to the trees.

☆993☆

 How can we keep cats and dogs from lying in our flower beds?

 Those same repellents might work. You can also take old socks and fill them with moth balls. Sometimes the odors will drive the pets off. Hardware stores and home centers sell low-voltage shock fences that scare the pets away. These are very effective and don't harm the pets. Once they get the gentle shock the first time, they leave the fence alone. You can unplug it and leave it in place for a while, then remove it once you think things are safe. If they return, re-install it for a week or two. You can also bury cables in the ground and put special collars on the pets. When they get near the cables an alarm alerts them to retreat before they receive a shock. Several companies around Texas install these systems, and veterinarians and gardeners report that they work very well.

994

We have rabbits eating our flowers. What will run them off without hurting them?

The animal repellents can help, but you probably also will need other ideas. Most of their damage will be done during the winter, so try planting winter rye somewhere in your landscape. They actually will prefer it to the pansies and other cool-season flowers. The low-voltage fences will help, and there are humane traps that might be useful.

995

Q I'd like to kill a bunch of spiders that are in my plants. What would be best?

A You may not like the answer, but spiders are beneficial. They're out there making a living by eating insects that are devouring your plants. Only if they appear to be threatening you should you try to kill them. Conventional insecticides will do the job, but please limit their use.

996

Q What effects will creosote or pressure-treated pine have on my plants and me?

A Creosote is the more harmful of the two, both to plants and to people. Don't use any wood timbers with fresh creosote oozing out of them. The pressure-treated pine, on the other hand, should present no problems around the landscape or garden or even in the greenhouse.

☆997☆

Q My lawn is being ruined by armadillos. They're probably going after grub worms, but I don't see any grubs at all. They're also plowing up my groundcovers and flowers. What will control them?

A Armadillos are very difficult to eliminate, and they usually move in families, so your work won't be finished when you catch the first one. While they may be looking for grub worms, they really seem to have no method to their digging. The best way to eliminate them is with a humane trap. There are several on the market, or you can make one yourself. It will need to be large enough to hold a mature armadillo, and you'll need some type of triggering mechanism that will drop doors at each end of the trap. Raw bacon makes a good bait, but be sure you don't have dogs that will come in after it. It really helps to build some type of temporary "fence" to act as a funnel. Use chicken wire, for example, to make a low fence on either side of the armadillo's run. It will hit the fence and be guided directly into the trap. If you release the armadillos elsewhere, take them 5 to 10 miles away and free them away from anyone else's landscape, garden or farm area.

998

Q How can I tell if I have gophers or moles in my lawn? What will eliminate them?

A There is a great deal of confusion in identification and control of these two damaging animals. Both will be most common in areas with sandy soils. Here are the details on each pest.

Gophers. Gophers have small external ears and eyes. Their front incisor teeth are always exposed. Gophers are rodents, and more closely resemble squirrels in their head and facial features. Gophers feed on roots which they encounter while digging. They may also feed on above-ground vegetation that is very close to the openings of their tunnels, and they may actually pull plants into their tunnels from above. They feed on all manners of plants, from grasses and annuals to shrubs and even trees. Gopher mounds are generally kidney-shaped and made of finely sifted soil. Gophers usually have larger mounds, and they often are in line with one another. Control them with poison baits that are placed into their tunnel systems. Remove any bait that spills on the surface of the ground. Locate the main tunnel, place the bait within it, then seal off any opening you made.

Moles. Moles have hairless, pointed snouts extending nearly 1/2-inch in front of their mouth opening. Their small eyes and the opening of their ear canals are concealed in fur, and there are no external ears. Moles are insectivores, related to bats. Moles are generally found in cool, moist and shaded soils that are populated by earthworms and grub worms. Moles leave volcano-shaped hills that are often made up of clods of soil. Moles are best controlled using traps that are implanted into depressed portions of the surface tunnels. As the moles push up to re-open their tunnels, the traps are triggered.

For the record, commercially available sonic devices that claim to scare gophers away are reportedly ineffective. So are the plants, gopher purge and castor bean, both of which have been claimed to drive the animals away.

☆ *999* ☆

Q What can we do to eliminate fleas on our pets? They're coming indoors, too.

A Spray the lawn, groundcovers, low shrubs and the sides of your house with a conventional insecticide such as Dursban. Treat the inside of your house with one of the aerosol bombs labeled to kill both the immature forms and the adults. Your veterinarian has products which can be put on the pet's back to kill the fleas within its coat. Make all of these treatments at the same time, to keep the fleas from migrating from one place to another.

1000

Q How long will my garden chemicals be good if they have been kept in the garage?

A It depends on the product and the conditions under which it has been stored. Some will tell you on their labels how quickly you need to use them. Once they have been opened, that shelf life starts decreasing quickly. If they're stored in hot Texas summer temperatures, the shelf life starts plummeting. If they're exposed to even one hard freeze, they may be rendered immediately useless. Some chemicals even become more toxic when they break down. The best advice is to buy only what you can use in one season. Store any extra carefully, and don't use it if it appears to have separated at all. Dispose of empty containers and any extra pesticides, whether they're organic or inorganic, according to your county's disposal plan. Your county Extension office will have all the details.

1001

Q I really don't want to use pesticides. Are there good alternatives to insecticides and fungicides? What about using things like detergent, pepper sprays, baking soda and vinegar?

A Use them on a trial basis. If they seem to help, and if you're comfortable with the results and any risks that may be associated with them, use them by all means. Most are relatively harmless to people, but you definitely need to think twice when you're dealing with the more toxic home products and remedies. Conventional insecticides and fungicides have gone through millions of dollars' worth of testing and proof before they could be sold for pest control. You can trust them to do what they claim they will do, and to do it efficiently and safely. As always, though, you need to read and follow label directions explicitly. Before you get to the spraying stage, however, try all other possible avenues of control. Use only resistant species that are known not to have serious pest problems. Use mechanical and biological controls whenever they are available, and use recommended organic controls as they are appropriate. When all of these means fail, and before the problem is at a crisis level, treat confined areas with a labeled insecticide or fungicide.

INDEX

Note: Numbers are question numbers, not page numbers

(Boldface number indicates that the indexed topic is the primary subject of that question)

—A—

Arborvitae:
 pruning, 209
 spider mite damage, 131
Aristocrat pear. See: pears,
 ornamental (*Pyrus* sp.)
Arizona cypress, as living Christmas
 tree, 85
Armadillos, elimination of, **997**
Ashes (*Fraxinus* sp.), Arizona, thin
 and weak, **117**
Asian jasmine. See: jasmine, Asian
Asparagus:
 bermudagrass in bed, **748**
 cutting brown stems, **750**
 fertilizers, **747**
 harvesting, **744, 745**
 planting, **719, 743**
 small spears, **746**
 soil preparation, **742**
 transplanting, **751**
 using rock salt around, **749**
Aspidistra elatior. See: cast
 iron plant
Asps. See: caterpillars, stinging
Asters (*Aster* sp.):
 fall, staking, **543**
 pruning, **543**
 roadside (weed), **434**
Astilbe, 538
Aucuba japonica. See: aucubas
Aucubas (*Aucuba japonica*):
 black leaves, **222**
 sunscorch, **222**
Avocados, **898**
 growing indoors, **897**
 keeping compact, **897**
 planting outdoors, **898**
 starting from a seed, **896**
Azaleas (*Rhododendron* sp.):
 fertilizers, 204, **225**
 iron deficiency in, 16
 life expectancy, **226**
 losing branches, **227**
 need acidic soil, **127**
 peat moss in soil, 192
 planting, **223**
 pruning, **224**
 soil preparation for, 11
 soil requirements, **223**
 toxicity, 218

—B—

Bacillus thuringiensis ("B.f."), 761,
 765, 768, 773

Bacterial leaf spot, in plum trees,
 180, 706
Bacterial soft rot:
 on irises, **579**
 on tomatoes, **841**
Bacterial stem canker:
 on junipers, **265**
 on plum and peach trees, **182,
 676, 707**
Bagworms, in junipers, **264**
Baking soda, as alternative to
 pesticides, 1001
Bald cypress (*Taxodium distichum*):
 in wet areas, 81
 iron deficiency, **118**
 spider mite damage, 131
 turning tan, **119**
 yellow, **118**
Bamboo, **569**
Banana trees, over-wintering, **462**
Barberries (*Berberis* sp.):
 losing color, **228**
 low varieties, 216
Bark. See also: mulches/mulching
 damaged with lawn trimmer, **98**
 falling off trees, **173**
 for houseplant soils, 863
 for indoor orchids, 927
 regrowth inhibited by sealant
 paint, 38
 scratching to check health
 of tree, 75
 splitting, **97**
 to improve clay soil, 7
Basil, 785, 788
Beans, 716
 Castor, toxicity, 218
 cold-sensitive nature of garden
 beans, 6
 harvesting, 738, **754, 755**
 nematodes, **757**
 planting, 719, **752**
 spider mite damage, **756**
 Texas varieties, **753**
 watering, 733
Beets, planting, 719
Begonias, 494, 889
 best types for indoors, **899**
 brown leaf edges, **474**
 insect damage, **473**
 lighting, **474**
 started from leaf cuttings, 966
 over-wintering, **475, 476**
Berberis sp. See: barberries

—I—

—U—